GROUPS:
THEORY AND EXPERIENCE

GROUPS:
THEORY AND EXPERIENCE

Rodney W. Napier
Department of Psychoeducational Processes
Temple University

Matti K. Gershenfeld
Formerly Visiting Professor
Department of Educational Psychology
Temple University

Houghton Mifflin Company · Boston
Atlanta
Dallas
Geneva, Illinois
Hopewell, New Jersey
Palo Alto

Printed in the U.S.A.

Library of Congress Catalog Number: 72-5641

ISBN: 0-395-12658-4

editor's introduction .

The significance for the helping professions of working with people in groups has probably been the most prominent development of the past decade. Some professionals, of course, see the growing attention given to behavioral conditioning and behavioral counseling as equal or superior to what is achieved through group movement. Be that as it may, it is clear that the developments known variously as group therapy, sensitivity training, encounter groups, or group counseling (the various terms overlap in meaning) have touched the lives of a great many people. During the 1960's over 100,000 people participated in weekend or longer seminars at Esalen (Big Sur, Calif.) alone, and additional hundreds of thousands attended workshops at NTL Institute (Bethel, Maine) or its regional training centers throughout the country. These are but two of the larger organized approaches to group work; others of more recent origin are the Parent Effectiveness Training groups, the Transactional Analysis groups. Beyond these are hundreds of less organized groups in schools and colleges, churches, hospitals, and community organizations.

This book is designed to help spread the values of group interaction, in which people learn from each other about themselves under the guidance of a group leader or "facilitator." The facilitator may be a teacher, counselor, mental health worker, graduate student, or community leader. The book is based solidly on an understanding of the group process and the dynamics of group interaction, and each chapter presents exercises which contribute to skill in *performance*. This is a unique contribution. The exercises within each of the eight chapters have been validated through use in classrooms and other settings. Only the most important and workable of the "tried and true" exercises are included here.

I think that the chapter on Perception and Communication is as powerful a statement on the subject as I have seen anywhere in the literature. I also think that the unique contribution that the exercises make to the understanding of the content of each chapter is an extremely useful teaching and learning device. Although much stress is given to *understanding* of the group process as opposed to the mere use of techniques, the Appendix deals with the basic skills that must be possessed by the group facilitator. The skills deal with such practical matters as timing, use of various techniques, feedback, etc.

The authors are giving the reader *tested* material, carefully organized for both understanding and use. I commend the book to the reader as one from which he cannot help but learn a great deal.

C. Gilbert Wrenn

became a legitimate area for widespread study and examination; as the centrality of small groups in a variety of settings became recognized as a basis for exploring group productivity, decision making, and leadership; and as findings of small group studies and laboratory training were seen to be relevant in areas ranging from increased personal growth to enhanced organizational effectiveness. Formerly the domain of therapists and social workers, involvement in the study of group life is presently an integral part of many religious, educational, and business communities. With this reality in mind, we have directed the text to populations such as students interested in the psychology of small groups and experience-related laboratory learning, teachers beginning to work in the area of affective education, community leaders working with volunteer groups, professionals working with community and service organizations, mental health workers involved in the community or in institutions working with groups, counselors working with students, business groups and organizational trainers.

Organization of the Book

The text is organized into "theory" and "experience" sections as follows. Each chapter contains two parts. The first part attempts to provide the individual with a conceptual framework that will give him a language for observing groups as they operate. Once he has gained a firm grasp of the conceptual learnings related to such areas as communication, leadership, group standards, and membership, the reader is then prepared to tackle the applied training exercises which follow in the "experience" section of each chapter. Each of the exercises applies to the subject of that particular chapter. Thus, if the reader's aim is to facilitate a group in understanding its own communication process, he will find a series of exercises ranging in complexity but which are all directed to some aspect of communication within groups.

When presenting training exercises, group facilitators often face a variety of problems. The Appendix of this book focuses on the practical skills a facilitator must acquire before he should begin to intervene in groups with the use of skill exercises. *It is essential that this section be read prior to using the exercises.* Techniques for observing groups are discussed, along with how to prepare a group for role playing and methods for diagnosing and evaluating group behaviors.

preface

This book is aimed at providing experiences directed at imp[...] the reader's understanding of group process and his skills as a [...] member or facilitator. As the authors, we feel we have crea[...] comprehensive study exploring the major aspects of group pr[...] Our intention is to reach diverse populations in many profes[...] fields. We believe that by combining theoretical and empirical [...] cepts with experiences derived from our own work in the fiel[...] reader will be encouraged not only to learn the concepts of [...] dynamics, but also to make useful applications of them.

By definition, the study of groups cannot be defined narrow[...] terms of particular areas of academic learning. However, it is [...] that the primary source of interest in this book will be generate[...] organizations and groups which are interested in human rela[...] training, planned change, leadership development, and decis[...] making processes. With its accompanying instructor's manual [...] book ideally can be used as a primary text for courses in guid[...] and counseling, social work, community organization, teacher trai[...] and supervision, mental health, and group dynamics. It may be [...] as a supplementary text for courses in social psychology, busi[...] administration, communications, sociology of small groups, psy[...] atry, and training of counselors and therapists.

Until quite recently, persons who conducted courses on small gro[...] were highly-trained behavioral scientists, usually educated at [...] doctoral level and based at universities. They designed and conduc[...] workshops (or laboratories, as they are frequently called) or serv[...] as consultants to industry. This small coterie developed, and son[...] times shared, diverse training designs and methods. Frequent[...] however, the effectiveness of the training design depended as much [...] the charisma of the trainer as on the validity of the design. Typicall[...] facilitators or trainers in one region were unfamiliar with the wo[...] and techniques of their peers in another part of the country.

Through the years, the number of people who required a knowledg[...] of small groups increased significantly, as studying small grou[...]

It is felt that while practice and experimentation are the most important factors in increasing the skill of the facilitator, he can also learn a great deal simply by becoming aware of the many pitfalls that can undermine an otherwise appropriate skill exercise.

In addition, an overview of the book's contents may prove useful to the reader before he begins. Chapter 1 discusses how groups communicate, focusing on the concept of selective perception and stereotyping. The ways in which our personal needs help to determine what we see and hear and eventually what we expect is analyzed in terms of both research and theory. The verbal and nonverbal cues that lead to a breakdown in personal communication within a group are examined. Chapter 2 looks in depth at what it takes to become a member of a given group. An individual's performance in a new group will, in part, be determined by his past experiences, which must be understood from a social, cultural, and idiosyncratic perspective. In Chapter 3 the pressures and internal dissonance that help determine acceptable standards of behavior are explored, focusing on the forces at work which create the ground rules present in any group. Chapter 4 deals with the motivational forces which influence members' productivity and sense of achievement. In Chapter 5 the notions of leadership and power are considered as they affect individual and group performance. Related to this is the study of the types of roles which evolve in a group and how these roles involve both task and maintenance concerns.

Thus, given some understanding of group membership, the determination of group standards, and the various leader-follower relationships that develop in a group, the reader is ready to interpret the relevance of these phenomena in terms of the decision-making process, as discussed in Chapter 6. What theory and research say about how successfully to minimize disruptive influences in that process is the major thrust of this chapter. Chapter 7 explores the field of group dynamics from an overview perspective and defines its value for a wide range of students, practitioners, and social scientists. Special attention is given to the characteristics of successful groups, which function as cohesive and productive units. The aim is to make the reader aware of the complex relationships that exist below the surface in any group, the implicit and explicit needs that govern behavior, the patterns of communication that exist, and the personal and organizational goals that decisively move or restrain the group. The proliferation of groups, and the corresponding fears and rumors as to the dangers of various groups, are examined in Chapter 8. Frequently asked questions are then answered directly.

The key to using this book effectively is the understanding that what is appropriate for one group may not be for another. The facilitator, whether student, counselor, teacher, or other professional, should have a large "vocabulary" of diagnostic and applied skills to cope effectively with a wide range of happenings within a group. Our aim is to provide some of the understanding and some of the alternatives. It is for the reader to provide the flexibility and awareness to put these findings into appropriate application.

We are grateful to many individuals for their help in this project, including the members of our own families. Students in our classes in the Graduate Department of Psychoeducational Processes at Temple University were particularly generous in their comments, suggestions, and enthusiastic support. We appreciate especially the efforts of Selma Laskin, for her careful editing, as well as the help provided by Winona Moseley, Sarah Engel, Alice Johnson, and Jerri Ball. We have seriously attempted to trace and give credit to all authors and originators of exercises; the result is incomplete, and we feel a need to express our gratitude to those who contributed whom we do not know. Finally, many of those at Houghton Mifflin provided encouragement and a sounding board for us at all times. We thank our Consulting Editor, C. Gilbert Wrenn.

Rod Napier

Matti Gershenfeld

contents

William B. Finch

1 perception and communication

They stood together waiting in front of the large plain door, each realizing what awaited him on the other side. The shorter, less physical of the two felt the gnawing grind in his stomach, the cold, sweaty palms, the panic of near flight. But he remained waiting patiently in the calm before the inevitable storm. The taller one was also tense, but more out of anticipation than desperation. He could hardly wait.

The door opened and they were ushered in amid a smog of cigarette smoke and an atmosphere of strained socializing. Although there was hardly a noticeable pause in activity, it seemed that every eye moved in their direction, every drink held off at the lips, every cigarette poised as the two new guests slowly gravitated toward the organized din and confusion. There would be no introductions, since it was an informal affair and there would be time for everyone to get to know one another. For the moment, the choices were few. One could continue to stand and be conspicuous, or he could move into one of the clusters of people and submerge himself quickly in a cover of introductions and superficial talk. Or, one might tread more gently, create a diversion by circumventing the group and "casually" looking around, getting a drink, perhaps looking with "curiosity" out an unoccupied window.

The tall one, after momentarily scanning the room, moved with apparent ease to the most animated group, and in what seemed like a second was indistinguishably a part of the mixture. Almost chameleon-like he had adopted the gestures, the humor, the language of the group.

Amazed at his friend's easy success, the short one began a ritualistic excursion around the room. There were so many questions pricking him. Could he possibly look as relaxed and casual? Could he create an image of "belonging" when he almost never felt that way? Would one of those staring faces provide him with the friendship he so desired but which his behavior belied? Would his message be heard?

We have all been there, standing on the threshold of a new group, carefully screening our own behavior and trying to communicate what we believe will be most acceptable. And, in turn, we select from

1

that narrow world of experience what we believe to be an unsullied, spotlessly perceived piece of information about the group facing us. We take the data projected at us and after a process of filtering, sifting, and refining, we respond to the distortion we have created. The ideas and information become alloys of our own making. Thus, one new member of a group may see eight potential friends while another sees eight sources of potential rejection. One may observe dress, tone of voice, and posture, while another may focus immediately upon evidence of influence and power . . . perhaps the direction of word flow or the movement of eyes toward a source of approval. Whatever the processes and needs of the individual, the view that eventually enters the "mind's eye" will be, to some degree, a distorted version of what is actually taking place, reduced by some and expanded by others (Berelson and Steiner, 1964; Sebald, 1962).

Selective Perception: Distortion of the Mechanical

That we see what we need to see is not merely a psychologist's whim —it is reality. An ink blot reveals the wide range of responses among different individuals that can be lured from an ill-defined or nebulous stimulus. Each perception and its interpretation of virtually any event is based on a combination of historical experiences, present needs, and the inherent properties of the scene being perceived (Wrench, 1964; North, 1957).

It is necessary to begin with the assumption that we distort and proceed to build on these distortions. Even with the most objective task, it is nearly impossible to keep our subjective views from altering that which really exists. If, for example, I present the following dia-

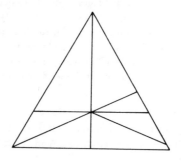

gram to a group of 100 people and ask them to simply count the number of triangles in the diagram, it is almost certain that there will be anywhere from 15 to 20 different responses ranging from perhaps a few to as many as 25 or more from each individual. How is this possible among a representative group of "normal," "well-adjusted," and "intelligent" people? The task is clear and easy enough (the fifth grade would not be too early); yet it is entirely possible that of the 100 participants, no more than 8 or 10 would have the same response.

Following are only a few of the possible reasons for the differences in the perceived realities of this group.

1. One individual vigorously defends the "fact" that there is only one triangle in the diagram. Somewhere in the far reaches of her memory, she sees a triangle as having "three equal sides."

2. Another person somehow discovers 43 by counting "every possible" angle in the diagram.

3. A number of people count six triangles moving from left to right around the diagram but not counting the figure in the lower right-hand corner.

4. Others find seven since they assume the figure in the lower right-hand corner to be a triangle.

5. Some people find seven, eight, nine by combining a few of the lines to form other triangles. Others push on and discover 13, 14, 15, 20 triangles.

Later it is discovered that some who stopped short of discovering all the possible combinations did not like puzzles, or did poorly in geometry and still carried the fear with them. Others saw the whole thing as a game, perhaps a trick—so why bother to try? Still others felt that they were being tested and thought it wiser to find fewer triangles and be correct than to have many and be wrong. Then, of course, there were the "competitors," some of whom managed to see triangles that were not even there. One lady's husband was an engineer, and she was determined to outdo him, at least on this one problem. She found 19 while he, under no such compulsion, found 11. Thus, even in a simple, straightforward task, among a responsible group of participants, one is able to ferret out unreasonable suspicion, fear of inadequacy, competitiveness, distortion of the instructions, and perhaps 40 or 50 other variables that make such an enormous variety of responses predictable. Since there are so many factors involved in one's choice on such a simple problem, imagine what happens when we add the additional variables that occur whenever we introduce the factors surrounding another human being.

Selective Perception: Adding the Human Dimension

In one way, our senses are overwhelmed by a thousand cues from the world we are attempting to understand. What we eventually perceive is the result of a complex sorting process that arranges stimuli in a manner most easily digestible, a process that facilitates our own self-maintenance for security. Colors, sizes, shapes, textures, smells, sounds, rhythms, and gestures as well as the essence of time, place, and history impinge on us and are woven into a pattern of responding behavior. It becomes even more complex when we add what we think others think or feel about our behavior. It is little wonder that what we communicate and what we in turn receive back is so often dressed in grays and obscured by shadows we ourselves cast. Often, past distortions are infused into the present and compounded in such a way that the real and imagined, the past and the present, intertwine and form the present reality (Fabun, 1965; Nylen et al. 1967).

In many ways this process is similar to the one a member of Congress experiences. His picture of the "facts" behind any one bill is far more complex than the view held by an average citizen. Even the simplest issue may be confused by innumerable subtle pressures that began to encroach upon his perceptual field. Lobbyists, personal biases, favors that must be repaid—these are all drawn into the picture, confounding what might have appeared to be a relatively simple and straightforward issue. To make matters worse, only some of these pressures may be conscious and under his control.

Often the most powerful influences on our perception are never realized. A group of people represents various degrees of acceptance and rejection, likes and dislikes, pleasant memories and distasteful ones, and it is from this complex assortment of stimuli that we conjure up a picture of our "reality" and build what appear to be appropriate responses—again, to maintain our own position and integrity within the group. Our needs may be so consistently present that nearly every perception is flavored in a similar fashion and our responding behaviors take on a consistency to match (Davison, 1959). A need for recognition or a need to control will probably not alter greatly from one situation to the next. Thus, we become predictable within a group. Similarly, groups become predictable in their perceptions and their responding behaviors. Following is a sketch of two such groups:

Like a person, an advertising company must sell much more than is visible to the naked eye. It must sell confidence, and an aura of competence that may or may not be justified. Communication is the key to the entire enterprise. The Standish Agency is no exception. One walks through the door and immediately loses sight of his shoe tops in four-inch carpeting. He is surrounded by rich wood paneling and beautiful women, the latter looking busy indeed. An atmosphere of coolly directed business among the immediacy of copy deadlines pervades the office. The visitor is attacked from every sense: visually, tactilely, emotionally. Taken into the unbelievably plush offices of the directors, he is surprised by their youthful dress, their easy manner, and their good humor amid all the work that is obviously being done. One is totally submerged in a feeling of efficiency, youth, up-to-dateness, and, above all, success. Just being there raises one above the ordinary, and one almost believes he belongs in this atmosphere.

But what kind of communication lies behind the fantasy world of the front office? Actually, there are two worlds: the businesslike, efficient, Madison Avenue world of the directors and account executives who sell and maintain the advertising product; and the freewheeling, loose-hanging, liberal world of the creative team upon whom, eventually, all success depends. The two groups, each numbering about 12, need each other and theoretically work closely together in creating meaningful "concepts" and designing means of expressing them. Whereas the creative group tend to be liberals, the executives are conservative; whereas the executives tend to *act* and *look* young, the creative staff tend to *be* young; whereas the executives reflect an unabashed desire to make profits and succeed, the creative people live in a world where the clever, artistic, and creative job is itself enough reward. They constantly find themselves justifying their own existence in such an "artificial" and "materialistic" environment and extol their own pure motivations in a system that owns neither their souls nor skills.

When members of the executive group sit down with members of the creative team (artist or writer), it is almost impossible for them to communicate except along clearly defined job lines. Usually such meetings are avoided until the last possible moment, when the pressure of time becomes an added factor in the tension that permeates the session. The executive desires a product that will sell, while the writer wants a product that clearly represents his own abilities and creative thoughts. The executive expects a product in the shortest possible time, while the creative person resists (overtly or covertly) any attempt to push what must be by its very nature a spontaneous and unstudied process. The executive has talked with the client, but often the creative person has not, since he might prove an embarrassment with his long hair, outlandish clothes, and lack of understanding of the business aspects of advertising. Conversely, the writer or artist regularly interjects the feeling that it takes a "creative person" to effectively take part in the creative process. Moreover, the executive has more prestige, makes more money, and receives the visible appreciation of a job well done. Although the creative group is relatively well paid for their services, they constantly feel the tensions inevitable in a "master-slave" relationship.

It is within this environment that ideas have to be communicated. The carpeting, the paneled walls, the beautiful secretarial artifacts mean little if effective communication fails to exist between these two groups. In a way, the problems here cut across the human life line of every group: status, influence, control, philosophy, dress, acceptance and personal worth, goals—each one in itself a potential source of tension. Together they succeed in stifling the potential of each to help the other. A dozen times a day stereotypes are reinforced, jokes and strategies generated at the expense of the other. Individual and group separateness is insured as each views the other through the jaundiced eye of personal needs. Each group and each individual must justify its existence.

In a group it appears that individual stereotypes feed on themselves, and we rapidly turn for support to those we believe share our own views (Kelley, 1951; Slater, 1955). The screening is quick, lightning fast, as we size up the opposition, gently test the climate, and feed the "vibrations" of other members into our own sorting system. We seek structure and support for our own insecurities in any situation we fail to understand or control. Especially in a group, where our roles are not determined clearly in advance, it is natural to seek confirmation that we are not alone, that there are potential allies among the strange faces (Festinger, 1950; Loomis, 1959). It takes but a few minutes to scan the superficial cues and sort out those with whom we can feel either safe or threatened, those with energy, anger, insecurity, power, softness, frayed nerves, or humor. We make our predictions and then spend a good part of our energy proving that we are correct. The tapping fingers, nervous smile, loud talk, tightly folded arms, cultivated friendliness, reading in the face of potential conversation, unabashed sharing of one's self to a stranger—these and a thousand pieces of instant information are sifted, labeled, and shelved for later use in our effort to confirm our own identities and understand others in the group. They are used as evidence and, in the long run, can be just as destructive as helpful in the development of the group and our relationships within it.

Unless we are ready to test the untested assumptions upon which we base our perceptions, it can be assumed that there will be many breakdowns in communications. The problem, of course, is that if we attempted to test many of our assumptions about people, we would find it very difficult to classify them, stereotype them, or pigeonhole them. We would feel so much less secure much of the time because we would constantly have to adjust to "other realities." Life would be so much more complex. The fact is that a person is a thousand things, but, first and foremost, he is what we want him to be in relation to our own needs. He is fat, hostile, irrational, Jewish, lethargic, smart, black, paranoid, handsome, homosexual, militant. We take a very specific word with a very narrow definition and frame another complex human being.

In the eyes of many blacks and some whites Malcolm X was black, militant, angry, heathen, bearded, a convict and revolutionist. The superficial data available about him easily fed the narrowest of stereotypes since in many cases it was the only information accessible or, just as often, the only information sought. However, to millions of blacks, Malcolm X was also a sensitive speaker, a person who had raised himself from the miseries of a cancerous ghetto existence to a new life, to a role of leadership and influence. He neither drank nor smoked and was devoted to his religious beliefs. He was articulate and emotional and provided a clear avenue of insight into the lives of thousands, maybe millions, of blacks in this country. His own perseverance and brilliance pushed him far beyond the reach of a ninth-grade education and into a role that was an expression of freedom and potency for some and fear and intimidation for others. Which set of data a person chose is based upon a complex maze of inner forces resulting from one's experience, personal history, and access to the man.

For many a white man to accept the words of Malcolm X about the course of life, it would require a recognition of realities so difficult to face and so long ignored that it could shake his very ability to accept himself. It would mean that there might be hope for so many of those wild youth of the ghetto who go about killing themselves. It might mean a recognition of the fact that doors have been closed, that responsibility lies outside the ghetto. And what does a man do with the guilt that he generates?

For the black man it can also create dilemmas since it forces many to reappraise their own anger, to persevere among their people, to act out of black brotherhood rather than in terms of white hatred, to take pieces of life and fit them into a pattern of action and personal constraint with dedication to living. And what does a man do with the guilt that he generates?

If either a black or white man can infuse into his own stereotype of the black man the essence of hope, potential, and integrity that is being communicated, it would have profound implications for that individual. Every group has such a man—a person who appears distorted, but who is really manipulated by the eye of the beholder. He may intimidate through flaming rhetoric or piercing silence. And we may create an image out of expectations and fail to sift through the defenses of our own seared egos to find the real message—the real man who may be a builder and not a destroyer. How many heard the message of Malcolm X when he said:

> I believe that it would be almost impossible to find anywhere in America a black man who has lived further down in the mud of human society than I have; or a black man who has been any more ignorant than I have; or a black man who has suffered more anguish during his life than I have. But it is only after the deepest darkness that the greatest joy can come; it is only after slavery and prison that the sweetest appreciation of freedom can come.
>
> . . . My greatest lack has been, I believe, that I don't have the kind of academic education I wish I had been able to get—to have been a lawyer, perhaps. I do believe that I might have made a good lawyer. I have always loved verbal battle and challenge. You can believe me that if I had the time right now I would not be one bit ashamed to go back into any New York City public school and start where I left off at the ninth grade, and go through a degree . . . I would just like to study. I mean ranging study, because I have a wide open mind, I'm interested in almost any subject you can mention. . . . (Malcolm X, 1964, pp. 379–380)

A Theoretical Viewpoint

Just as we select and organize simple physical stimuli in a manner that is easiest and most convenient for us, so too we organize the complexities of human behavior in similar ways. A number of simple concepts developed by the Gestalt psychologists in relation to physical stimuli can be used to help understand what occurs when people get together in a group (Kohler, 1947). For example, we tend to create figure ground relationships. In any one perceptual field (all the stimuli we are able to see at one time), certain figures are drawn forward into positions of dominance while others recede to form the background of the scene. In many cases, which objects are reduced to the background and which are drawn forward is dependent on the immediate needs of the viewer. For example, in the famous picture of the old lady–young lady composite a person will "allow himself" to see one figure while the other forms a part of the background for the former. Similarly, in a group certain individuals will form a natural backdrop while others, for a variety of reasons, remain a clear part of the foreground. (A facsimile of the old lady–young lady composite is included in the Instructor's Manual.)

Following this line of thought, there is a tendency to group objects into a "natural order," thus making it easier to establish relationships out of the immediate confusion in a scene. The mind struggles to achieve order by grasping similarities that appear to be present or by perceiving certain continuities in the stimuli presented. This process of organization may take place when looking at dots on a piece of paper or individuals in a group. Using size, sex, clothes, tone of voice, posture, and many other cues, we proceed to subtly organize the group into a variety of composite groupings. This ordering is merely a convenience, a way of handling the enormous amount of data that suddenly confront us at any one moment in time.

Another concept discussed originally by the Gestaltists concerns the tendency to take incomplete data and organize it into a meaningful whole. Thus, an incomplete circle will more often than not be seen by people as a full circle rather than a curved line. Apparently, we have a need to bring "closure" to objects within our perceptual field. In looking at the participants in a group we will take the data they put forth such as voice, verbal gestures, and dress, then add our own stereotypes, and in this way develop a "complete" picture of the person. We bring closure on the incomplete object (in this case a person) and, in a sense, fill in the missing pieces so that we can more easily contend with the previously unknown commodity. By putting all the clues together into a meaningful package, we are better able to have a relationship that is consistent and comfortable to us. It provides a means of gaining a measure of safety for us in what is, perhaps, an incomplete, strange, and uncomfortable situation.

It has also been suggested that there is a tendency to take the various stimuli and focus on one set of stimuli which appears to be "good" in terms of similarity, continuity, closure, and symmetry. According to this concept, for example, we will immediately be attracted to those in a group who tend to "fit" our perception of a "good" group member, those who are least threatening to us and tend to create the least dissonance in terms of our own values and goals within the group.

If we were not able to impose this kind of order on the group and certain of its members, the situation might prove to be unbearably tense and difficult. Thus, if we are quiet and shy, we may seek order and some relief in the group by discovering those who are the least abrasive or dominating and those who show the greatest restraint. In this way we can bring harmony to a dissonant situation; we can seek allies and support in fact or in fantasy.

Our propensity to organize a group in a manner that is most comforting to us can prove to be a distinct liability to effective communication. It often generates inflexibility, restricted routes of information, and a need to verify and then justify our initial perceptions. As a result, we often begin with two strikes against us in our efforts to achieve understanding and insight into group processes. A first step, of course, is to confront the significance of our own feelings and uncover some of the untested assumptions and stereotypes that are helping to influence our behaviors.

The fact that we hear what we wish to hear and draw on assumptions to support the view we wish to follow is vividly portrayed below.

Even in modern Mexico, the relations an adolescent girl develops with young men is severely restricted by numerous family rules and careful chaperoning. Between organized religion and the extended arm of the family, it is the rare girl who will risk disgrace among these groups and break the cultural norms surrounding sexual behavior. Nevertheless, the Mexican male, perhaps because of these very restrictions on his avenues of conquest, often perceives himself as an invincible lover.

In recent years many young American girls in their late teens have been visiting Mexican cities during summer vacations. They have proven to be most vulnerable to the bravado of the Mexican male, which among the Mexican girls is accepted with some equanimity and good humor. When the Mexican male tells the young and eager American lass of her great beauty, his undying love and passion, he is responding as much to the demands of *his* role as he is to the young lady. But the poor girl, so unaccustomed to such energetic pursuit, rapture, and the *machismo* of the Latin lover, hears only the words and the love she desires. And, again, for him there is the forbidden fruit, an opportunity to prove his real style in a field of combat usually closed to him. The result is often disaster for the unsuspecting girl who is left crushed by the sudden realization of just what the words meant.

In this example, illusions were created out of words and dreams—two of the greatest sources of misinterpretation in the communication process.

Language = Words; Communication = Men

It has often been said that only men and not words have any meaning in people's attempts to communicate (Fabun, 1965). Unless a person is able to probe behind the easily flowing façade of words that screen us from one another, he will remain confused and often out of touch. So often it is the gesture, tone, inflection, posture, or eye contact that holds the key to the real message, while the "clear," seemingly unambiguous words merely provide false starts and dead ends to the unwary listener. Even when we think we understand the meaning behind a word, there are usually three or four possible variations in meaning that could fit nicely into the sentence. Usually we draw upon the intent we believe the speaker has in mind. It's "hard" to imagine that a simple word such as *hard* has 17 possible definitions (Webster, 1953). Among other things, that one word can describe the solidity of coal, the earnestness of a student, the difficulty of a test, the severity of a man's disposition, the penetrating power of an x ray, or the parsimony of an old man. There are so many subtle innuendoes that flavor language and require a personal definition before they can be translated into the context of a particular statement. Often what we end up with is nothing more than a makeshift assemblage of words spiced with half-known definitions and a variety of feelings. What eventually transpires depends upon the web created out of past experience, definitions, language skills, expectations, speed and clarity of the words spoken, and the general psychological climate that exists. How often we are led off the trail because we simply do not have enough information and drift further away rather than closer to the actual meaning. On the other hand, when history and experience are on our side, when we are familiar with the nonverbal communication that accompanies the words, then the group in which we are participating may respond in near unison to a message which to the casual listener may mean just the opposite. The following is an example of how predictable patterns of behavior resulted in very specific communication that was just the opposite of the message intended.

A principal of a large junior high school had a sincere desire to involve his faculty in more of the school's decision-making process as well as in the implementation phase of numerous school programs. Periodically he would help sponsor a program to show the faculty his good intentions. The usual pattern was that after a brief flurry of activity on the part of those faculty involved, the effort would slowly lose momentum and 6 months or a year later the responsibility would again, somehow, be in the hands of the administration.

On one occasion it was decided that something had to happen to help control the uproar that occurred between classes. Students would enter the hall shouting, dancing, laughing, and occasionally fighting. It was difficult for teachers to even move from one class to another until after the final bell had rung. The decision was made that the faculty had to develop the necessary manpower controls among themselves and take the full responsibility to insure discipline during these times. Thus, teachers were assigned to proctor areas in close proximity to their classes at various times during the school day. The task was clear, and the faculty support for the idea was nearly unanimous.

For a week the system worked to near perfection. But then, strangely, there were defections in faculty responsibility and complaints began to filter into the principal's office. In an effort to save the situation, the principal and his three assistants began to patrol the halls between classes. Five more days and the program was in shambles. The pattern that eventually developed was one in which the principal, his three assistants, and a few teachers on the school faculty discipline committee would patrol the halls and, with vigorous use of authority, they developed a somewhat better (less noisy) solution than had previously existed.

But, what was the message communicated that made the failure of the program so predictable? The faculty liked the principal and knew he had good intentions. They also knew that he was absolutely compulsive about his involvement in nearly everything that took place. He simply could not leave well enough alone. The faculty knew that regardless of the well-worded statement of purpose, regardless of the

elaborate proctoring schedules, regardless of the articulate pro-
nouncement of his good intentions, it would only be a short time
before he would intervene. On the one hand, many of the faculty
were willing to give up the added burden of responsibility, thus reinforcing the principal's feelings of indispensability and the faculty's
dependency on him. On the other hand, there was a quiet but immediate resentment at his constant involvement in their affairs, in his
unwillingness to let the faculty stand accountable and suffer the
consequences. Between the dependent and counterdependent factions,
the program collapsed. Actually, it collapsed before it started. For
the faculty, the message, born out of experience, was clear. The man,
not the words, was heard.

The Impact of Conditioning on the Group

People desire to be liked and accepted. In some ways it is our
Achilles' heel, since it leaves us vulnerable to the subtle influence and
control of those from whom we seek approval. Often the pressures
pushing one to adjustment and compliance and eventual favor in the
eyes of another are not even discernible by us or the other person
(see Chapter 3 relating to group norms). There is no longer any
doubt that in our efforts to be accepted we become sensitive to the
minute behavioral clues that suggest degree of approval on the part
of the other person (Greenspoon, 1955; Verplanck, 1955). Indeed,
we are as keen as any bloodhound in ferreting out and following these
clues to acceptance. A nod of the head, the slightest murmur, a smile,
a frown, or a seemingly innocuous "mm-hmm" can put us on the
track. Although most of the research in this area of communication
has been within the context of the one-to-one relationship, there is
little doubt that the same holds true within any group where people
are concerned with their image and acceptability (Slater, 1955;
Asch, 1956; Strodtback et al., 1957). In fact, if the need is to be
accepted by seven or eight people instead of only one, it is quite
possible that we will work overtime to discover the sources of reward
in the group as well as the favored behavior. This, in turn, alters
communication patterns and overt behavior within the group. A
group of 10 counselors who had worked for 3 weeks in a wilderness
setting developing communication and leadership skills provide a
helpful example.

During the first hour of their stay together the 10 strangers were
confronted with a 10-foot wall and told that they had 1 minute to
plan how they were to get all of their members over the wall in the

shortest possible time. This was a harrowing thought for a group that spanned an age difference of 25 years, came in all assorted shapes and sizes, and had previously done little more than shake hands with one another. After 30 seconds of stunned disbelief and nervous laughter, the group managed to mobilize itself in some fashion. Then, by pulling, pushing, shoving, twisting, and turning, intermingled with appropriate grunts and moans, they successfully completed the task. The group was ecstatic over their triumph and at that moment seemed to become more than a collection of individuals.

Near the end of the program it was intimated that the group would again have to go over the wall on the final day—this time in competition with another group of counselors. That news was met with loud groans, but the group, by then, had been through so much together that they felt they were ready for nearly any challenge. They truly believed that they had worked through every possible communication problem. At this point a lone member (who was also the heaviest member of the group) quietly stated that he would not go over the wall a second time. The initial calm, almost courteous acceptance of the group, soon gave way to feelings of broken trust, being let down, rejected. Questions of true solidarity and support were raised. Worse for the group was the fact that the dissenting member had always been one of the most cooperative and helpful participants. Without ever confronting him directly with their thoughts, it was clear that nearly everyone was feeling, "How could he let us down like this?"

The issue was never resolved and after an hour of tense, indirect discussion, nothing more was said. On the final day at the moment of decision, the individual quietly capitulated and joined in. The response from the group was one of shared guilt and the wish that he had not participated. Many had come to the realization that while the group had developed tremendous internal strength and mutual cooperation, they had done it at the expense of individual opinion and free will. In discussing the problem it became clear that the group had subtly conditioned itself to negate dissonant ideas or opinions. They agreed that until they were free to accept all forms of communication, their very "groupness" was a hollow lie based on subtle coercion and manipulation.

Factors Inhibiting Communication in a Group

The communication patterns within any group can be greatly influenced by four factors (NTL, 1969). First of all, unless a person is extraordinarily selfless in a group, his primary aim is to "survive" without loss of personal integrity—if possible, to enhance himself in his own eyes and the eyes of others. Thus, each of us is forever bound up in the issue of our own personal needs and goals. They may have very little to do with the stated needs and goals of the group, but unless the group can provide vehicles to personal self-fulfillment, there will be a move by the individual to remove himself psychologically or physically from participation.

Secondly, and closely related to the issue of personal needs and goals, is the question of identity. Every participant in a group has to answer the questions, "Who am I to be in this group, what image am I going to project for these people, and what roles will I undertake to insure this image?" In some cases our behavioral response to these questions is very natural, while in others it is strategic. Usually we desire acceptance in the best possible light, although we all know individuals who actually try to generate a negative image and, thus, reinforce their own expectation of rejection.

A third issue faced consciously or unconsciously by every group member involves power, influence, and control. Who has power, how is it used, to what degree are others invited to share this power? All these questions are responded to in some overt or covert manner by the individual participant. Whether his response is facilitative or destructive to the group process depends again on an individual's particular needs and the realities of the particular group.

Finally, not only is personal identity important to establish, but the acceptance of one's self by other members is essential. A great deal depends on our willingness to risk ourselves intellectually and emotionally within the group. How intimate will I allow myself to become with these people? How much will I share my own limitations and strengths? Of course, much depends on how strong the group is, how much an individual wishes to be a part of it, and how vulnerable he will allow himself to become. The more an individual feels accepted, the more willing he will be to risk deeper and potentially more fulfilling involvement.

Thus, the issues of goals, personal identification, power, and intimacy will influence the developing communication patterns within any group. How much we speak, to whom we speak, whether we speak defensively or openly, and how much we hear will all be influenced by the emergence of these factors. If we feel controlled, limited in our own potency, inadequate, unable to fulfill our own needs, or unable to develop meaningful relationships among those present, communication will be influenced in several ways. We may passively withdraw resources that might otherwise be offered to the group. We may actively strike out against the source of obstruction to us, or, finally, we may attempt to forge relationships with individuals perceived as least threatening and a source of support. To deny the existence of these issues and their possible repercussions is to bury one's head in the sand of wishful thinking. They are present and must be dealt with if an effective climate for communication is to develop (Gibb, 1961).

Recently a group of executives met for 3 days to explore team building among themselves and how they might pass their own experiences along to subordinates in the plant. It became immediately evident that although the group seemed to have an extraordinarily good social rapport, they were enormously dependent on the director of the group. Seven of the eight members were young and fairly inexperienced in managerial roles. The director was perhaps 7 years older than the group average; he was personable, open, quick to learn, and clearly desirous of sharing the decision-making process and leadership within the group.

However, fully 75 percent of all verbal communication went to him, with much of the remainder going to the one person in the group he felt was most competent. This pattern of communication had developed over a period of a year and resulted (a) from the director's obvious knowledge of the company's technical operation and (b) from a tradition within the company of unilateral decisions from the top. After 3 days of working together and analyzing their own communication and decision-making patterns, considerable progress was apparent. New lines of communication had opened within the group and shared leadership was accepted more in fact than in idea.

On the final day of the workshop, the men were joined by their wives for a picnic. The director thought it would be helpful if the wives knew what had occurred during the long weekend and how the laboratory method of learning had been instrumental in this process. Thus, the wives, who had never been together as a group prior to this time, removed themselves for an hour and together explored briefly many of the concepts discussed by their husbands. At one point, all of the wives were asked to solve a mathematical problem individually and having once committed themselves to an individual answer, they were asked to agree to one answer among themselves. Speed was important, and it appeared that they were in some way competing as a group with their husbands—even in their absence.

Except in one case, the pattern of communication that developed during this brief period of group problem solving paralleled that which occurred in the husbands' group. Approximately 75 percent of all the verbal communication either came from or was directed to the wife of the director and the wife of the second ranking executive (although there was no official designation of such a hierarchy). Similarly, the two women who contributed least were wives of men who felt least secure or satisfied in the group and who communicated very little during the initial stages of the 3-day workshop.

The women were quite free to discuss the implications of the data. It was strongly suggested that each one of them was well aware of the presence of the "director's wife" and that they were willing to give her the reins. The fact that she was a strong person and willing to take them did not hinder the process. They were also aware of the general pecking order that existed among the men and were willing to defer to a similar pattern among themselves during this period rather than create any waves for their husbands.

For these women, even though the group was of the most temporary nature, the issues of personal identification (am I me or my husband's wife?), goals (do I push beyond the stated task?), power (do I fight the natural and inherited power of the director's wife?), and intimacy (do I wish to develop relationships outside the formal work roles defined by my husband?) were forced to the surface. As a group, they came with certain expectations, picked up cues of dominance and submission, and then proceeded to reinforce those attitudes almost immediately. The behavior and communication patterns that evolved would eventually create some of the same tensions and problems faced by their husbands. There is little doubt that had the women not known "to whom they belonged," the initial interaction would have been different just as it is fairly certain that, given more time, other needs would begin to take precedence as the fear of influencing their husbands' positions diminished.

How Tension and Defensiveness Arise
in the Communication Process

If an individual desired to create problems in communication, there seem to be certain tried and true behaviors that will most assuredly help him on his way (Gibb, 1961; Rogers and Roethlisberger, 1952). A first step would be to keep people from expressing their own ideas. People have a simple need to be heard, to have their ideas made visible. To have them accepted is desirable, yet not always possible. However, not to be even recognized or heard is an intolerable situation for most of us. Thus, there will be tension in a group if it is dominated by a few vociferous individuals while others listen passively. Whenever participants feel that a group is out of their control and in the possession of others, the atmosphere is likely to deteriorate.

Closely linked to this situation is one in which an individual responds with such certainty and force that only a full-scale verbal war would change his opinion. People naturally don't like to be pushed. Sometimes individuals in a group will attack a position in which they basically believe merely because one person has taken a "too certain" opposing viewpoint.

Even though we spend much time and energy evaluating people and events, if there is one thing that puts us on guard, it is the feeling that *we* are being evaluated by *others*. We are so used to judging the person along with the idea that we tend to become supersensitive to the same treatment. It is such a short step from the words: "Do you really believe that idea?" to the translation in one's mind: "How could you possibly be so stupid as to believe that idea?" In a group where our need for acceptance increases, the feeling that we are being personally judged is a sure way of developing internal friction. Similarly, if we feel someone is placing himself above us in some sort of superior position, an immediate response is to prove to the world that this individual is "not that good." Quite often we find ourselves responding on the inside to the sharp but barely perceptible cues of superiority from another person.

Communication is also damaged when individuals do not trust the group enough to share what they really feel or think. The problem, of course, is that when we fail to express our feelings, others tend to "read into" this lack of expression what they "believe" we are feeling or thinking. More often than not the small streak of paranoia in each of us translates this neutral behavior into a negative perception. This behavior as well as other strategies that hide one's real self from the group will predictably result in defensive reactions by those on the receiving end. The diagram on page 19 reveals the subtleties involved in this complex process.

Bill's response to John's statement is partly the result of the selection of words, the context in which they are spoken, and his image of John as well as all the nonverbal cues he gets from the tone of voice, gestures, and posture. Also, the nature of the statement is partly the

Statement by John: "Yes, but Bill, that's impossible. I've been here for 5 years, and I've never known that to work. Have you thought of the fact that . . ."

John feels:	*John as perceived by Bill:*
Reasonable	⟶ Evaluative, judging
Correct	⟶ Superior
Having heard Bill	⟶ Certain
I've got him backing up	⟶ Controlling
The group is with me	
He's probably angry; you never know with Bill	

Bill feels:	*Bill's eventual response:*
What's he mean "yes"?	⟶ Withdrawal
He never even heard me.	⟶ Neutrality
If it's impossible, I wouldn't have said it.	⟶ Passive hostility
Big deal—5 years—he doesn't know everything.	
It's impossible to be right against him.	
He can sure make a person feel stupid.	
Obviously I've thought about it.	
It's always a fact coming from him.	
I'll bet everyone agrees with him.	
I should just keep quiet—that's better than looking stupid.	

Impact on Group: Unresolved hostility
Other members afraid to venture out against John
Those sympathetic to Bill strengthen their protective subgroup.

result of John's response to Bill's particular behavioral strategy with him (in this case neutrality). The result is a predictable increase in what Jack Gibb (1961) would call "defensive communication." Part of the problem obviously lies in John's insensitivity to Bill and in Bill's tendency to read more into the words than was actually intended. Worse than this is the fact that the underlying issues build in a cumulative fashion, which results in increased tension, deteriorated communication, greater polarization among group members, and less inclination to resolve these emotional roadblocks.

Feedback: A Means of Reducing Distortions in the Communication Process

The more group communication is allowed to be spontaneous and open the more the participants will be willing to recognize the perceptual distortions that develop and the behaviors that cause defensive responses. At any given time we see ourselves communicating a particular "content" message as well as an image of ourselves. Just as we often fail to communicate the verbal message of our intent, so too we fail to communicate the person or image we wish to bring to the group. In most groups, however, neither of these two levels is clarified for us and we can only assume the degree to which we were effective. We like to think that we are effective in our efforts, and it can be quite threatening to discover how often we are not. We are torn between a real desire to confront ourselves with how we are actually perceived (both at content and image levels) and our desire to live with the image we think or would like to think we are projecting.

The *feedback process* (Leavitt and Mueller, 1951) within a group is nothing more than a concerted effort on the part of the participants to communicate in a manner that insures the least possible distortion between a person's intent and the message actually received by others. At one level it involves making certain that the technical information is reaching the receiver—which can occur if a listener paraphrases the essence of the message. This process of clarification not only involves the listener actively but also allows the speaker the opportunity to adjust his presentation. It is immediate, descriptive, and almost mechanical in nature. However, even this process requires an atmosphere of trust and support or else the speaker may hold off for fear of invoking criticism.

Expanding the process beyond the level of simple content and including more emotional aspects of the meeting, one begins to tread on softer and less reliable ground. In most groups the feedback process can be used to best advantage as a means of clearing the air, providing the opportunity to shift course or procedures, and raising important issues which could not easily be explored during the give-and-take of the meeting. It is possible to begin the process gently. For example, after a meeting the participants can spend a few minutes discussing what might be handled differently the next time in order to insure a more effective meeting. In this way the process can focus on future behavior and events and not just on the behavior that hindered the present meeting. It requires the participants to develop effective modes of future behavior and a constructive attitude toward their own efforts. Similarly, without becoming too personal, the participants might each jot down on a piece of paper a specific type of behavior they feel was facilitative in the meeting as well as one that inhibited the progress of the group. The use of such immediate information can prepare a group to accept more readily specific information relating to individual behaviors. It can also increase the members' desire to solicit information about their own effectiveness. It is out of this search for personal learning and improvement that a climate of increasing support and openness will develop. Eventually it is possible for the group to develop enough trust so that the feedback process becomes an integral and unobtrusive part of the entire meeting, with members responding at both a feeling and content level and checking out their own perceptions with others in the group.

There is, of course, the possibility that feedback can become of greater importance to the members than the task facing the group. There is no doubt that the process can itself become distorted, inappropriately personal, and an actual imposition if mishandled. One way to control this situation is occasionally to appoint a member of the group as observer and nonparticipant. A brief descriptive report after the meeting can provide a stimulus for the group to reassess its own working goals and priorities. Of greatest importance is that the use of feedback not be imposed because it will inevitably create even more tensions and divisiveness and actually inhibit the very communication channels that the group is attempting to open.

Poor Communication: The Rule, Not the Exception

If one would take a cross-section of American institutions, it is likely that breakdowns in communication are one of the primary sources of internal conflict and stress. Spend a day in a mental health institution and it soon becomes clear that the administration communicates badly with the staff, psychiatrists with psychologists, doctors with nurses, and nurses with day-care workers. Somewhere in the labyrinth of status, roles, job descriptions, and the multitude of internal conflicts that exist, help is given to the resident patient. There are, of course, those exceptional institutions where hierarchical power struggles are minimized, where role differentiation in terms of status is limited, and where, as a result, communication channels remain relatively uncluttered.

The same can be said in much of industry, although strange as it may seem to some, industry has generally provided leadership in areas of communication specifically and organizational development in general. At what appears to be the other end of the continuum (definitely a subjective perception), there are huge communication problems in organized religion. Between priests and bishops, religious and lay people, sisters and priests, and even between religious orders there are often fragmented lines of communication.

And then there are the schools. Perhaps nowhere is there a better example of tensions that exist because of the communication process. It touches every level, but most pointedly it is present in the classroom. Most of us have been part of classroom "groups" for between 10 and 12 years of our lives. How well the lesson is learned, how well the tradition is carried into other groups. And what a price is paid in terms of efficiency, motivation, and personal identity. There are some exceptions, but they remain exceptions. The following conditions in education do exist in other institutions, but the school system is something we have all experienced firsthand.

1. Communication is one way—from a source of information to the receiver who can ask for clarification, but he is seldom in a position to transfer his learnings to others be they younger students or age peers.

2. In the classroom group the goals of learning are seldom established by the participants or even with them, but, instead, by an outside power source.

3. Rather than being shared, leadership is usually held tightly in the hands of the "responsible" person.

4. The participants are held accountable only for content information—usually in the form of an evaluative examination which labels

individuals according to performance in terms of discrete letters or numbers.

5. While held accountable in content areas, the participants are seldom held accountable in other areas, such as discipline and decision making, which are relevant to them.

6. The faculty are not held accountable for their performance in terms of the student participants. This lack of a two-way evaluation increases distance between student and teacher.

7. Rather than being perceived as an important resource to be used effectively by the classroom group, the teacher is established as *the* resource person.

8. Often the internal climate is highly competitive and sets student against student rather than stressing the educational venture as a cooperative one.

9. The communication of information from the students to the teacher is usually, for a variety of reasons, through a relatively small number of students.

With a very slight shift in titles and certain terms, the situation described here could easily be transferred to small groups within a variety of institutions. Obviously, it would be simplistic to say that by changing communication patterns, all these conditions would change. Nevertheless, research in the area of small groups suggests a variety of logical alternatives that could make for a more open communication.

Factors Influencing Communication

Group leaders, for example, are often hesitant to spend (waste) time developing interpersonal relations in a group where the goals are clearly defined around specific tasks (Slater, 1955; Grace, 1956). Thus, a program director may have a regularly scheduled 3-hour meeting every week (150 hours over a year) for his staff and never spend any time strengthening the communication process or exploring ways to improve interpersonal relations within the group. Similarly, a high school history teacher may spend from 3 to 5 hours a week with the same students for an entire year.

Almost any new group will be charged with tension (Crook, 1961) as individuals test out their environment and observe the various

personalities involved. It is in this early period when most communication patterns develop. Among adolescents an enormous amount of
energy is spent worrying about or defining their self-images so that
time spent early in opening lines of communication would help
reduce initial personal anxiety and develop an atmosphere of greater
support later. Groups that are attractive to their members have been
shown to be better able to control deviant behavior by their members
and to stay focused more directly on the task than less satisfied
groups (Schachter, 1951; Back, 1951; Festinger and Thibaut, 1951;
Gerard, 1953). Furthermore, there is a tendency to submerge negative
feelings and a willingness to deal with them directly and aboveboard.
Finally, as members feel increasingly satisfied with the group there is
increased participation and more flexibility in the decision-making
process. Thus, it appears that time spent initially and periodically in
improving the communication process will pay dividends in terms of
greater work efficiency (see also Decision Making and Problem
Solving in Chapter 6).

Also relevant is the notion of competition and its place in a group.
There is little doubt that a group can be drawn closer together when
competing with another group. However, there is little evidence that
the seeking of mutually exclusive rewards even in the attainment of
more general group goals is effective in producing an efficient environment for work (Deutsch, 1960). It seems that when people enter into
a task with a predefined need to be cooperative and interdependent
there is more listening, more acceptance of ideas, less possessiveness
of ideas and, in general, more communication. Within this atmosphere, the group will also tend to create achievement pressure upon
itself. Furthermore, there seems to be more attentiveness to members'
ideas and a friendlier climate than in groups where interpersonal
competition is stressed to a greater degree. As suggested earlier, all
these conditions help to make a group more attractive to its participants and will generally lead to greater group productivity.

Small Groups: What Size? What Shape?

Two-person groups often result in considerable tension, since inevitably a dominant-submissive relationship is created. When one does
not feel that he has power over another, the tendency is either to
fight the person and his ideas or to withdraw into a passive pattern

of behavior. Whatever behavior is required to balance the control component within the group will be used.

A three-person group, on the other hand, may have less tension, but only because two people will usually join forces and push their ideas into acceptance. The recognition of power through numbers decreases the resistance of the third party and allows a quicker resolution of the problem under consideration. The person in the minority may not feel good about it, but he is better able to rationalize away his own impotence given the obvious power of the opposition. Similarly, communication in odd-number groups tends to be smoother since there is not the possibility of an equal split of opinion and the resulting struggle for power.

There appears to be no magic number for a successful working group (Berelson and Steiner, 1964) since so much depends on the topic, individual personalities, motivations, and the past experience of its members. Nevertheless, a group of five or seven seems to be optimal in a number of situations since there are enough people to allow for a diversity of opinions and ideas, yet the group remains small enough to allow everyone to be heard.

However, even when one has decided on the size of a particular group, he is still faced with the question of shape or physical structure. There are several factors that need to be considered (Shaw, 1964; Bavelas, 1950):

1. Total group morale will be higher in groups in which there is more access to participation among those involved—the more open the participation, the higher the morale.

2. Efficiency tends to be lowest among groups that are the most open. Since more wrong ideas need to be sifted out, more extraneous material is generated and more time is "wasted" listening to individuals even when a point has been made.

3. Groups that are most efficient tend to be those in which all members have access to a central leadership figure who can act as an expediter and clarifier as well as keep the group on the right track in working through the problem.

4. Positions that individuals take can have a definite influence upon leadership in the group as well as on potential conflict among group members.

5. Groups with centralized leadership (see 3 above) tend to organize more rapidly, be more stable in performance, and show greater efficiency. However, morale also tends to drop and this, in the long run, could influence its stability and even productivity (Hearn, 1957; Glazer and Glazer, 1961).

It is clear that communication and the decision-making process are influenced by the physical structure (communication nets) that develop in any group, and it, in turn, helps to determine the success of the group (efficiency) as well as how satisfied the participants are in the experience. This communication pattern influences behavior, accuracy, satisfaction, and the potential emergence of leadership (Slater, 1958; Heise and Miller, 1951).

If one selects a circle that insures a relatively high degree of openness (access to participation), behavior will tend to be more erratic, participation will be greater, organization will be slow, and errors greater. It is possible, however, that the satisfaction gained by the participants from being heard and having their ideas made visible may prove beneficial in the long run as members develop interest, trust, more attraction for the group, and, eventually, greater efficiency in their work efforts.

Groups where the lines of communication are clear from the beginning and where relations with authority are specified tend to be more productive in terms of completing task objectives. The price for this, of course, is a reduction in the amount of information shared and a subsequent increase in the dependency upon the person(s) in authority. In the short run, it is doubtful that tension and resentment in such groups would be inhibiting when the concern for completing a task is greatest. However, in the long run, such communication patterns may well create numerous problems as individual frustrations build up with no legitimate ways for venting them.

Thus, a dilemma. One may choose greater leader control and efficiency at the price of lower morale and participation. Or, it is possible to choose higher morale and group satisfaction at the price of efficiency. The answer would seem to be a combination of the two, but it seems to be the rare person who is able to encourage sharing and full participation and still impose the restrictions desired to help maximize the operation of the group. Such a role is by no means impossible if the individual is aware of the many difficulties and traps when, for example, some individuals demand more structure and guidance, while others seek absolute freedom from restrictions. That there are no easy answers is suggested in the following example.

A meeting was planned for about 40 individuals to help introduce them to one another as well as orient them for a large convention involving 20,000 people the next day. The room was capable of seating nearly 250 people and chairs were arranged in rows. In order to alter the sterile environment, the program director changed the chairs around in a manner that would be more conducive for informal talking and getting to know one another. Thus, the chairs in the front of the room were rearranged to form loosely grouped circles of about five chairs each. Barriers were then arranged so that the chairs in the back of the room could not be reached.

When the director arrived 5 minutes before the meeting was scheduled to begin, he found his efforts to no avail. No one was sitting in the front of the room, and, as a result of much effort on the part of a number of individuals, the chairs in the back were now accessible and occupied. It was clear that the participants came to be talked to, that they felt more comfortable in straight rows and with a minimum of contact with one another, regardless of the publicized nature of the meeting. To meet and listen in straight rows, to not interact, to remain strangers in the group until drawn together by the force of a task, and to remain "comfortable" while being fed information are all the result of past conditioning. For the director to have allowed the situation to remain as it was would probably have resulted in many of the participants' leaving dissatisfied with the formal and structured nature of the program. To have moved them out of their security would have risked incurring a negative reaction as individuals became less secure and more dependent on themselves and not the authority.

The Influence of Status and Power on Communication[1]

A meeting is about to begin and we look around and say to ourselves, "Say, isn't this an interesting looking group. I believe everyone from the janitor on up is here." And then the chairman of the meeting says: "This should be a great experience today having so many different people with so many diverse points of view to talk together. I hope everyone feels as free as I do to express exactly what's on his mind. After all, that's why we're here, isn't it?"

The uncomfortable silence that follows is unnerving, but it captures the mood of impending failure. Unless extraordinary precautions are

[1] See Hurwitz et al., 1968; Pepitone and Reichling, 1955; Mills, 1967.

woven into a carefully planned program, the expected will occur. And the expected is that communication among those present will be dramatically influenced by the perceived status of individuals in the group. It has been shown that when high-status individuals are present in a group, both high- and low-status individuals direct their communication to them (Hurwitz et al., 1968). It is the high-status individuals who will tend to be accepted more, and they will find it easier and to their advantage to speak more. Similarly, because low-status participants don't value acceptance by their own status peers, they will often avoid association with one another during the meeting. Rather, they will wait until later to express their own feelings and attitudes concerning the proceedings. Also, since there is a general fear of evaluation by those with power (Kelley, 1951), it can be expected that those lacking it will take few risks, generally speak inconsequentially, and avoid candidness in their statements. Because of this expected trend in behavior, it becomes even more difficult to contribute if one lacks power, since considerably more attention will be given to each contribution by a low-status person. This in turn will only increase his fears of intimidation and critical evaluation. The cycle is further extended by the probability that those with influence will hesitate to reveal any of their limitations or personal vulnerability among those with lesser influence, thus lending an artificial quality to the whole proceeding.

So it is that status and power talk to status and power, with others tending to become observers in the process. What appears to be voluntary silence may be subtly imposed by the group. Unless it is legitimate to "draw in" those pushed to the periphery by the sheer power present, they will tend to feel an increasing sense of impotence. This may not occur if the individual is able to share vicariously the ideas and influence of a person with high status. But even the individual who participates least in the group has feelings about what is going on, has ideas that could be a contribution to the discussion, and, most of all, a desire to feel worthwhile. However, just as certainly he may also lack the skills, trust, and energy to overcome the obstacles to his communication.

It is not forced participation that is essential, but an atmosphere in which an individual really feels his contribution is desired and his ideas perceived not as "interesting" but rather *with real interest*. It does not occur when a high-status person is suddenly aware that he has obviously avoided John throughout the discussion and now wishes to recoup with a condescending question like, "Well, John, what do you think?" And then John, called into action with no real choice, can only stammer (as expected) a few simple comments, more because he wants to get the group off his back than because the words really represent his opinion.

It is always amazing when a group of ten or so is involved in a heated discussion among three or four individuals with the greatest status and overt involvement and someone suggests that it might be helpful to spend a few minutes in twos and threes discussing progress up to that point. Usually the noise level in the group goes up tenfold, as individuals who have not talked but suddenly realize they have a brief time to express themselves in a less inhibiting situation, pour forth ideas and feelings. It is not that they had nothing to say previously, but the atmosphere in the group simply did not allow a free expression of their ideas. Even among individuals skilled in working with groups, it takes a concerted effort to push beyond immediate needs and sources of gratification, and, instead, seek and actually cultivate opportunities for participation. This process does not seem to evolve naturally—there are too many personal needs in the way.

Conclusion

The purpose of this chapter has not been to impart great wisdom concerning perception and communication in a group. Rather, it has been to focus upon the painfully obvious: an increased awareness of the *process* underlying group endeavors. It is not necessary to print great lists of "how tos" since the awareness of what is happening is the first and largest step in correcting some of the obvious problems that exist. It is an awareness of ourselves at both a feeling and behavioral level, and then an awareness of what is happening among other group members that is most important. Thus, the prescriptions are missing and so too, hopefully, is the moralizing. Communication problems do exist, but they are merely reflective of our own fallibility and the extent of our needs whenever we get together with others. For that very reason communication is difficult but very possible to improve.

Exercise 1
The Three-Stage Rocket:
An Exercise in Listening and Speaking Precisely

Objectives

To stimulate participants to listen more carefully

To develop skills in the feedback of verbal content

To help in the clear and succinct expression of ideas

To increase one's awareness of nonverbal cues in the communication process

Rationale

We are forever in a hurry to say what must be said and to be listened to in return. We expect instant attention on the part of others and an alert response to *our* responses. However, we are so busy formulating our own ideas, preparing rebuttals, and thinking beyond the person who is speaking (with the same expectations) that we often fail to hear the message he is sending our way. As a result, some people feel that expending energy in the conversation is senseless, and withdraw; others try to make their point by overwhelming the other person with words. Neither response is very effective.

Setting

The group is divided into sets of three persons. The facilitator may want this group to be with participants who are unfamiliar with one another, or with individuals who communicate regularly. There is a tendency for a structured activity to be more effective if the individuals who are working together in the skill session are not the best of friends. Among strangers the norm is usually to participate, while among friends it is easy to become sidetracked. Individuals within the three-person groups are labeled *A, B,* and *C.* The three stages of this session can easily take between 45 minutes and an hour including discussion. It is assumed that the participants have been having some difficulty communicating or in some other way have been readied for the exercise. This might be nothing more than talking with the group about the factors that make simple verbal communication such a difficult task (i.e., poor speech, saying too much, not listening). The facilitator then asks for two participants to demonstrate an activity that will help focus more directly on the problem, and a topic is selected in which they can comfortably take opposite sides. He then establishes the rule that each individual must recapitulate what the other has said to his satisfaction before he is able to express an idea or opinion of his own. Thus, person *A* opens with a statement and person *B* must capture the essence of the message and feed it back to *A* to *A*'s satisfaction (a nod of the head is sufficient). If the feedback is not satisfactory, *B* must try again until *A* is certain that he has grasped his message. *C* (in this case the facilitator) acts as a moderator to make sure both participants are listening and recapitulating before injecting their own ideas into the conversation.

Action

Stage One   *A*s and *B*s in all the trios now begin talking (it may facilitate things if a common topic is selected) with *C* as the moderator. The facilitator should float and see that the instructions are understood. After 5 minutes, *B* talks to *C* and *A* becomes the moderator. This continues for another 5 minutes (if there is time, the facilitator may want *A* and *C* to have a chance with *B* as the moderator).

Stage Two   Another rule is imposed on the participants. The process is to continue, but a time limit is added. *A* makes a statement to *B*. Now *B* must reflect the essence of the message to *A*'s satisfaction and introduce his own idea in no more than 25 seconds. If he is unable to do so, he forfeits his chance to add his own idea. The aim is to sharpen listening and recapitulating and, at the same time, to reduce *B*'s input to just what is essential. It is important that *C* be a strict referee or else this stage of the exercise will prove ineffective. After 5 minutes or so *B* and *C* interchange in this manner and *A* is the time referee. It is possible during this second interchange (and possibly a third—between *C* and *A*) for the facilitator to have the participants sit on their hands, thus adding another restriction.

At this point, it is possible to have a brief discussion among the members of the trio concerning what has occurred up to that moment. Some facilitators, however, do not like to break up the sequence of the activity and hold off the discussion until after the third stage.

Stage Three   Now the time restriction is removed and all three participants take part equally. They are all to discuss a particular topic (by this time they will easily select a topic of interest by themselves). They must, however, still reflect upon what the speaker has said and recapitulate to the speaker's satisfaction. The new restriction is that all the participants must keep their eyes closed during this entire stage. Thus, the conversation should be relatively natural since the recapitulating will be fairly natural by then. The rationale for this stage is to make the participants aware of their dependency upon many nonverbal cues in the process of normal conversation.

Discussion

The participants may talk together within their own trios about their learnings and the implications of the Three-Stage Rocket in their efforts to communicate. Or, it is sometimes helpful to establish new trios for the discussion with members from different groups helping them to focus on specific questions such as:

At which point in the exercise did you feel least comfortable? Why should this be?

What did you learn about yourself from this exercise that may have implications for you in your future efforts to communicate?

Did the exercise prove annoying to you at any time? Why?

What did the time restriction do to you? Was it helpful?

What did you learn about yourself with your eyes closed and how you listen and how you communicate?

With these types of questions in mind, the discussion should be profitable. It may be helpful to have the groups report specific findings to the entire group in an effort to begin closure to the exercise. Also, although feedback is held strictly to the verbal content level, it may be worthwhile to use this exercise as a first step in readying the group for a more in-depth analysis of the subject.

**Exercise 2
Communication Role Reversal**

Objectives

To make group members aware of how easily they "tune out" one another

To force people into a position where listening becomes expected at both an emotional (affective) level and at a content level

Setting

The large group is divided into subgroups or sets of four or five participants. Each person is given a rather large name tag which is pinned on him or placed in his lap so that every other person can clearly see it. This is to be done even if members know one another's names. Again, it is probably helpful if the members are not too familiar with one another, since it usually requires greater concentration and insures greater involvement (unless the members are voluntarily together where familiarity is one of the aims of that particular program).

Action

The subgroups are given a topic that insures some involvement on the part of all the participants. If possible the topic should be of such a nature that opposing views will be presented. After 5 or 10 minutes —at a point when the discussion has developed to a considerable degree—the facilitator requests that each individual give his name tag to the person across from him. They are then asked to continue the discussion as if they were the person whose name tag they now have. After another 5 minutes, the facilitator asks the group members to begin expressing the views of the person on their right (another exchange of tags).

Discussion

If the participants have really been listening to one another and the discussion is moving with most individuals participating, the exercise will not prove difficult. However, if a person has not been participating for some reason, this poses questions for the person playing him, and it poses questions for the group. Why was he not involved in a topic about which he must have ideas? The group is also asked to discuss whether the switch made them uncomfortable or made the task particularly difficult. Also, what was present in this situation that is present in most group communication? Was it easy to pick up the emotional as well as the content information of the person you were playing? Did the learnings from the first switch carry over into the second switch?

Exercise 3
The Blind Builder:
A Task in Interdependent Communication

Objectives

To observe how different individuals give direction

To observe how different individuals receive direction

To gain a better understanding of what happens when communication occurs under stress conditions

Setting

This exercise is limited to some extent by the availability of materials and space. Groups consisting of four participants are established. Two of the four are to be observers. Each group must have the following materials:

A blindfold

A hacksaw or other small handsaw

Odd-sized pieces of wood board (perhaps 5 or 6)

A hammer

Between 10 and 20 tacks or small nails

A 3-foot piece of rope or twine

The participants are told the following story:

Two men flying across a group of islands in the South Pacific were forced to crash-land on a small, uninhabited island. The temperature is extremely hot and, although the land is quite arid, it appears that there will be rain sometime during the day. The two men fully expect to be rescued in a few days and have enough food for 5 days. However, their water supply was lost in the crash and they haven't even got a container for holding water should it rain. Because of the heat and their fear of dehydration, the two survivors feel it is essential to build a water container and then wait for what looks like an inevitable thunderstorm. They find some wood and tools and are ready to set about their task. The only problem is that during the crash one of the two men received a heavy blow on the head and is now both blind and mute. The second man burned both his hands while pulling the tools from the burning wreckage and is not able to use them at all. But, together they must build the container—and before the rain comes. A few drops begin to fall.

Thus, the hands of one individual are to be tied with the twine securely behnd his back, and the eyes of the other are to be blindfolded.

Observer Roles

Both observers are to take notes on the more general aspects of the activity, but each is responsible for a more detailed observational report concerning one of the men in the activity. How does the second man give directions? Is it possible for the blind man to understand him? Do they establish a basic nonverbal system of communication so that the blind man can communicate? What signs does each of the men reveal as the task becomes increasingly difficult? How is this frustration communicated to the other, and what is the other's response? What could have been done to facilitate their communication?

Action

The task will take between 15 and 30 minutes. The observers may wish to observe other groups for the sake of contrast. When the task is completed (or not completed), the facilitator consolidates the two groups of four into one group of eight for a discussion of (a) the observers' data and (b) the feelings of the two participants. He then has the group of eight try to draw together some general learnings and implications to be shared with the large group.

Exercise 4
One-Way versus Two-Way Communication[2]

Objectives

To illuminate problems inherent in any communication between one person and another or a group when the aim is to give specific directions or information

[2] Design is based on one developed by Harold J. Leavitt in *Managerial Psychology*, Chicago: Univ. of Chicago Press, 1958, pp. 118–128.

To explore the feelings generated from two very different approaches of transferring information to others

Action

It will probably facilitate the experience if this particular exercise is carefully outlined step by step since there are many phases which, if discussed in a general format, might prove confusing.

1. The facilitator makes a few warm-up comments relating to the problems facing individuals who must transfer information or directions to others. The exercise provides some insights into this process as well as some possible behavioral alternatives.

2. It is important that each individual is facing the person who is to be designated to give him certain information. This person or the *sender* should be selected from volunteers. It is also important that the person selected have a clear and distinct speaking voice. Each member of the group should have a pencil and paper.

3. Then the facilitator informs the volunteer that he is to give the group members all the verbal information necessary for them to reproduce the figures in Diagram I exactly as they are drawn on the page. He is to begin with the top figure and then describe each figure in succession as he moves down the page. The group members must reproduce each figure in the same relationship to the one above it, as shown in the diagram. The volunteer should have his own copy of Diagram I. It is important that the sender follow certain specific rules in his presentation. They are:

   a. Sit with your back to the group. You are not to face them during this phase of the exercise.

   b. There will be no questions. Simply give the group as much information as you feel necessary to transmit the information necessary for them to reproduce the Diagram I.

4. A large chart similar to the one on page 37 should be prepared. The facilitator may not wish to put it up until after the final phase. However, it will be necessary to gather some data in the meantime. First, the facilitator notes the time it takes for the sender to give the group the information necessary for reproducing Diagram I. Next, he asks the group to write down the answers to the following questions:

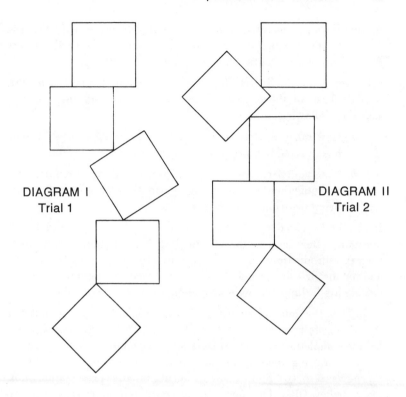

DIAGRAM I
Trial 1

DIAGRAM II
Trial 2

a. How many squares in the diagram do you believe you have correctly reproduced on your paper?

b. Note your feelings as you took part in the exercise. Be as specific as you can, using descriptive adjectives.

The responses to these questions will be collected and posted on the chart following the final phase of the exercise.

5. Now, the sender is given a copy of Diagram II and tells him that his task is the same. He is to study the figures in the diagram and then describe the diagram to the group so they can reproduce it on their paper. Again, he is to begin with the top figure and then describe each figure in succession as he moves down the page. The group members must reproduce each figure in the same relationship to the one above it, as shown in the diagram. The sender should follow certain specific rules during this phase of the exercise.

a. He must sit facing the group.

b. He may answer any questions that will help clarify the task to the group. The facilitator may help them verbally in any way but of course should not show them the diagram.

6. Again, the facilitator should note the elapsed time during this second phase of the exercise. When it is completed, the group is asked the following questions:

a. How many squares in the second diagram do you believe you have correctly reproduced on your paper?

b. Note your feelings as you took part in the exercise during the reproduction of the second diagram. Be as specific as you can, using descriptive adjectives.

It should be noted here that the sender is also to respond to the questions after each of the phases. But, he is to guess how many correct reproductions the group (or average person in the group) had for the first diagram and later for the second diagram. He is also to note his feelings during each presentation and record them.

7. Then the data are collected. On the large chart, the facilitator is to note the following information: First, he records the elapsed time for the completion of each presentation. Second, he asks the group to show by raising their hands how many believe they were able to reproduce zero (0) figures correct during the first presentation; how many believe they had one (1) correctly reproduced; and so on through five (5). He repeats these same questions for the second phase or trial in Diagram II.

	Elapsed Time	Guessed Correct Trial I						Feelings – Trial I
		0	1	2	3	4	5	
Trial I Diag. I		Actual Correct Trial I						
		Guessed Correct Trial II						Feelings – Trial II
Trial II Diag. II		0	1	2	3	4	5	
		Actual Correct Trial II						

8. At this point, Diagram I is presented to the group and each person calculates how many he actually had correct. A show of hands again allows the facilitator to record these responses on the chart. The same is then done with Diagram II and the data recorded. A cross-sampling of the feelings generated during the first trial is then posted, followed by a posting of feelings from the second trial. (It is possible to actually collect these data and make a more accurate tabulation, although this will probably not influence the impact of the information.) Now, the guesses of the sender during each trial are noted alongside the other data as well as his feelings during each presentation.

9. In analyzing the data and discussion, there are many possible procedures for drawing significant information. The facilitator could lead a general discussion of the results, asking key questions in relation to the data. For the most part the data will lead to some natural conclusions relating to time, accuracy, and feeling dimensions. One possible design would be to:

a. Present the data in an objective fashion—drawing no conclusions.

b. In groups of about five, have the participants analyze the data and draw specific conclusions in terms of the communication process.

c. Post these conclusions in a session with the total group supplementing the implications they have drawn if necessary. Total time set: 1½ hours.

Exercise 5
An Introductory Micro-Laboratory Experience

Objectives

To hasten the development of interpersonal communication within a group

To help establish a norm of openness within a group in which both content and feeling level statements are appropriate

To begin exploring perceptions of one another among the participants

Rationale

A micro-experience is designed to move group members through a variety of activities in a relatively short period of time (1 or 2 hours). By reducing the amount of time spent on any one activity a wide range of ideas and experiences can be developed and then built upon later. The objectives of each micro-lab will differ according to the particular aims of the facilitator and the needs of the group. This particular design is directed at helping to open channels of communication in a new group of individuals or in a group where channels of communication have been restricted or narrowly defined. Of course, a key in this approach is the knowledge by the participants that they are free to communicate at any level that is comfortable for them and that the various activities are merely meant to help provide a structure within which to relate. This approach has met with considerable success, since people basically desire to be known and enjoy talking about themselves and others. An opportunity to do this in an atmosphere of fun and goodwill can be most satisfying and may build innumerable personal bridges among individuals in the group.

For the facilitator, it is important that the activities build on one another in a sequential fashion and make sense in terms of the stated objectives. Too often the approach is misused and individuals are submerged too rapidly into personal areas which bring on later feelings of guilt or anger.

The following design sequence lasts about 90 minutes but could easily be extended to 2 or 3 hours by adding other activities. (Many of the exercises in the section on Selective Perception could be integrated with little difficulty, if these proved appropriate in terms of the aims of the program.)

1. Getting to Know You

(Time: 15–20 min.) The group divides itself into pairs, in each case with people they do not know. They have 5 minutes to get to know each other in any way they wish. The facilitator has a blackboard or newsprint available and after 5 minutes asks members of the group to call out the topical areas that were being discussed. He posts these quickly.

He then says something like this to the group: "In each of our lives there are usually a handful of individuals that we can call true friends. These are the people in whom we could have complete and ultimate trust. If this person to whom you are now talking were to become one of these very special friends, what would you have to know about him? What would be the most important thing to discover before you could have a relationship with the kind of trust necessary to sustain it?" The group members discuss this for about 5 minutes with their "potential" friend.

Again, after 5 minutes or a bit longer, the facilitator asks the group to share the topical areas they were exploring together. He lists these next to the original list developed after the first talk. The difference should be apparent. The second list should be much less superficial, more personal, and with much more involvement. In this period of 10 minutes, the participants will probably have shared more about themselves than they ever have in many of the "friendly" relationships they now have. How simple it is to go a little deeper, if only the two participants agree that it is all right to venture into these areas. Both usually like the experience. There is no need for much discussion of the data outside, only perhaps a few expressions of feelings from the group. The point is too self-evident to lose in a "superficial" discussion.

2. *Discussion of Communication with a Person Like Yourself*

(Time: 15–20 min.) The facilitator has the members of the group look around and find someone that, for some reason, they believe is like themselves. He has them sit with that person. This may take a little encouragement and pushing on the part of the facilitator, but once individuals see others doing it, it becomes much easier. These new pairs are to spend a few minutes discussing what it was about themselves that caused them to get together and what else they have in common.   (5–10 min.)

At this point, the group is asked to listen to a record carefully (e.g., "Sounds of Silence" or "Dangling Conversations") and discuss the implications it has for their own participation in a group. The aim is to get the individuals involved at a content level, thus using different behaviors than when they first began talking.   (5–10 min.)

The pairs are to discuss some apparent dissimilarities they have now noticed about themselves, things that were not apparent when they first began to talk, and also whether the original similarities were just as apparent at this point.   (5–10 min.)

3. *Discussing a Critical Event in Life with a Person Unlike Yourself*

(Time: 15–20 min.) The facilitator now has the members of the group look around and find someone that, for some reason, they believe is unlike themselves. Again, the new pairs are to spend 5 or 10 minutes discussing what it is about themselves that they perceive as probably different.

Then the facilitator asks the two individuals to share an experience in their lives that proved to be absolutely crucial in shaping "who they are" today. The experience can be positive or negative but must have been essential in their development as a person.

The participants discuss once more the initial differences they perceived. Are they the same? Are there others they have since noticed during the course of their conversation?

4. *Childhood Fantasy with a Person You Would Like to Know*

(Time: 20–30 min.) This particular experience can be rich in a variety of learnings and, if taken naturally along with the other events, will not be perceived as threatening to the participants. Evaluation or analysis is not the key. Rather it is the pulling together of a wide variety of verbal and nonverbal cues that can communicate to each one of us an enormous amount of information about the other person.

The facilitator might introduce this section by giving everyone a final chance to meet someone else in the group. He has everybody seek out another person they would simply like to get to know better and gives them 5 minutes or so to talk about the kinds of things that usually keep people from getting to know others. What keeps people from being personal with one another and allowing much more information with which we can all relate and bring to the surface?   (5 min.)

The facilitator continues by saying: "Now, knowing just what you have been able to learn in these few minutes, let's see how much more we can discover about the person with us. Think for a few minutes about this person and imagine him when he was an eight-year-old. Try to draw a picture of him at that time in his life. For example, try to imagine him at play, how he played, with whom, his types of friends in school, how he enjoyed it, what he liked about it, his family, wealthy or poor, how many children, oldest, youngest, his relations with his family, how he expressed anger, etc."

The facilitator can close by saying: "There are a thousand possible avenues you might want to focus upon. Try to be as thorough as you can so as to obtain the most complete picture possible. Now, after thinking about all this, share it with the individual. Then let him share his picture of you. After that tell him how accurate he was and what the *real* picture was. You may want to know why certain things were pictured."

It should be stressed that the most a person can be is absolutely wrong. After at least 15 minutes or when it appears that most of the pairs are through conversing, it might be useful to have two groups of pairs come together and share why they believe they were able to be so accurate or why they were so inaccurate. Also, why go through this exercise in the first place among relative strangers? It is always interesting to have a show of hands among the total group to discover how many individuals were very accurate in their descriptions. Often as many as 80 percent feel their partner hit the mark. Why? Because we are the product of our past. For most of us, our behaviors at 30 are remarkably similar to those at 8. We are open books to the world, though we seldom realize it.

A general discussion of the significance of the micro-experience for the participants and its relation to the rest of the program can provide a useful conclusion to the total experience.

REFERENCES

Asch, S. E. Studies of independence and conformity: I. A minority of one against a unanimous majority. *Psychological Monographs,* 1956, *70*(9, Whole No. 416).

Back, K. Influence through social communication. *Journal of Abnormal and Social Psychology,* 1951, *46,* 9.

Bavelas, A. Communication patterns in task oriented groups. *Journal of the Acoustical Society of America,* 1950, *22,* 725.

Berelson, B. and Steiner, G. A. *Human behavior* (Short ed.). New York: Harcourt, Brace and World, Inc. 1964.

Crook, R. Communication and group structure. *Journal of Communication,* 1961, *11,* 136.

Davison, W. P. On the effects of communication. *Public Opinion Quarterly,* 1959, *23,* 342.

Deutsch, M. The effects of cooperation and competition upon group process. In D. Cartwright and A. Zander (Eds.), *Group dynamics.* (2nd ed.) New York: Harper and Row, Publishers, 1960, 414–448.

Fabun, D. (Ed.). Communications. *Kaiser Aluminum*, 1965, *23* (3).

Festinger, L. Informal social communication. *Psychological Review*, 1950, *57*, 271.

Festinger, L. and Thibaut, J. Interpersonal communication in small groups. *Journal of Abnormal and Social Psychology*, 1951, *56*, 92.

Gerard, H. The effect of different dimensions of disagreement on the communication process in small groups. *Human Relations*, 1953, *6*, 249.

Gibb, J. R. Defensive communication. *Journal of Communication*, 1961, *11*(3), 141.

Glazer, M. and Glazer, R. Techniques for the study of group structure and behavior: Empirical studies of the effects of structure in small groups. *Psychological Bulletin*, 1961, *58*.

Grace, H. Confidence, redundancy and the purpose of communication. *Journal of Communication*, 1956, *6*, 16.

Greenspoon, L. The reinforcing effect of two spoken sounds on the frequency of two responses. *American Journal of Psychology*, 1955, *68*, 409–416.

Hearn, G. Leadership and the spatial factor in small groups. *Journal of Abnormal and Social Psychology*, 1957, *54*, 219–272.

Heise, G. A. and Miller, G. Problem solving by small groups using various communication nets. *Journal of Abnormal and Social Psychology*, 1951, *46*, 327.

Hurwitz, J., Zander, A., and Hymovitch, B. Some effects of power on the relations among group members. In D. Cartwright and A. Zander (Eds.)', *Group dynamics*. (3rd ed.) New York: Harper and Row, 1968, 291–297.

Kelley, H. Communication in experimentally created hierarchies. *Human Relations*, 1951, *4*, 39.

Kohler, W. *Gestalt psychology*. New York: A Mentor Book—The New American Library, 1947.

Leavitt, H. and Mueller, R. Some effects of feedback on communication. *Human Relations*, 1951, *4*, 401.

Loomis, J. Communication, the development of trust and cooperative behavior. *Human Relations*, 1959, *12*, 305.

Malcolm X. *The autobiography of Malcolm X*. New York: The Grove Press, Inc., 1964.

Mellinger, G. Interpersonal trust as a factor in communication. *Journal of Abnormal and Social Psychology*, 1956, *61*(52), 304.

Mills, T. M. *The sociology of small groups*. Englewood Cliffs, N.J.: Prentice-Hall, Inc., 1967.

North, A. Language and communication in group functioning. *Group Psychotherapy*, 1957, *10*(4), 300.

NTL Institute of Applied Behavioral Science. *Laboratories in human relations training.* Washington, D.C.: NTL Institute of Applied Behavioral Science, 1969, 23.

Nylen, D., Mitchell, R., and Stout, A. *Handbook of staff development and human relations training.* Washington, D.C.: NTL Institute for Applied Behavioral Science associated with NEA, 1967, 71–74.

Pepitone, A. and Reichling, G. Group cohesiveness and expression of hostility. *Human Relations,* 1955, *8,* 327–337.

Rogers, C. and Roethlisberger, F. J. Barriers and gateways to communication. *Harvard Business Review,* 1952, *30*(4), 46.

Schachter, S. Deviation, rejection and communication. *Journal of Abnormal and Social Psychology,* 1951, *46,* 190.

Sebald, H. Limitations of communication—mechanisms of image maintenance in the form of selective perception, selective memory, and selective distortion. *Journal of Communication,* 1962, *12,* 142.

Shaw, M. Communication networks. In L. Berkowitz (Ed.), *Advances in Experimental social psychology.* Vol. I. New York: Academy Press, 1964.

Slater, P. Contrasting correlates of group size. *Sociometry,* 1958, *211,* 129.

Slater, P. Role differentiation in small groups. *American Sociological Review,* 1955, *20,* 300–310.

Strodtback, F. et al. Social status in jury deliberations. *American Sociological Review,* 1957, *22,* 713–719.

Verplanck, W. The control of the content of conversation. *Journal of Abnormal and Social Psychology,* 1955, *51,* 668–676.

Webster's new collegiate dictionary. Springfield, Mass.: G. & C. Merriam Co., 1953.

Wrench, D. The perception of two-sided messages. *Human Relations,* 1964, *17,* 227.

Mark Josephson

2 membership

Membership is a central concept in thinking about ourselves, from birth with our initiation into our first group—a family membership—through the myriad tensions, fears, stresses, joys, and pleasures subsequent memberships will bring us throughout our lives.

The middle- or upper-class couple anticipating their first child is a phenomenon. From the parents' point of view, the event is only slightly less spectacular than man's first walk on the moon. For many couples there is the pride of becoming a real family, the ecstasy of having their own child, and the subsequent attention to every phase of the process. There are many decisions to be made: on the obstetrician, the hospital, the color of the baby's room, the kind of furniture, a nurse, and endless equipment—from long-forgotten diaper pins to a bathinette. All these decisions are discussed and planned and talked about with never ending interest. And the baby is born to a mother whose life now centers on him, a father who proudly hands out cigars, and grandparents who will "coo" him and "bounce" him. His arrival will be heralded for weeks. Gifts arrive almost daily, and there is a procession of friends and relatives who reverently view him and pay him homage.

Contrast this joyously awaited arrival with the coming of the eighth child in a migrant's family. In this case the event is a grudging acceptance of "God's will." The mother thinks of losing time from work, the father worries about another mouth to feed, and when the baby is born there is the problem of making more room in an already decrepit, overcrowded house. From the beginning what can this baby's image be of himself and his position in his first group?

Description of Memberships

Membership is a central concept in groups. From the beginning, the group is perceived as the environment within which an individual moves; it provides his primary source of reference (Thelen, 1954).

Although membership is taken for granted, it describes the quality or relationship between an individual and a group. First, there is the quality of being in or out, and in a family this boundary condition is rather clearly defined as to who is a member of the family and who is not. The first-born child may be only newly born, but it is patently evident that he is not only a new member of the family group but maybe its most important member—in terms of the extent he is listened to, the rapidity with which his needs are met even at the inconvenience of other members, and the interdependent relationship which exists. The infant is dependent on the other members for survival and nutriment, and the parents depend on the infant for a link to the future and an opportunity to test their theories of human development.

Another fundamental factor in groups is that membership can be defined, and members know who belongs and who does not. Also, individuals think of themselves as constituents in a group and have a definitive image of the group as a whole as well as its individual members. Although the boundaries are quite apparent in the simple illustration of a first membership, i.e., a child's birth, the concept applies in other relationships. The dues-paying, card-carrying, addressograph-plate individual is formally recognized as a member of a group as within the boundary condition. His affiliation places him within the boundary of that group, he perceives himself as part of it, and he has an image of the group and the purposes generally shared by the other members. Another kind of relationship is that of the "aspiring" member. The aspiring member is not formally within the boundary of the group. He is not a member, but he acts as if he were.

A boy's father had gone to Princeton, his older brother had gone to Princeton, and as long as he could remember, he had planned to go to Princeton. The family had season tickets to the football games, he always went to Alumni Day, and he followed the news of Princeton's progress in sports more avidly than his high school scores. His books had Princeton covers, his Princeton sweatshirt was a new one because the other was too small. He felt "his" school had made a disastrous mistake to admit girls.

If asked, the boy would readily admit that he was not a member of the Princeton student body, but Princeton greatly influences his dress style, his activities, his aspirations for the future. He frequently feels like a member when he walks around campus in his sweatshirt with his brother, and psychologically he is a member. In terms of formal membership, however, he is outside the boundary, at least for the present. In contrast, consider the following situation:

> A senior at Princeton is being interviewed for jobs for next year. He doesn't attend the football games or get involved in sports scores. He disdains Princeton covers and Princeton sweatshirts, or for that matter any Princeton emblems. He dashes for the train to New York immediately after his last class and returns in time for his first class on Monday. He belongs, he is a member of the Princeton student body, but neither the school nor its members influence him to any degree. He identifies much more with people "making it" in New York; college is already in his past. He could be termed a "marginal" member.

Membership might be conceived then as if the group were a circle on a piece of paper. Those who belong are within the circle. Those who are actively involved and influenced by the members may be seen as being in the center of the circle—or conceptually, they are centrally involved, such as the first-born child and his parents. The marginal member may be seen as within the circle (the boundary), but close to the edge (the Princeton senior). The aspiring member is outside the circle. Full psychological membership occurs when a person is positively attracted to membership and is positively accepted as a member.

That a person is a member does not mean it affects his entire behavior. Membership may only involve a limited personal investment—such as membership in a bridge club, P.T.A., union, church group, scout troop committee, or neighborhood association. However, the degree to which the person is involved will affect both the functioning of the group and its significance for members.

Voluntary–Nonvoluntary membership

In speaking of memberships, we are often considering participation of a voluntary nature. Should we join the bridge club, the P.T.A., the church group, the scout committee? Often it is forgotten that we are members of many groups in which we have no choice, i.e., nonvoluntary groups. There are a variety of reasons for membership in nonvoluntary groups. For example, membership in the family (birth), Miss Turner's sixth grade class (age, address), a prison population (court order), whites (race) are all compulsory memberships. Obviously, compulsory memberships are not necessarily unattractive.

Sources of Attractions

So much for compulsory groups about which there is little we can do. The important question seems to be: Why do people join the groups they do?

> The number of memberships was a political issue in a recent campaign for mayor of a large city. One candidate was a member of over 40 organizations. There was a question about whether these memberships were for political show or represented personal interests. In the campaign, his detractors utilized the memberships to point him out as a dilettante, and his seeking the mayoralty as a passing fancy which he would not take seriously. His advocates used the same memberships to refer to him as a Renaissance Man, a man of broad interests and knowledge, whose familiarity with such a diversity of groups and organizations especially qualified him for the post.

Some people seem to have a "need to belong," which is interpreted by outsiders as a desire to be in the limelight—the "politic" way. It may be. It may also represent an interest in the goals of these organizations. Others, who are not outgoing, may also seek memberships.

> A certain faculty member of a large urban university is painfully shy and finds it difficult to make "small talk." He has learned to talk to a few friends on a one-to-one basis. Usually he is seen alone and most of the members of his department consider him antisocial. However, he is active in the large professional societies. These societies have rigid criteria for acceptance, and appointment to committee membership or chairmanship involves a great deal of work. He is rightly seen as an expert, and by working hard on the formal committee he is liked and accepted. He may even have a feeling of being loved at the formal level when the relationships at the personal, informal end of the continuum are difficult to attain or elusive.

An understanding of why people join is complicated (Quey, 1971). However, there seem to be three major reasons:

1. They like the task or activity of the group. For example, people join Women Strike for Peace because they hope to further efforts toward peace, the tennis club because they like to play tennis, the local civic association because they would like to improve neighborhood conditions, and a consumer's club because they would like to pay lower prices for food.

2. They like the people in the group. This is a most prevalent reason for social activities, i.e., a sorority, a fraternity, a luncheon club, a country club (for nongolfers), etc. Frequently people join because they like both the task and the people. They may want to be in the League of Women Voters, but may often travel some distance to a chapter in which they feel they will "get along." People may join an organization initially because of an interest in the task or activity, and then find they enjoy the people as well. Often they will continue their membership long after their task interests have waned, in order to participate in the pleasant personal associations. The reverse situation also occurs. A person may join an organization because of the pleading of a good friend—and he joins only to please the friend, although later he may become genuinely interested in the activity.

3. A third reason for joining is that being in the group can satisfy needs lying outside the group. In this category, the group itself does not satisfy the person's needs directly, but is a *means* to satisfying his needs. There has been some interesting research which illuminates the "means to" reason for joining. Willerman and Swanson (1953) found that girls joined sororities because of the prestige accorded them as sorority members. Rose (1952) found that people joined unions not because they enjoyed union activities or working with other union members, but because the union got them higher wages and job security. Schachter (1959) found that under conditions of experimentally induced anxiety, people wanted to be with other people. His results showed that a state of anxiety leads to arousal of affiliative tendencies.

Kurt Back (1951) was intrigued by the following questions: Does it affect the group as to *why* a person joins? Does it really make any difference whether he joins because he is interested in the task, or likes the other people, or because the group is a means to meeting his needs? If it makes a difference, how? What kind? Back designed an experiment to get answers to these questions. He arbitrarily paired subjects, but told them that, on the basis of previous tests of personality and other measures, they had a special relationship to each other. He told some pairs that their personalities were similar and that they would have a great deal in common (the liking condition). He told another grouping of pairs that they had common goal interests in the project (interest in task condition). In the third grouping, he told each of the partners that the other would be an important person to know and could be influential (the group as a "means to" condition).

The results indicated that it did make a difference. Those primarily attracted as friends interacted at a primarily personal level—they had long conversations, were pleasant to each other, and expected to influence each other. In those groups attracted primarily by the task, members wanted to complete it quickly and efficiently and discussed only those matters they thought relevant to achieving their goals. In those groups attracted by potential prestige from membership, members acted cautiously, concentrated on their own actions, and in general were careful not to risk their status. When there were none of these bases of attraction, members of a pair acted independently and with little consideration of each other.

The Back experiment leads to the generalization that the nature of group life will vary with different sources of attraction.

Multiple Memberships

The complexities of membership are compounded when it is remembered that an individual belongs to a multiplicity of groups. Some he may join for task reasons, some because of the people, some to meet needs beyond the group; in some he is an involuntary member—and to each he brings his unique self and behavior to meet his needs in that situation. Is it any wonder, then, that having multiple memberships offers another dimension to membership experience? It carries with it a number of assets. There are advantages in the variety of contacts, in a "reality" based on experiences in different kinds of groups, in the ability to have liaison with other groups, and this very diversity can be a source of creativity and innovation. In some instances problem-solving may be simplified when all the members of one group are also members of another, as when the citizens of a playground advisory council are asked to make recommendations for recreational programs for youth in their area. The members of the advisory council, who have worked together before on a regular basis, now work in a related area on a different problem. Another example might be a training staff who work together in the implementation of training programs and are then assigned the task of making recommendations to a national agency for future training programs. In both these illustrations, the fact that all the members of one group involved in one issue were also involved in another issue facilitates problem-solving—they know one another, have worked together before, and have developed working procedures.

Sometimes, and in many areas, multiple memberships "coexist" in the person. Memberships in a family, a professional association, a P.T.A., a bowling club, a faculty journal club, and a church can exist in a person's life with little conflict. There may be an occasional time problem—everything is scheduled for the same Tuesday night—but this conflict is minor and resolved with little tension.

Sometimes, however, multiple memberships can be the source of serious conflicts. *The Lonely African* gives an example not soon forgotten.

> In Africa today, many young men leave their families and the sharing within the tribal community to attempt to enhance their futures in the city. They learn, with difficulty, to begin to accept new standards. First, they are alone and it is not the tribe which mattters but the individual. If there is to be success and achievement, it is the individual who must achieve and earn his own success. Painfully he learns—to accept a loneliness, to strive by these new standards, to become successful. His new success brings with it increased pain, loneliness, and conflict. Soon tribal members learn of his success and come to visit their kinsman. They remind him of the rules of the tribe —of sharing his wealth and his possessions with all of them as they would with him in the community. The conflict of his memberships both in the tribe and in an individualistic, achievement-oriented society provoke dire consequences for him. Many decide to totally cut themselves off from their tribal community. They change their names, move to a different address, and become the "lonely African." (Turnbull, 1963)

Generally people do not join organizations or groups with conflicting norms or values. A person is not likely to be a member of the National Association of Manufacturers and also a member of the Socialist Party; nor of the Catholic Church and the Planned Parenthood Association; nor of the Republican Party and S.D.S. Although a person will attempt to avoid membership conflicts, sometimes they cannot be avoided. The businessman who believes that—as in a "jungle" environment—survival and eventual success depend on taking advantage of the situation, may have difficulties on Sundays in church as the minister discusses ethical behavior. He may resolve this by not going to church, changing his business practices, or compartmentalizing his memberships—one kind of behavior is appropriate in the business world dominated by "business" ethics and another kind of behavior on Sunday that is compatible with "Christian" ethics.

Some multiple memberships result in conflicts that present serious problems, where the dilemmas created cannot be resolved to the person's satisfaction. Frequently he feels that the choice has negative consequences regardless of the decision. Examples are: the career woman and mother; the salesman father away from home much of the time; the student wife or husband; the busy doctor who was called out on an emergency when he had promised to take his son to the movies.

Yet another kind of multiple membership conflict is common whenever a coordinating committee or representative committee is composed of representatives of subordinate groups. The conflict that occurs creates intrapersonal dilemmas as the individual vacillates between representing the subordinate group, acting in a way which seems appropriate to him and his needs, and being open to the discussion as it takes place in the coordinating committee. In this case, there can be a conflict of interests.

> Whether religious habits should be retained or rules on their necessity be modified is a source of discussion and stress in some religious communities. One governing board, made up primarily of older sisters who have spent a lifetime in habits, considered the change to the modified habit adventurous and more than sufficient. Young sisters, who make up the majority of the order, would prefer wearing a still further modified habit for professional use only. Those in their thirties and forties prefer a further modified habit to be worn at all times.
>
> The dilemmas for a thirty-one-year-old governing board member are real and agonizing. As a representative of her convent she should vote in accord with what most of the members indicated as their preference; they are older and favor retention of the present habit. Yet, as one of the youngest members of the board, she identifies with the youngest group who are not represented—shouldn't she be their spokesman and speak out in favor of limited wearing of a further modified habit? And within herself, she prefers (as her age group) the further modified habit to be worn at all times. How does she respond to the discussion taking place? How can she vote when she knows that whatever she decides will be considered "traitorous" by one of the three groups?

The resolution of conflicts of multiple membership is often attained at great personal cost and with much anxiety. Often these conflicts are resolved in accord with the standards of the group that are most salient at the moment.

Reference Groups

Of the many groups to which a person belongs, which are the most salient for him? Which influence how he typically feels about things? To which do his attitudes most closely relate? Membership in a group implies the right to influence others in the group; it also implies an agreement to accept influence from others.

An Eagle Scout certainly considers the Boy Scouts a reference group. He has attended patrol and troop meetings for years, accepted varying degrees of responsibility, and influenced boys younger than himself as well as his peers. He has risen through the ranks in advancement programs, acquiring numerous merit badges to become an Eagle. Scouts have obviously been an important reference group for him. There are also "candidates" who attend a few meetings and never achieve the beginning rank of "Tenderfoot." The weekly meetings are too frequent, they don't like the boys, they may not be as agile or competitive as others—and so for them the Boy Scouts never becomes a referent group.

Those groups an individual selects as his reference groups are the ones which will influence his behavior and the ones whose influence he is willing to accept.

Consider the following illustration:

A black college student undergoes 15 weeks of pledging prior to admission to a prestigious black national fraternity. He wears his hair in a handsome, well-cultivated "bush" style. The final ordeal, if he is serious in his intent of becoming a member, requires that, as in slave times, he submit to having his head shaved. There are no exceptions.

Reference groups have been described (Kelley, 1952) as serving two distinct functions. First, they serve a comparison function. "A group functions as a comparison reference group for an individual to the extent that the behavior, attitudes, circumstances, or other characteristics of its members represent standards or comparison points which he uses in making judgments and evaluations." This is the concept of social influence on an individual's perception, cognition, and level of aspiration (Sherif, 1936; Festinger, 1957; Asch, 1956).

Second, reference groups serve a normative function. "A group functions as a normative reference group for a person to the extent that its evaluations of him are based upon the degree of his conformity to certain standards of behavior or attitude and to the extent that the delivery of rewards or punishments is conditional upon these evaluations." This concept would be viewed as social pressure (Mirande, 1968).

Both these functions may be served by the same groups. A person's reference groups may greatly influence his attitudes toward himself and will affect his relationships with other groups. Thelen (1954) distinguishes different sorts of groups in which an individual may hold membership and to which he addresses his behavior:

1. *The actual group.* It is in the actual group that a person can interact, test ideas, hear the responses of others, get feedback on his own behavior, and learn. It is only in this actual group where he can have the experience on which to build understanding of his behavior and attitudes. In a given group, there are only some people who are referents, those whom he attempts to influence and who in turn influence him. These people represent the effective group for that individual. The effective group is determined subjectively for each member—those who "make sense" to him, those who seem to be in touch with reality, those with whom the subject identifies. These few, perhaps only 8 to 10 in a group of 30 (and their composition may change over time), are the total group for that person. It is they who influence him, and they to whom he can relate.

2. *The group we represent.* There are two levels of reference groups in this concept. At one level are the groups that appoint or elect a member to represent them in another group. There are numerous examples of a representative from one group serving in a coordinating committee for a specific purpose, or in a general coordinating committee. Examples are representatives of various faculty departments at a university who study and make recommendations on grading; representatives of the professional staff of districts of Girl Scouts to plan the regional "camporee"; representatives of the community who are members of the city citizens' poverty action boards. Here the group the person represents is thought of as "his" group, whom he must speak for, fight for, and defend. In defending his representative group, he believes or comes to believe that their approach and position is the one he advocates. He strives for goals that favor his group —these are his vested interests. A member relates to the group he represents, and this for him becomes a reference group.

At another level are the groups he represents when he is not officially delegated to do so. In a classroom discussion on the value of sororities, a sorority member may feel a need to enter the discussion in heated terms as she defends the worth of sororities. In a meeting on school enrichment programs for Saturday mornings, a Jewish teacher may state quite vehemently that this would conflict with the Jews' observance of the Sabbath. Some say that when people defend their vested interests almost blindly it is because these groups are important reference groups in their lives. Another theory holds that it occurs when a person is anxious about his membership in that group; he defends the group to assure himself that he does belong—and that it is worth belonging. Festinger's (1957) theory of cognitive dissonance may be helpful here.

In both cases, the person reacts to the actual group as well as the group he represents (formally or in subjective terms). The group he represents influences his behavior.

3. *The abstracted group.* Here the person is influenced by groups from his past, although that influence is not specifically remembered. He might have found that a stern, "no nonsense" teacher accomplished the most in a classroom; he might have worked for a direct, authoritarian employer whom he found to be very efficient. He may be influenced by these dimly remembered models, and feel that the ultimate goal of all groups is to function in this way. His behaviors are influenced by this abstracted group. It should be noted here that when values abstracted from these "forgotten" groups come into conflict with the values of the current group, the former should be examined to determine whether the circumstances and goals are similar to the present situation. ´

4. *The "hangover" group.* Unresolved membership anxieties and problems in important reference groups may be continuously dealt with in other groups. For example, the child who was the "little brother" in his family—the last to be heard, the most frequently disregarded, the one allowed almost no responsibility because he was "young" even at voting age—may in other groups strive for leadership or be antileadership. Some feel that many of the problems of leadership are not legitimate problems of the actual group, but are unresolved "hangovers" from previous groups—unresolved family relationships which influence behavior in the present group. It is as if the same conditions are being repeated all the time. Thus the hang-

over group can be a person's referent, and it is to this group that he still addresses his behavior, either consciously or unconsciously.

5. *The fantasied or constructed group.* This is a kind of group that may give one the emotional support he is not receiving from the actual group. A person who has read some legal materials may argue a legal point and think of himself not as addressing the actual group, but as representing the "legal point of view." Consultants brought into groups often fantasize themselves as being ultimate authorities on questions of organization. Often consultants fantasize themselves as speaking with graduate students rather than with clients, and theorize or speak in "ivory tower" terms. When a person does not accept and address his behavior to the actual group, he will use some other group or mixture of groups, or even a constructed group. Some people recognize that they are addressing their behavior to groups other than the actual ones; to others these hidden groups remain in the subconscious.

Finally, it is evident that there are actual groups which influence us and to which we address our behavior. However, when there is a perplexing situation in the actual group, it is as if there were other groups overlapping. Groups that overlap at a particular time are the ones that have special salience for us in the particular situation. Frequently, cues in any actual situation remind us of groups in which we are anxious about our membership role.

It seems that there is even a hierarchy of reference groups, since whenever a decision is reached in an overlapping or conflicting membership situation, membership in some groups is enhanced at the expense of others.

Factors Increasing Attractiveness of Membership

An understanding of the problems of membership is important, but the ultimate goal of behavioral scientists is to be able to predict which groups will be attractive, or unattractive, to their members, and on what basis. One real goal of the behavioral sciences is to provide the skills for adequately describing a group at work, and also provide the facility to make groups more attractive and thus more productive.

Generally, we know that the attractiveness of a group can be increased if a member (or potential member) is aware that he can fulfill his needs by belonging to that group. Since it is difficult to change the member's needs, it is a more feasible approach to emphasize the properties that meet members' needs or the gains to be derived from belonging. Some of the properties that increase attractiveness are as follows:

1. *Prestige.* The more prestige a person has within a group, or the more that appears to be obtainable, the more he will be attracted to the group (Kelley, 1951; Aronson and Linder, 1965). People who are placed in a position of authority over others are more attracted to the group than those low in authority. This is especially true of those in authority who expect to remain in that position. For example, the group or organization will be attractive to a principal who is appointed "for life," army officers who may be promoted but are rarely demoted, or chief executives who are appointed and remain in that position until a bigger executive position is available.

However, those in a position of high authority who may be demoted to one of low authority are attracted to a lesser degree. Those of low authority who expect to remain in that position are not attracted to the group. The shipping clerk, the member of the telephone squad, and the "envelope licker" are not attracted. Yet those of low authority who envision being moved up can also find the group attractive; for example, the telephone squad member who sees herself as a potential officer or committee chairman.

Those most attracted of all are members of high prestige who see themselves remaining in that position or those of low prestige who perceive themselves as rising in the group. High authority members who can be demoted (the president after his year of office) and low authority members who cannot rise (frequently women in a business enterprise) are not attracted to membership. In addition, persons who are valued members are more likely to be attracted to a group than those who do not have much social worth (Jackson, 1959; Snoek, 1959; Lott and Lott, 1969).

Imagine a questionnaire being passed around to a group in which members are asked to rank members on who is most important to the group. Suppose also that a questionnaire is distributed in which each member is asked how attracted he is on a scale from 0 (not attracted) to 10 (highly attracted). It is likely that when the data are tabulated and analyzed, the results will indicate that those seen as most valued or most important in the group will be those who are most attracted to it. Thus, when we feel that our ideas are listened to and acted upon, we are more attracted to the group.

2. *Milieu.*   A cooperative relationship is more attractive than one which is competitive (Deutsch, 1959). If a group works together as a team to develop a product (solution or procedure) and if it will be rated on the basis of team effort, the members will be more friendly than in a competitive situation. However, when members are rated on the basis of individual performance, there is less interpersonal relationship, more withholding of information or not volunteering information, fewer influence attempts.

The classroom teacher can easily test this finding. He can set up a class project in which half the class is divided into work groups and graded as units, while the remainder of the class, although working in groups, are individually evaluated. The results may not only be illuminating but also a basis for reexamination of the class norms. Another illustration is to observe the feelings of swim team members in a relay to accrue points for their school. How different it is from members in individual swim competitions. The group is more attractive to members in the cooperative situation.

3. *Degree of interaction among members.*   Heightened interaction among members may increase the attractiveness of the group (Homans, 1950). Participating, or enjoying some of the members, or making some good friends as a by-product of belonging to the group increases the attractiveness to its members—it offers increased opportunities to continue these pleasing relationships. Research here includes some contingency conditions. While pleasing interaction increases attractiveness of membership, if the interaction is unpleasant (if members disregard each other, bore each other, or if there are members who are considered repulsive), attraction to membership will be decreased (Festinger, 1957; Aronson, 1970; Amir, 1969).

4. *Size.*   As most of us have experienced (Seashore, 1954), the size of a group greatly influences our attraction to it. Smaller groups are likely to be more attractive than large ones (Wicker, 1969). In a small group it is easier to get to know the other members, to discover similar interests, to have dedication to the cause, to have a sense of being a significant participant in the group. As the group increases in membership there is a corresponding heterogeneity of interests. Feelings toward each other become less personal, concern with the "cause" is often less intense, and there is a reduction in the degree of individual participation, intimacy, and involvement (Tsouderos, 1955). Rela-

tionships with *other* groups are also a factor. Groups are more attractive if their position is improved with respect to other groups (Deutsch, 1959; Stotland, 1959).

5. *Success.* The maxim that nothing succeeds like success applies to groups also. Members are more inclined to join groups or continue in groups that have been successful or prestigious (Jackson, 1959; Shelley, 1954).

If a group struggling along in fund raising, for example, suddenly receives a large gift so that it is more successful than other units of the organization in fund raising, membership in that group is more attractive. If one team in competition with other teams proves more competent or more successful, membership in that team is more attractive. Even if people are told that a unit may be *potentially* successful, the group takes on new prestige and members are more attracted to it. Task success is an important determinant in members' reactions to the leader and the group (Ninane and Fiedler, 1970).

It is interesting that if a person desires membership and it is difficult to obtain, he will value the membership more than if it were easy (Aronson and Mills, 1959). As if to reduce a dissonance within himself he says, "This membership had to be worth it for me to go through such an ordeal—of course it's worth it—it's a great group— I'm lucky to be a member" (Festinger, 1957).

There is no evidence, however, to indicate that the same situation prevails if a person does not desire membership. Then the difficulty of the ordeal simply becomes another reason the membership is unattractive.

Factors Decreasing Attractiveness of Membership

When does a person consider leaving a group? He will consider leaving when the forces of attraction are decreased or negative, when his own needs for satisfaction are reduced, when the group becomes less suitable as a means for satisfying existing needs, or when the group acquires unpleasant properties. He will actually leave when the forces for remaining in the group are less than the forces for leaving (there are also forces against making a change and, instead, just letting the existing conditions continue). It is possible for a group to retain members (as all of us are aware) when attraction is zero or near zero. In such cases the group is inactive, exerts little influence over its members, and the members in turn provide little internal support. Members in this category—in conceptual terms, borderline members—are pushed over (and out) when the precarious balance is disturbed—as when the meeting time is changed or dues are raised even a small amount.

Research findings indicate that groups can lose their attractiveness for several reasons:

1. A group disagrees on how to solve a group problem. Some will walk away from the discussion, or not attend the meetings at which such a problem is on the agenda; others withdraw by working on private problems or become "turned off." Members may sense real personal frustration in such instances and the group is viewed as a source for precipitating feelings of personal inadequacy and impotency.

2. If the group makes unreasonable or excessive demands on a person, or the person feels inadequate in the group situation, the group is less attractive and he will leave (Horowitz et al., 1953). If a person is assigned a job that is too difficult for him (like arranging a program) or if the person feels inadequate in the group situation (which requires his giving verbal reports at meetings and he might feel he is an inadequate speaker), the group will be less attractive and he will leave, often without stating or being fully aware of his reasons.

3. Groups that have members who are too dominating or who have other unpleasant behaviors reduce attractiveness of the group.

4. Staff conferences in which there was a high degree of self-oriented behavior were viewed as less attractive to the staff (Fouriezos et al., 1950). Members who dominate the discussion and severely limit the opportunities for participation by others reduce attractiveness.

5. Some memberships may limit the satisfactions a person can receive from activities outside the group. For example, women who are Black Muslims are not permitted to drink, dance, wear make up, or wear miniskirts (sleeves and skirt lengths must reach the ankles). Membership as a Black Muslim clearly limits satisfactions which might be derived from going to dances, or being "stylish." Policemen on rotating weekly shifts or nurses on night duty are also limited in their outside activities.

6. Negative evaluation placed upon membership in a group by people outside the group (which gives the group low status), also

reduces attractiveness of the group. Teenage boys who enjoy scouting and become Eagle Scouts rarely tell their schoolmates of their scouting activities, nor even consider wearing their uniforms to school during Boy Scout Week because of the derisive comments anticipated. Being a member of the school discipline committee is not a sought-after appointment because of the reactions of peers to members of such committees.

7. Competition among groups also reduces attractiveness unless the person has reason to believe he will be with the "winners."

8. A person will leave one group to join another if the second is better able to meet his needs or if he has a limited time for participation. For example, a member may belong to an organization and then move to another part of the same city. He may join a branch of the organization closer to his new home. Or, he may instead join a similar, but different, organization since he is moving and planning new relationships.

Consequences of Attractiveness of Membership

How a group functions, then, does depend on how attractive it is to its members. This will be reflected in how easily the group reaches its goal as well as how satisfying the product is. There is evidence to suggest that if a person is attracted to membership, he is more likely to accept the responsibilities of membership (Dion, Miller, and Magnan, 1970). He is likely to attend meetings more regularly (Sagi, 1955), he is more apt to participate readily in meetings (Back, 1951), and he is more likely to accept responsibilities in the organization (Larson, 1953). In addition, he will be more persevering in working toward long or difficult goals (Horowitz et al., 1953).

If the group is attractive, he is more open to interpersonal influence. It has been found that when a member is attracted to the group, he is more willing to listen to others, he is more flexible in accepting other opinions (Rasmussen and Zander, 1954), and he will attempt to influence others more (Schachter, 1951). It is especially worthy of note that an attracted member will change his mind more often to take the view of fellow members.

There is also an effect on productivity. When members are attracted to the group, they adhere more closely to the group's standards (i.e., the group's procedures for doing things), and are more likely to exert pressure on those who would ignore the group standards. It is not only the *way* the group does things that is valued, but *what it is doing* that is especially valued. With groups in which the members are attracted, greater value is placed upon the group's goal than in groups in which membership is not attracted (Zander and Havelin, 1960).

Finally, it seems to make a difference in the state of the person's well-being. Attracted members develop a greater security in the group in that they are less likely to be "jumpy" or nervous in group activities and more often may even find release from tension in their membership activities (Feldman, 1969).

In conclusion, membership issues are complex and the range of problems affected by membership is extensive. Increased understanding of membership variables may increase our awareness of factors influencing the effectiveness of a group and provide insight into ways of facilitating greater task efficiency and member attractiveness.

Exercise 1
Multiple Memberships:
Representative Group—Member Role

Objectives

To experience the conflicts of multiple memberships

To understand the conflicts of representative memberships in a familiar community situation

Setting

A table with five chairs is placed in the center of the room.
The facilitator asks for five volunteers to play various roles in a discussion of sex education.
The roles assigned are:

A parent, a representative of the P.T.A.

A conservative businessman, a representative of the Chamber of Commerce

A middle-aged lawyer, a representative of the Citizens' Association

The principal of the high school, a representative of the faculty

The executive director, representing the Mental Health Association

Situation

The setting is a suburban community in the Midwest; there are 30,000 inhabitants. The community is conservative and incomes are above the national median. The facilitator describes the situation as follows:

An anonymous benefactor feels there is a need for sex education in this community. Such education has never been part of the budget; the benefactor will donate $10,000, which would be sufficient for an excellent program—the community will determine the program. He would like to see such a program instituted this year, but there is a stipulation that we must let him know our decision at the end of the month. If we agree to the program, we can have the funds immediately. If not, the benefactor has made plans to use the funds for a project in another community.

During the past month we have brought the situation to the attention of groups within the community. Opinion has been divided. Your groups are the major ones involved. We must make our decision promptly because today is the last of the month. You have been appointed by your groups to help arrive at the final decision; the other groups will follow your decision.

The following developments have taken place during the month: the P.T.A. has not made a commitment due to disagreement within the organization; the Chamber of Commerce was opposed; the Citizens Association unfortunately had their meeting canceled due to the elections; the faculty want to represent the wishes of the whole community although they themselves feel it is a desirable project and a special opportunity; the Mental Health Association strongly supports the project and might have been influential in finding the benefactor.

Each role player is told to think about his role and how he will act in the situation as a representative of his organization. If possible, each player should have a "coach" with whom he can practice his role. The coach may help the individual to magnify certain aspects or modify others. The coaches would take about 5 minutes with role players.

The facilitator announces, "The meeting will begin with the representative of the Mental Health Association as chairman."

Action

The meeting begins. Nonparticipants watch the role playing, the discussion, and the decision.

Discussion

To the nonparticipants:

At the beginning how accurately did the representatives speak for their organizations?

Who changed from his organizational position? How?

What conflicts in membership did you see? For whom were they greater?

Who remained unchanged? How could you interpret this? (Observers might be asked to look for egocentric behaviors, i.e., deflating others, sarcasm, building up of self, defensive replies, withdrawing or nonparticipating behaviors.)

To the role players:

What conflicts did you feel? When? What influenced your decision?

Exercise 2
Conflicting Memberships

Multiple memberships are situations in which one person has membership in a number of groups simultaneously. These may or may not be in conflict. In conflicting memberships or conflicting roles, there is conflict within the person as to which membership or role should be a determinant of his behavior at that moment.

The conflicting memberships can be experienced readily in a number of situations. Take, for example, the family situation wherein a woman plays a dual role of wife and mother.

Setting

The facilitator asks for volunteers to be a family, i.e., a mother, father, oldest child, middle child, youngest child. He assigns each his role and explains the situation. A number of situations will be presented. For example, one situation might begin with the wife-mother saying: "My husband and children pull at me constantly. My husband wants me to go downtown with him, and my children want me to be home

when they come out of school." (The issue of conflicting memberships—her two roles—is evident.)

The situation is staged with a woman in the center with her arms
stretched out at shoulder height. On one side her "husband" will be
pulling her in his direction. On the other side her children will be
lined up pulling in their direction. The youngest might be pulling at
the mother's knees or the bottom of her skirt. The middle child might
be pushing the youngest away and pulling the mother at the waist, the
oldest might be pulling the mother's shoulder or arm in his direction.
Once the family knows its roles, the facilitator says, "Act out." The
father pulls and entreats, "Come on, honey." The youngest pulls and
may say, "I want my mommy," the middle one may pull with determination silently, the oldest may plead, "Please, listen to me." Each is
pulling, and the mother is feeling pulled and swayed and harassed
and inadequate. She may simply be moaning, or she may say, "Stop
pulling so hard, you're hurting me. Please stop, I feel as though I'm
caught in a vise." (In acting out the situation, participants are encouraged to actually pull, indicate their feelings nonverbally, or with
just a few words.) After a few moments of this, the facilitator calls,
"Stop." All relax their holds.

Discussion

Then the "family" is asked: How did it feel? How did you like your
role? What were the relationships with the other members of your
"family"?

Some questions are also put to the audience:

What did you notice?

How did the central person feel?

What behaviors might have helped reduce the conflicts?

What could have been done so that members could be accepted or
respected?

There are other possibilities for acting out role conflict in a family
situation.

The "husband" might say: "My wife, my children are strangling
me—I can't move, they're clutching me so tightly. I want to get
ahead, but how can I if I have to be home every night for dinner at
six, if I have to spend every free minute playing with the children?"

One of the children might say: "I'm being pulled in all directions—my parents want me to be one way, my boyfriend wants me to go another way, my best friend wants me to do other things."

After several possibilities are decided upon, the "family" may reenact these new situations, observe the effects, and then both actors and audience discuss the same questions posed the first time.

Exercise 3
Reference Groups:
"Who Am I?" Composition

Objectives

An understanding of reference groups

An understanding that reference groups, groups to which a person can relate, are subjectively determined

An understanding that groups which may be referent groups for some are not referent groups for others

Setting

Members are divided into groups (four to six per group). Each member should have a pencil and paper.

Action

The facilitator asks each person to write a 100-word composition explaining who he is so that "people will know what you're like." The compositions are written, and each person reads his to the group. Members are then asked to determine from the composition who that person's reference groups are.

Discussion

How were reference groups different among members?

What difference does it make to the person?

What will be the effect in the group, or in other groups?

Exercise 4
Increasing Attractiveness of Membership

Objectives

To understand that cooperative rather than competitive relationships can increase attractiveness of the group

To understand that increased interaction increases attractiveness of the group

To understand that interdependence can increase attractiveness of the group

Setting

Participants are divided into tens (approximately) and seated five at a table. Each participant is given a piece of paper. At one table each person is given a crayon. At the other table the entire group is given one crayon. The members at the second table are instructed that they can hold the crayon only 20 seconds and then must pass it to the next person. The groups are instructed to "draw something from your life which is characteristic of you" or "draw something characteristic of you in the group." The facilitator may call out at the end of each 20-second period or have a "timekeeper" at the table do it.

Action

The groups draw as instructed. In one group each person works with his crayon on the drawing; in the other, members pass a crayon to the next person every 20 seconds.

Discussion

How did you feel about the process?

How do you feel about your product?

How do you feel about your group? Talk about the experience.

Variation

This can be done as a group drawing. Each group is given one piece of paper. In one case each member is given a crayon; in the other group, one crayon is to be rotated. This variation heightens interdependence and cooperative relationships in the passed-crayon group.

The exercise is as described through the action phase. Then, before the discussion, individual evaluation sheets are distributed. These evaluation sheets permit those who worked individually to compare their evaluations with those who worked cooperatively. Some questions in the evaluation sheet might be:

1. Did you enjoy working in this way?

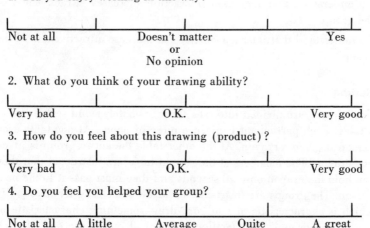

Not at all   Doesn't matter   Yes
                            or
                      No opinion

2. What do you think of your drawing ability?

Very bad   O.K.   Very good

3. How do you feel about this drawing (product)?

Very bad   O.K.   Very good

4. Do you feel you helped your group?

Not at all   A little   Average   Quite   A great
                                           a bit   deal

Sheets should be identified either by the color of the paper (white to groups who worked individually—colored to cooperative groups) or a coding designation (I, individual; II, cooperative). Rating sheets are frequently utilized to obtain opinions along a range. Sometimes they are numbered (1–5) and results tallied with presentation of the lowest, highest, and median scores for each question. Data should be tallied, comparisons made by questions, and results reported.

Discussion

See objectives as a basis for discussion.

Exercise 5
Factors Influencing Attractiveness of Membership

Objectives

To understand personal sources of attraction in a group

To become aware of and experience the problems of having new members in a group

To become aware that changed membership in a group influences not only relationships with new members but also the relationship of older members with one another

To understand that changed membership influences sources of attraction to the group

To understand that increasing the size of a group has advantages as well as problems

Action

The facilitator says, "Select a partner. Get acquainted. Be aware of how you feel in this pair." Pairs talk for 15 minutes. While they are talking, the facilitator assigns each pair a number. After 15 minutes he tells them to stop talking and asks, "How do you feel about this dyad? Would you like to continue in this group? *Think* about your answer." Then he says, "Would groups 2, 5, 8, 11, etc. [every third group] split? One member go to the group on one side of you; the other go to the group on the other side of you. There will now be a series of triads or three-person groups. Get to know one another."

Discussion

One person comes alone and must develop a whole new set of relationships. How does he feel? How is he treated?

Others were in a pair which was or was not satisfying. How do they feel toward one another with the newcomer? How do they respond to the newcomer?

How do members of the triad feel in comparison to how they felt in the dyad?

Variations

Discussion can be within triads rather than with the whole group, or two triads combined.

There can be progressions in the size of groups. Triads 2, 5, 8, 11, etc. disband. One person goes to the group at the left, the pair goes to the group at the right. The feelings of one person going into an existing group (newcomer joins trio) are examined; the same is done with a pair going into an existing group (pair joins trio).

Exercise 6
Increasing the Attractiveness of a Group:
High Talkers—Low Talkers

Objectives

To present an opportunity for "high talkers" and "low talkers" to develop empathy for the other

To recognize the limitations of either behavior

To present low talkers an opportunity to recognize that their situation is not unique

To afford an opportunity for high talkers to practice listening and for low talkers to speak

To experience how group membership can be determined by certain behavioral patterns.

Situation

This exercise is appropriate after the groups have been working together for some time and usual behavior patterns are known by the members. The facilitator asks each person to categorize himself as a high talker or a low talker. (This can be written down, and there can be a perception check among the members.)

Action

A "fishbowl" is set up with the low talkers sitting in the center, and the high talkers standing around the outside observing. The low talkers discuss the problems of being a low talker.   (8 min.)

Then the groups switch. The high talkers go to the center and discuss why they talk a great deal, and the problems involved. (8 min.)

Both groups come together and talk about their feelings and observations.

Variation

Instead of action in a fishbowl setting, action occurs in "mixed quartets," i.e., two low talkers and two high talkers in a group. In each there is a discussion of the problems of being a low or high talker. (20 min.)

The entire group comes together and discusses their feelings and observations.

REFERENCES

Amir, Y. The effectiveness of the kibbutz-born soldier in the Israel defense forces. *Human Relations*, 1969, *22*(4) 333–344.

Aronson, E. and Mills, J. The effect of severity of initiation on liking for a group. *Journal of Abnormal and Social Psychology*, 1959, *59*, 177–181.

Aronson, E. and Linder, D. Gain and loss of esteem as determinants of interpersonal attractiveness. *Journal of Experimental and Social Psychology*, 1965, *1*(2) 156–171.

Aronson, E. Who likes whom and why. *Psychology Today*, 1970, *4*(3), 48–50, 74.

Asch, S. E. Effects of group pressure upon the modification and distortion of judgments. In D. Cartwright and A. Zander (Eds.), *Group dynamics* (2nd ed.), Evanston, Ill.: Row, Peterson, 1960, 189–200.

Back, K. Influence through social communication. *Journal of Abnormal and Social Psychology*, 1951, *46*, 9–23.

Deutsch, M. Some factors affecting membership motivation and achievement motivation. *Human Relations*, 1959, *12*, 81–85.

Dion, K. L., Miller, N., and Magnan, M. Cohesiveness and social responsibility as determinants of group risk taking. *Proceedings of the annual convention, American Psychological Association*, 1970, *5* (Pt. 1), 335–336.

Feldman, R. A. Group integration and intense interpersonal disliking. *Human Relations*, 1969, *22*(5), 405–413.

Festinger, L. A theory of social comparison processes. *Human Relations*, 1954, *37*, 184–200.

Festinger, L. *A theory of cognitive dissonance*. Evanston, Ill.: Row, Peterson, 1957.

Festinger, L. and Kelley, H. *Changing attitudes through social contract*. Ann Arbor, Michigan: Research Center for Group Dynamics, 1951.

Fouriezos, N., Hutt, M., and Geutzkow, H. Measurement of self-oriented needs in discussion groups. *Journal of Abnormal and Social Psychology*, 1950, *52*, 296–300.

French, J. P. R., Jr. The disruption and cohesion of groups. *Journal of Abnormal and Social Psychology*, 1941, *36*, 361–377.

Homans, G. *The human group.* New York: Harcourt, Brace, 1950.

Horowitz, M., Exline, R., Goldman, M., and Lee, R. Motivation effects of alternative decision making process in groups. ONR Tech. Rep. 1953, Urbana, Ill.: University of Illinois, College of Education, Bureau of Educational Research.

Jackson, Jay M. Reference group processes in a formal organization. *Sociometry*, 1959, *22*, 307–327.

Kelley, H. H. Communication in experimentally created hierarchies. *Human Relations*, 1951, *4*, 39–56.

Kelley, H. H. Two functions of reference groups. In G. E. Swanson, T. M. Newcomb, and E. L. Hartley (Eds.), *Readings in social psychology.* New York: Holt, Rinehart, and Winston, 1952, 410–414.

Larson, C. Participation in adult groups. Unpublished doctoral dissertation, University of Michigan, 1953.

Lott, A. J. and Lott, B. E. Liked and disliked persons as reinforcing stimuli. *Journal of Personality and Social Psychology*, 1969, *11*(2), 129–137.

Mirande, A. M. Reference group theory and adolescent sexual behavior. *Journal of Marriage and the Family*, 1968, *30*(4), 572–577.

Ninane, P. and Fiedler, F. E. Member reactions to success and failure of task groups. *Human Relations*, 1970, *23*(1), 3–13.

Quey, R. L. Functions and dynamics of work groups. *American Psychologist*, 1971, *26*(10), 1081.

Rasmussen, G. and Zander, A. Group membership and self-evaluation. *Human Relations*, 1954, *7*, 239–251.

Rose, A. *Union solidarity.* Minneapolis: University of Minnesota Press, 1952.

Sagi, P., Olmstead, D., and Atlesk, F. Predicting maintenance of membership in small groups. *Journal of Abnormal and Social Psychology*, 1955, *51*, 308–331.

Schachter, S. Deviation, rejection and communication. *Journal of Abnormal and Social Psychology*, 1951, *46*, 190–207.

Schachter, S. *The psychology of affiliation.* Stanford, Calif.: Stanford University Press, 1959.

Seashore, S. *Group cohesiveness in the industrial work group.* Ann Arbor, Michigan: Institute for Social Research, 1954.

Shelley, H. P. Level of aspiration phenomena in small groups. *Journal of Social Psychology*, 1954, *XL*: 149–164.

Sherif, M. *The psychology of social norms.* New York: Harper and Row, 1936.

Snoek, J. D. Some effects of rejection upon attraction to the group. Unpublished doctoral dissertation, University of Michigan, 1959.

Stotland, E. Determination of attraction to groups. *Journal of Social Psychology*, 1959, *49*, 71–80.

Thelen, H. A. *Dynamics of groups at work*. Chicago: University of Chicago Press, 1954.

Tsouderos, J. Organizational change in terms of a series of selected variables. *American Sociological Review*, 1955, *20*, 207–210.

Turnbull, C. M. *The lonely African*. New York: Anchor Books Edition, 1963.

Wicker, A. W. Size of church membership and members support of church behavior settings. *Journal of Personality and Social Psychology*, 1969, *13*(3), 278–288.

Willerman, B. and Swanson, L. Group prestige in voluntary organizations. *Human Relations*, 1953, *6*, 57–77.

Zander A. and Havelin, A. Social comparison and intergroup attraction. *Human Relations*, 1960, *13*, 21–32.

ADDITIONAL REFERENCES

Although the following books are not specifically cited in the references, they were helpful in developing this chapter.

Cartwright, D. and Zander, A. *Group dynamics*. New York: Harper and Row, 1968.

Kemp, C. G. *Perspectives on the group process*. Boston: Houghton Mifflin Company, 1964.

Knowles, M. and Knowles, H. *Introduction to group dynamics*. New York: Association Press, 1959.

Maier, N. R. F. *Problem-solving discussions and conferences*. New York: McGraw-Hill Book Company, 1963.

Miles, M. B. *Learning to work in groups*. New York: Teachers College Press, 1967.

Shepherd, C. R. *Small groups*. San Francisco: Chandler Publishing Company, 1964.

Michael Leary

3 norms, group pressures, and group standards

To a new member, group norms are unclear, confusing, ambiguous, arbitrary, and restrictive. He despairs of finding any sense of order in a group, and is bewildered by group procedures. For example:

1. A person goes to a meeting scheduled for 8:30 p.m. He arrives promptly only to find the janitor wearily arranging the chairs; no other members are present. Subsequently, others arrive, and the meeting begins at 9:00; the new member senses that the chairman has opened, but is stalling. The meeting really begins after another group of people enters, at 9:15.

The next night he goes to a second meeting with another group but is less compulsive about being there on time. He arrives half an hour late and discovers half the agenda has already been covered. When do meetings start? What are the rules?

2. He plays basketball with a group. At practice, the leader fouls pretty regularly, and no one seems to notice. But when he fouls, the others give him angry stares; or he gets a quick elbow; or there seems to be a reluctance to pass the ball to him. How come it's O.K. if some people foul, but not others?

3. He attends a meeting at which time the "budget will be discussed and passed"—so it states in the notification. At the meeting the budget is read, and the chairman asks, "Is there any discussion?" He raises his hand. The chairman ignores it. The person next to him explains that if there are questions on the budget they were to have been asked at the previous open executive meeting, not at this general meeting—here there will be a "rubber stamp" passage of the budget as worked out. The question of discussion is simply a rhetorical gesture; no one even hears it as the budget chairman continues with, "Do I hear a motion for passage of the budget as read?"

How do you find out when they do discuss what they say they are going to discuss? It isn't written; how do you find out?

4. He joins a professional association. The president asks for a volunteer to be chairman of a committee to investigate an issue brought before the group. He raises his hand to volunteer (if he is

going to belong, he might as well get involved). The president again asks for a volunteer chairman; his hand remains raised. The president pleads, "Won't someone volunteer to be chairman?" There are no other volunteers. The president suggests that the matter will be dealt with after the meeting.

Is one of the rules that new members cannot be appointed chairman of a committee even if help is needed desperately? Where does it say that? Why? Wasn't he deemed professionally competent when he was accepted as a member? (See preceding chapter on Group Membership.)

The examples are endless. The variety and complexity of norms within various groups are indeed sources of confusion to new members and to outside onlookers; and yet those same norms are sources of order and stable relationships among members and those who understand that group. It is within this framework of order and stability, interlaced with uniqueness and variability, that an understanding of group norms will be developed. One must understand a group's normative structure in order to comprehend its development or current behavior.

The Concept of Group Norms

Within a university department there were severe internal problems. The issues involved time spent at the university as opposed to time in consultation; additional income for those in consultation; and the perennial conflict of the relative importance of research as opposed to teaching. Casually, one faction would meet in an office, close the door, and discuss their frustration and feeling of impotence: "What can we do about them?" Another faction, with more power and status, was comfortable in its belief that research was more important than teaching, that student popularity was equated with easy courses, and that rigor and scholarship were the prime criteria for a successful university program. Still other faculty members, who saw the polarizations develop, were eager to preserve both factions in the department. They felt that the combination offered the best resources, and in addition, they enjoyed their relationships with the dissident faculty. They were attempting to reduce extremes and seek out alternatives in subtle ways. However, the way the situation was progressing, there could be a split in the department.

All this was occurring at an informal level. The norms at the formal level were:

1. We are all one happy department, the image of unity is to be preserved.

2. We are civilized and always greet each other in the halls.

3. At university committee meetings, we represent the department. The image must be that of a strong, cohesive department.

4. Students should not know of any faculty differences within the department (just as children should not know their parents are fighting).

5. At faculty meetings we discuss only the issues and pretend to ignore who supports whom as factions line up.

6. Items for faculty agendas must be presented to the chairman in writing a week in advance so that we may be informed (so that each side may have time to align).

One need not have been employed by a university department to identify with both the stressful situation and the norms which operate to enhance an image that there are no problems and that all is well.

Group norms, at an individual level, are ideas in the minds of members about what should and should not be done by a specific member under certain specified circumstances (Homans, 1950).

When the norms are expectations for the behavior of a particular person, these are termed "role expectations." For example, if someone asks who will take notes at a meeting and all eyes turn to one member who has unofficially taken notes at several previous meetings, there are readily visible role expectations. It is important to understand that norms are not only rules about behavior in the group but also ideas about the patterns of behavior. Rarely can the ideas be inferred directly from behavior; rather they must be learned. For example, a new faculty member learns "not to bring up" the subject of stress, or to overtly state that there are difficulties. Or, in another situation, a new member learns that in basketball fouling in practice is frowned upon by the group, but fouling by the leader is not. He also learns that "ratting" to the police is disapproved by members no matter who does it. Thus, through his experience, he learns that the significance of an act is not the act itself, but the meaning the group gives to it. He learns that the meaning may change according to who commits the act and the circumstances under which it is committed.

This experience results in what is called shared ideas among members about what should or should not be done by a specific member under certain circumstances. A shared idea means that an illusion of cohesiveness and harmony must be preserved; that no one should foul a fellow member during practice, but because of his position, the leader has a special privilege in this regard. It is another shared idea that new members should be given inferior or disagreeable tasks.

At a group level, norms (or more correctly the normative system) are the organized and largely shared ideas about what members should do and feel, about how these norms should be regulated, and about what sanctions should be applied when behavior does not coincide with the norms (Mills, 1967). Group norms function to regulate the performance of a group as an organized unit, keeping it on the course of its objectives. They also regulate the differentiated but interrelated functions of individual members of a group. Norms in some cases specify particular behavior, while in other situations they merely define the range of behaviors acceptable. In some areas, no transgressions are permitted; in others, wide variability may be practiced. Similarly, norms range from those formally stated to those held by group members at an unconscious level, and they are realized only when they are somehow transcended. Thus, at all levels there are implicit or explicit standards which have important implications for the feelings and behaviors generated in the group.

Classification of Norms

It is understood that norms are a set of standards groups develop for themselves, but is there a way to classify them? Are there dimensions along which these norms develop? Is there a way to understand a group in terms of its norms, and can this method also be a means to contrast groups? Sociologist Talcott Parsons (Parsons and Shils, 1951) believes there are. He feels that norms in any society or group must provide answers to questions relating to at least four dimensions:

1. *Affective Relationships* How personal are the relationships? Are relations among members to be based upon expression of feelings they have toward each other, or are feelings to be suppressed and controlled? For example, is an expression of emotion considered legitimate and appropriate, or is it understood that any expression of emotion is "personal" and will hamper the movement of the group?

In the university illustration personal issues are inappropriate at faculty meetings, and only within subgroups are personal feelings expressed.

2. *Control, Decision Making, Authority Relationships* Is the involvement with one another to be total and unbounded (as with a parent and child), or is it to be restricted and specific (as with a driving instructor and a pupil)? Within a department, where certain decisions are made by the department chairman, they obviously apply only in a work relationship.

3. *Status—Acceptance Relationships* Is the relationship with another due to the uniqueness of the other (a brother, a cousin, a friend), or is it due to the fact that he represents a status or position (a servant, an employer, a client)? For some, the relationship in the department is an acknowledging nod, while with others there develops a colleagueship and personal friendship.

4. *Achievement—Success Relationships* Is the significance of the other due to his personal qualities (intelligent, trustworthy), or is it due to his professional skills (as a scientist, as an athlete)? Within the department some are respected for their professional contributions, while with others there are varying criteria for what is considered success. To all, rank is an important factor.

One way to compare norms across groups might be with regard to answers members give to the questions above. A great variety of combinations is possible. It may prove a simple, meaningful way to contrast the difference between primary and secondary groups. It may also clarify the difference between members' wishes for norms and the actual existing norms. It may also make it possible to reduce stress for the members or to precipitate action toward changing the norms.

Students, prior to entering a university, frequently believe that they can discuss issues or ideas with teachers, but after awhile they are sometimes disappointed. It is difficult to make appointments, or they are casually kept, some faculty rush out just as class ends to avoid being trapped by a student. To the dismay of students many faculty members are willing to discuss only issues specifically related to the course content and are not receptive to discussions of opportunities in the field, interesting developments on campus, or personal matters —and sometimes the faculty member may not even know the student when he sees him.

An understanding of these norms may help the student clarify the differences between his wish level and the reality level, with a consequent reduction in stress, an increased ability to function appropriately at the reality level, and perhaps some alternatives leading to a modification of the norms, at least with some faculty members.

Kinds of Norms

It is the infinite variety of norms which most impedes an understanding of the concept. Norms must be learned, and some are more readily learned than others.

Formal Norms   Some norms are codified as in bylaws and code books. They may be formal, written statements intended to be taken literally as group rules, and they are enforced by organizational sanctions (i.e., actions to insure compliance). They are stated and presumably available to members who are willing to examine the constitution or corporate policies. But, there are complications.

Sometimes statements in code books are not adhered to as stated. For example, it may be stated with regard to procedures for promotion for university faculty that teaching skill, service, and publication will be weighted equally. However, since publication is easier to measure and more prestigious, it takes on greater weight. The norm then is that publication is most important; teaching skill and service become secondary factors.

Sometimes there is a tacit understanding that formal laws can be ignored, much like old statutes that remain on the books but are not enforced, a classic example being the old Connecticut statute which makes taking a bath on Sunday unlawful.

This distinction between norms and formal rules is an important one, for as some of the formal rules are weighted differently than perceived, as some are adhered to and others are not, a new set of rules is established; these are the formal norms of the group. Frequently those unfamiliar with this distinction will examine a copy of a group's constitution and believe these are the procedures by which that group functions; yet, there may be almost no similarity between such official pronouncements and what actually occurs in practice.

Explicitly Stated Norms   Some norms do not appear in the codifications or in formal written form, but may be explicitly stated verbally or may easily be recognized by members. In being hired, an employee may be told, "Everyone gets here by 9:30." (the explicitly stated norm being that you're late if you arrive after 9:30.) Although nothing may be said about attire at work, the new employee may notice that all the men he has encountered in the office are wearing suit jackets and ties; there is the easily recognized norm that he will be expected to wear a suit jacket and tie in his work.

However, as previously stated, the explicitly stated norms may not be the actual norms. The Catholic Church is an example. In the early training of priests and nuns, the Church clearly advocates ideas of love, charity, and responsiveness to others. However, until recently, there were internal norms of the strongest kind prohibiting close relationships among religious of either sex, and it was improper to show physical affection (in some orders a nun would keep her hands in her habit so that a child could not take her hand, nor would she be tempted to reach out to a child). The explicit norm stated was not the actual norm practiced. The explicit norms were, rather, that love, charity, and responsiveness were ideas to be nurtured, but without close relationships or physical contact, which were considered deviant behaviors. This conflict between explicitly stated norms and actual norms has been a special area of stress, as nuns have questioned the disparity between being dedicated to love and humanness and yet being required to wear a religious habit which sets them off as distant occupants of a "nonhuman" role.

Nonexplicit, Informal Norms   Within each formal group there may be nonexplicit or informal norms that influence member behavior. For example, it may be understood that when the boss asks for a report by Monday, it is not expected to be submitted until Wednesday; or, although there are no assigned seats at committee meetings, the chairman generally sits at the left end of the room and the vice-chairmen flank him.

Sometimes norms become known only when they are violated. For example, a minister may preach about justice and racial equality; he may urge his congregation to live according to these principles. However, when he marches in a picket line, he may be rebuked by his congregation as transcending his position. He may be sanctioned with a statement to the effect that ministers can preach about justice and equality, but action on social issues is for others. Here, the fact that a norm had been violated (for that congregation) was not known either by the minister or the congregation until an action took place which was contrary to the norm; the congregation made known the violation by the threat of sanctions.

Unconscious Norms   There are even norms that are unconscious, as in the case of some taboos, which are in themselves unthinkable ideas. It goes without saying that the League of Women Voters will not advocate the overthrow of the government by revolutionary means; church groups will not promote incest; the Boy Scouts will not teach boys to become professional thieves.

The process by which a group brings pressure on its members to conform to its norms, or by which a member manipulates the behavior of others, is the process of social control. If the norms of the group are compatible with an individual's norms and goals, he will conform to the norms of the group. However, if he finds that his behavior deviates from the group norms, he has four choices: to conform, to change the norms, to remain a deviant, or to leave the group.

Forces Toward Conformity or Acceptance of Group Norms

Why does a person bother to learn the norms of a group, and is it worth the effort? Why should he be governed by the norms of a group? Why would he conform to group expectations, rather than his own? How do members get other members to conform?

Basically, there are two kinds of forces that induce an individual to conform. One set of forces may be viewed as internal forces, i.e., those based on intrapersonal conflict; the second may be viewed as external forces, i.e., forces induced by other people who seek to influence him directly.

Internal Forces Based on Intrapersonal Conflict   Intrapersonal conflict occurs when a person experiences an event under the same circumstances as others whom he perceives to be like him. The conflict within him occurs when he must make a judgment or opinion that is different from the others. Suppose, for example, five people are waiting at a corner for a bus, and while standing there, an accident occurs between a black car and a green car. The police, investigating the accident, ask the five witnesses to describe what they saw. The first witness states that the black car sideswiped the green car; the second gives similar testimony; the third and the fourth give similar reports. How is the fifth witness to report if he thinks he saw the green car changing lanes without indicating it with a turn signal (in his judgment the green car came into the path of the black car) ? Will he render a judgment similar to the others? Will he question his own perception in the light of the reports from four other people? Will his personality influence his report? He doesn't know the others; there are no overt pressures for him to give a judgment similar to theirs. Where is the pressure for uniformity? The intrapersonal conflict occurs as he questions whether he should trust his own senses or whether he should be influenced by the unanimity of the others.

Asch (1952) attempts to explain the situation as follows: The individual comes to experience a world he shares with others; events occur which he sees and which they see simultaneously. He understands that the environment includes him as well as others, and that he is in the same relation to the surroundings as others. If it rains, it rains on him as well as those standing beside him; if an automobile in which he is a passenger stops suddenly, he as well as other passengers will be shaken. He knows (in the basic internal sense of knowing) that he, as well as others, is in a similar experience and responds to certain identical properties (they all are wet due to the rain, the smoothness of the ride is interrupted because of the sudden stop). Since the person is aware of similarity of experience and similarity of response, which seem the inevitable direct response to an identical experience, the intrapersonal conflict situation arises for him. In these circumstances the "pull" toward the group becomes understandable. Since he knows he experiences a shared reality with others, there is an internal tension to "hear" what they are saying, even if it is not what he thinks he saw.

However, it should be noted that this situation occurs only in making a judgment based on internal conflict. It does not occur in all cases, as for example, a judgment on personal preference. In this case, the individual does not perceive himself as being in a situation similarly experienced by others; he perceives himself as having idiosyncratic preferences which are his alone. If he is standing on a corner with some other people, and a surveyor should question each person as to his favorite flavor ice cream in a study on preferences of Americans, the internal conflict does not occur. The first person may answer, "chocolate," the next may also say, "chocolate," and even if the third and fourth reply "chocolate," the fifth will answer without hesitation, "coffee" or "tutti-frutti," as the case may be. Personal preference replies are perceived as being in a different category from judgment replies in which each member sees himself as responding to a common environment.

External Forces Based on Direct Influence by Others   Usually the person is influenced by those who seek to pattern his behavior along certain paths under certain circumstances. These are direct influence attempts. There are a number of reasons why people attempt to influence others to comply to certain norms. One is that it will help the group to accomplish its goals, another is that it will help the group maintain itself, both functions which must be developed with strong supporting forces if the group is to succeed. At another level, in some ways similar to the conflict over intrapersonal forces mentioned earlier, a person is open to other influences in an effort to determine a social reality for himself.

Norms are sustained to help the group achieve its goal (Festinger, 1950). If a group is attempting to raise funds, norms will develop as to standardized pledge cards, procedures for assigning members to districts to be solicited, procedures for turning in money, for reporting results, etc. All these procedures will develop, because they will help the group achieve its ends. But how will members respond to the member who turns in his pledges on the corner of a menu or the back of a shopping list? How will they respond to the member who solicits people in someone else's territory? How will they respond if the campaign ends and a member doesn't turn in the money? People exert pressures on others to follow approved procedures that are directed toward achieving the group goal. These are sources of uniformity which are seen as legitimate.

Another example of norms developing to help achieve a goal can be seen in a library. The procedures for owning library cards, determining which books may or may not be taken out, setting the length of time a book may be held—these are all procedures developed to attain the goal of servicing books to the community.

If a football team is to win, members are expected to learn the plays and execute them. The maverick who disregards the rules (pressures toward uniformity) will be ridiculed—"So you thought you were the whole team, or better than the whole team?"

Members are expected to adhere to the norms viewed as necessary to help the group achieve its goal; any member who does not adhere will be seen as a threat to that end, and efforts will be made to induce him to return to the group procedures.

Norms are also sustained to help the group maintain itself (Stock et al., 1958). Procedures for paying dues, pressures for attending meetings regularly, norms of waiting for enough members to come before starting the meeting may all be viewed as norms or standards which are conducive to maintaining a group or organization. Pressures may be put on members to adhere to these norms in order to sustain the organization.

Frequently, other norms develop in an effort to sustain the organization. For example, conflict areas may be avoided in discussion (for fear that those who "lose" may leave), areas of tensions may be ignored, and information that may bring disgrace on a member (and perhaps the group) is not to be brought up. On the other hand, norms develop for announcing honors to the group, awards to members, or prestigious events in order to enhance the attractiveness of membership. These norms will also be enforced as members are solicited to report these events, and they will be reprimanded for not reporting an honor (a speech, a publication, a promotion). These pressures toward uniformity are also deemed legitimate as a means of sustaining the group.

In addition, norms are a means for creating a consensually validated social reality within which members can check their perceptions (Festinger, 1954). Whereas in the first two sections, norms and procedures arise and are enforced so that the group may achieve its ends, this aspect of norms—a social reality—develops so that an individual may better understand and judge himself, and he does it through a group and its norms.

Suppose an individual is faced with an issue about which he must make a judgment, but there are no objective criteria with which to make the determination. In this instance he cannot depend on logic, or objective reality, or information from his senses. He is most likely to seek out others whom he perceives are like him. (See the section on Reference Groups in Chapter 2.) He will make a judgment based on their norms, their procedures, their standards. In the course of comparing his opinions, beliefs, or emotions (Schachter, 1959) with others like him, he will be exposed to pressures for establishing the "correctness" of an opinion, the "goodness" of an ability, and the "appropriateness" of an emotion. Discussion groups, bull sessions, and identity seminars help develop a social reality for their participants.

These forces toward uniformity may exist singly or in combination. The norms developed may help the group achieve its goal or maintain its membership, or the norms may be impediments restricting the members' use of their resources.

Conformity to Norms: Under What Conditions?

Under what conditions does a member act like other members and conform to the norms of the group? He is most likely to conform when one or more of the following circumstances are a factor.

Continued Membership Is Desired   If membership is desired, he is more likely to be influenced by other members of the group. (For a further discussion on attractiveness of membership see Chapter 2.) If the group is a reference group for him, he will be especially influenced by the norms of the group (Gould, 1969; Buchwald, 1966). In the university illustration presented earlier, the fact that membership in the department was desired is what made each member adhere to presenting a cohesive front and continuing the established norms. Otherwise the person would leave.

Salience of Membership Is Heightened   Imagine a research experiment designed to acquire information on attitudes toward birth control. Let us assume the population to be studied is divided into two groups. One group will be asked their opinion on birth control. For the second group, the design will be changed slightly. One additional question will be asked prior to the central one; each person will be asked his religion. How will the responses differ? The question on religion heightens the salience or cues of membership, and the respondent is more likely to remember "how one of us is expected to feel." When a member receives cues that he is an American Federation of Teachers' member, a professional, a Christian, or a Boy Scout leader, he is more likely to accept the pressures toward uniformity for that group.

The Group Is Cohesive[1]   A cohesive group is one that members find meets their needs, or one in which they desire to remain for some other reason. The more cohesive the group, the greater the likelihood that members will conform to the group norms, and the greater the pressure the members exert on others to conform (Janis, 1971). It is

[1] Festinger and Thibault, 1951.

often said that management or administration should help their lower staffs or employees become cohesive units. The dilemma here is that management might not be induced to work in this direction unless they could be sure that the norms to be created would be compatible with their goals. A highly cohesive work group can restrict production by bringing the "eager beavers" and "rate busters" into line.

Sanctions Are Expected   Norms exist for specific purposes, and if these purposes are valued by members, those who are deviant can expect to be sanctioned. The sanctions may be fines (for lateness, swearing, etc.), a negative comment, sarcasm or ridicule, or even exclusion from the group. If membership is desired, and sanctions can be expected in response to deviance from norms, members will be more likely to conform to the pressure for uniformity.

> Some blacks who have high church attendance and strong commitment to the "paths of peace" find violence abhorrent. They believe time will bring a change for the better. And, in the Martin Luther King image, many believe that an activist stand is necessary—but that rock-throwing, abusive name-calling, virulent repudiation of the system by burning and looting is not the way.
>
> A new generation of blacks is increasingly frustrated by emulating "whitey's" ways, by trying to work in a system that is unresponsive, by not being heard because of a lack of economic, social, or political power. A hundred years of "trying patiently" is more than enough; for them the time is Now. At meetings in which young militant blacks are active, older or more conservative members are quiet and squirm. From the late Whitney Young down, the sanction of being an "Uncle Tom" is understood.
>
> "Black is beautiful" was for many middle-class nonviolent blacks a return to primitivism, but the sanctions were felt. Women who had their hair straightened were seen as not "with it." How could blacks identify with a leader who opted for imitating a white man's ways? (Witness the change in Julian Bond's hair style—Bond is the first black to be elected to the Georgia legislature in recent years and is seen having national political potential.) Blacks who two years ago ridiculed the wearing of African garb now accept or are even proud that more and more university professionals, entertainment stars, and urban leaders have the courage to wear it even though as middle-class blacks they do not.

Although the sanctions with regard to clothes were originally negative, it seems that now the sanctions are positive. Black leaders are expected to be identified as blacks first, and then as leaders in housing or law.

Although the term sanction is frequently used with a negative connotation, it is important to note that sanctions can be used for positive reinforcements, as in the previous illustration. The sanctions may also be a name on the honor roll, the "good citizen of the week," a raise, a bonus (to the person with the best safety record in the plant), or a promotion.

Another notable aspect of sanctions is that they carry two messages, one about present behavior and another about future behavior. For example: "That was quite an error [present]; you'd better watch it next time [future]." Or, "You're doing great [present]; keep it up, and you'll be president of this place [future]." Or, "If you are a black leader, you have to look like a black, now and in the future." Sanctions can be expected to influence both present conformity and future conformity.

Deviance from Norms

What about those who do not conform to norms? An act which violates a shared idea about what should or should not be done on that occasion is termed a deviant act. It is deviant to "rat" to the police, to leave during a fight, to "not show" when your team is in competition. However, every behavior that departs from the expected is not deviant. The quiet member may become more active; the active member may take an unpopular position in the course of discussion; one member may change his feeling toward another member. (None of these are deviant acts unless the group has norms pressuring that quiet members remain quiet, that no opinions other than the traditional may be discussed, that members maintain the same relations with others.) What happens when a person is deviant?

Interaction with the deviant increases when the group first recognizes a member's deviancy; there will be efforts directed toward amplification and clarification of his position, opposing information will be directed toward him in an effort to lessen his deviancy. If the pressure brings the deviant to return to the norms of the group, the discussion will continue with the deviant in his usual role. If, however, the deviant continues in his behavior, the group may redefine its boundaries to exclude him by ignoring him in discussions. This is most likely to occur in a cohesive group, and if the area of deviance is relevant to the purpose of the group (Schachter, 1951).

However, if the member is a respected and valued member, the situation may be different. There is a theory (Hollander, 1960) that prestigious members have "idiosyncrasy credits," that is, a kind of credit for helpful behavior in the past which allows them leeway in following the norms of the present. It is as if their previous work for the group entitles them to some rewards in the form of increased flexibility of behavior and immunity from punishment for deviance. A prestigious member who deviates from the norm may be dealt with in a number of ways. One is that he may be purposely misinterpreted or "not heard." Another is that his behavior may be perceived as idiosyncratic ("You know he has these bad days; disregard anything he says; he doesn't mean it"). Or nonconforming acts are now approved rather than disapproved. (A recent article noted that Mrs. Henry Ford enjoyed attending luncheons in blue jeans. She commented that all others arrive in chic luncheon dresses; but they accept the fact that she is "comfortable and prefers to come in jeans.")

Until recently, deviance from norms was regarded only as a negative function, a behavior requiring reinterpretation and individual or group pressures to return to accepted norms. Researchers (Dentler and Erikson, 1959) currently view deviance as also serving a positive function. Deviance helps members to master norms (it is a demonstration of what should not be done) and helps them to be more articulate about these norms. In addition, it helps them to comprehend what their group is and what their group is not (to feel offended by an act and to see others similarly offended provides information on oneself and the group which could be gained in no other way).

Deviance or nonconformity has become an interesting target of research from yet another viewpoint (McDavid and Harari, 1968, Grinder, 1969). A number of studies call attention to the importance of distinguishing true independence (indifference to the normative expectations of other people and groups) from rebellion (direct rejection of the normative expectations of other people and groups). While both represent nonconforming behavior, it is important to recognize that they are very different in both the attitudes they represent and the consequential behaviors. Conforming behavior (to norms) is a consequence of a person's awareness of expectations held for him by others or as a member of a group, coupled with a decision to adhere to these expectations. Rebellion against norms is a consequence of awareness of the norms coupled with a decision *not* to adhere to them. True independence represents indifference to the norms and expectations of others—personal criteria for behavior are seen as motivators of behavior rather than expectations of others. In some cases norms may be adhered to, in others, disregarded. In some ways rebellion and indifference are alike, in that both represent nonconforming behaviors. However, it should be noted that conformity and rebellion are in some ways alike—both represent behavior dependent on norms and expectations of others. This is important to understand with regard to some of the radical movements on many college campuses. Many of the dissidents are rebelling against some institutionalized issues—against the "military-industrial complex," against "computerization," against the "establishment"—rather than being for some alternative. The adolescent who sees himself as independent is often more likely to be rebelling than to be truly independent (Willis and Hollander, 1964).

Norms for the Future

John Kenneth Galbraith (1970), in a *Time* magazine article, refers to regulatory bodies, but the phenomena he describes is familiar: "the fat cat syndrome."

> Regulatory bodies, like the people who comprise them, have a marked life cycle. In youth they are vigorous, aggressive, evangelistic and even intolerant. Later they mellow, and in old age—after a matter of ten or fifteen years—they become, with some exceptions, either an arm of the industry they are regulating or senile [p. 88].

The analogy to youth and vigor in young people and organizations is apt.

Group norms are basically conservative mechanisms: they tend to preserve the status quo. Procedures which at one time might have been appropriate and helped the group achieve its purposes may still be in existence long after their appropriateness has diminished. Procedures developed at a time when there was only one organizational structure (the formal hierarchical model) may still be in effect for lack of consideration of possible alternatives. Other rules and procedures may be appropriate for some tasks but not for others. The overwhelming tendency is to consider what is as what should be. Of course, there may be problems; progress is "part of the times," but it should be considered only within "our policies, our framework, our image."

Yet these very resistances to change which promulgate increased difficulties and problems in a differentiated society comprise some of the group's prime assets. Norms and pressures toward uniformity create a security and order in interaction. Members know the rules and procedures for working in that group; they know what is expected; they hope to be rewarded for conforming to group norms.

In working with groups, the question with regard to norms is not whether they are good or bad. Rather, the questions are: Which norms help the group achieve its purposes, and which are harmful or inhibiting? Which norms are compatible with the goals and values of the group and under what conditions? How can the norms be changed or reconsidered to permit the group to achieve its purposes under conditions of maximizing its resources? (Schmuck et al., 1969; Gardner, 1963; McGregor, 1967)

Changing Group Norms

Norms are developed by the group as procedures or statements of expectations which are perceived as appropriate by that group. They are highly resistant to change. Lewin (1947), in his force field theory (see Chapter 7), indicates that when forces are increased for change in a given direction, counter forces in the other direction may also occur, bringing behavior to the prior position. Change involves not only enhancing the forces in the direction of the desired change but also holding the resistant forces constant or reducing them.

Homans (1947) has a similar equilibrium model. For example, following a research investigation, a school may decide that the procedures for student grading should be changed to be more in keeping with the goals of the school. Perhaps a new system of credit–no credit rather than traditional grades may be advocated. The administration may favor the new system and approve it (an example of a changed norm for the organization). However, the administration may say that each department shall implement the new system in ways appropriate to that department. Those departments who prefer the previous system may simply "sit it out," may make no changes, or never get around to implementing the new system. The resistant forces have effectively maintained the old norms; the result is no change in norms except at the "formal" level. (See earlier section on Norms.)

Another illustration is the highly touted community or urban university concept. At the formal level, the president may make compassionate pronouncements about the need for the university to revise its procedures in the direction of increased community participation at every level, yet the system maintains its own status quo intentionally.

The classic illustration, of course, is the Brown-Topeka 1954 Supreme Court decision, which stated that segregation was by definition unequal with regard to schools; the situation 19 years later speaks clearly with regard to changed norms and the resistance of some organizations to that change.

Norms will be changed more readily by those of high status who have earned their idiosyncrasy credits—those who have previously worked hard for the group, have achieved positions from which they can be "listened to," and are perceived as striving to enhance the productivity and values of the organization. Even for them, this will represent a high risk venture with the possibility of being considered deviant if the norms to be changed are too drastic. It will be attempted first in areas of peripheral importance, more slowly in central areas. Many school districts have been willing to discuss and review dress codes (peripheral norms) in the direction of increased variability more readily than changes in curriculum.

For new members, the risks are even greater. They have not yet earned status or idiosyncrasy credits. For them the risks of non-acceptance, perceived deviance, or rejection are greater; however, they are not committed to the vested interests or the knowledge of the status quo as the way. Especially when new members represent a significant number, there is an opportunity for a change of norms not perceived with the impact possible.

It may be that norms will be changed by "outside consultants" who are trained in studying organizational structure, communication, human relations, and goals (Schmuck, 1968). Their view of the organization from an objective perspective, and their knowledge of a variety of alternatives, may be the impetus toward developing norms that are more compatible with the organization's goals and also reduce the risks for members. Or trained "internal consultants" may be specifically delegated to review norms and procedures in the light of organizational goals; this could increasingly become a new area for behavioral scientists. These internal consultants may develop specialization in "operationalizing" because they have an understanding of the timing and centrality issues unique to that organization.

It would seem that a statement could be made to the effect that those norms most central to that group's purposes are most resistant to change. Frequently, however, one encounters norms which seem peripheral to the group, yet are adhered to rigidly. Which norms can be changed and under what conditions are questions to be examined for their explicit meaning in a particular group.

Since social progress is intimately connected to changing norms, considerable research has focused on methods for inducing changed norms. Some of the methods attempted have been to influence through lectures, by fiat, through discussion without decision, or by discussion with decision. Lewin (1947) and his colleagues, in their "action research" during World War II, conducted some of the classic research on changing norms. In one study Lewin sought to change the eating habits of families so that they would buy low-priority foods to which they were not accustomed. He determined that the housewives were the "gatekeepers," those who exert major influence with regard to food in their families. Some women were given lectures on the value of eating these new foods; others participated in a discussion. More changed their behavior and attitudes after the group discussion than the lecture. Once there was public agreement on the new standard, it was easier to change individual behavior in accord with this new standard.

Another experiment dealt with lecture and group discussion on changing the pattern of giving orange juice to newborn babies. The findings were similar; there was greater change among the women who had participated in the group discussion, and in the follow-up, it was found that more women continued in the new behavior.

There is extensive research to support the previous findings over a wide range of behaviors: in community problems (Dean and Rosen, 1955; Lipsitt and Steinbruner, 1969), in raising productivity (Jenkins, 1949; Hall, 1971), and in improvement of group skills (Bradford and French, 1948; Hall and Williams, 1970).

In attempting to understand why group discussion seems to be an important element in change, there is evidence pointing to a number of factors. One area of research indicates that breaking down the old value system prior to adopting a new one is a crucial element in changing norms (Rokeach, 1971). It is an emotional as well as an intellectual process; for this reason group discussion is most effective (Alpert and Smith, 1949; Watson, 1967).

Others feel that what produces the changed behavior is not so much public decision making and commitment, but, rather, a consensus on the decision (Bennett, 1955). It seems that the desire for group conformity is stronger when there is unanimity on an issue.

On yet another level, members change norms frequently. If they belong to multiple groups having a variety of norms in a multiplicity of settings, they may adapt readily to the present group, unaware of inconsistencies in their behavior.

This last statement returns us, once again, to the new and rather confused member faced with the multiplicity of norms in a variety of settings. Thus, as described earlier in this chapter, he will enter the new group confused, the norms will seem ambiguous, and he will feel his behavior is restrained—he can't behave as he would like until he can determine what is appropriate behavior and what is expected of him. As he talks with others, the rules become less absolute and more flexible. They appear not only as constraints but also as a guide. The newcomer is then better able to see the norms as the outer limits within which he is free to operate. When he learns what is allowed, he gains both a sense of confidence and greater latitude in his behavior. Thus, from his experience in the group and his interaction with others, he learns how to interpret what is happening and how to conduct his own behavior.

Exercise 1
Awareness of Norms

Objectives

To develop an awareness of norms by changing the norms

To develop the understanding that norms function to create an order in the group and regulate the interaction among members

To note the changes in the group when the normative structure is violated

Setting

The following exercise is illustrated within a classroom setting, but the procedures would be equally applicable in a variety of other situations.

Action

The exercise should not be used until after the group has met for some time, then the teacher (facilitator) examines a number of norms of the class (group) and for one session purposely changes them. This need not continue for more than 15 minutes of the classroom period.

An example, as the authors have used it, may be helpful. A course in group dynamics is taught to college students. Typically, the chairs are arranged around tables; smoking and drinking coffee in class are accepted; attendance is not taken; observer's reports are returned at the beginning of each class; examinations are not given unless scheduled. The teacher is available for questions or problems which have occurred since the last class; sometimes there are a number of questions and class does not begin promptly. All these norms are purposely broken.

The students enter the class one day and encounter the following:

Chairs are set in rows.

A pile of examination blue books are on the desk (no examination had been announced).

The teacher (could be a substitute) sits at the desk and appears to be busy reading; she answers no questions, nor has discussion.

The class starts promptly.

The teacher announces the observer's reports not ready to be returned.

The teacher calls the roll.

The teacher makes a sarcastic comment to someone smoking and to someone drinking coffee.

The teacher answers no questions on her strange behavior and appears not to notice the confusion in the class.

Blue books are distributed.

Members of the class are asked to write one or two sentences on how they feel at this moment.

The teacher explains that the norms of the class were purposely violated.

Discussion

What are the feelings you had? Why?

What are norms?

What is the value of norms?

What are the norms in this classroom? How many can you name that were violated? What are other norms of this class?

What effect do norms have on behavior of members?

What is the effect of the norms in the class? Are they appropriate?

Could they be modified to be more appropriate to the goals of the course?

Variation

A stranger may come in to teach the class that day, purposely breaking the norms under the guise of not knowing them. Students will attempt to make his behavior conform as they indicate the "rules."

Discussion

What are the problems of a substitute, or a new member?

How are they dealt with? How can they be dealt with?

Are the norms of the group appropriate to its goals?

Are there alternatives as the newcomer sees them?

Exercise 2
Survey of Dress Norms

Objectives

To understand that norms develop uniquely to a particular group

To develop the understanding that the "character" of a group can be determined from observation of its norms

To collect data in order to determine whether there are differences in the norms of groups, and to explore the reasons that might be behind these differences

Situation

It is sometimes thought that norms are not developed by a group itself. Rather, they may exist for a variety of reasons, that is, they may be imposed by exterior forces, they may be common to the environment, they may be typical of all people, etc. This reality can be the basis for a simple research project. For example:

> Among the colleges in the Philadelphia area are University of Pennsylvania, Temple University, LaSalle College, Drexel Institute of Technology, Beaver College, Philadelphia Community College, Philadelphia Textile Institute. One hypothesis is that college students in the Philadelphia area will dress reasonably alike, because all the students will conform to the dress codes of large eastern cities. They will wear what college-age students wear at an urban eastern college, and there will be no difference in dress among the colleges. (A student at Penn will be dressed similarly to a student at Drexel or one at Temple.) Another hypothesis is that each school will have its own norm for dress and that typical dress will be different and recognizable among the schools.

Action

The class is divided into work teams of 4 to 6 on a team. Teams stand at places on the various school campuses where they can observe the dress style of the students. Each team views a sample of 50 students. Each team visits the various schools at their convenience in no special order over a common 2-week period. Team members tally their observations on specific items (see categories of dress, below) by a simple categorizing system. Each team tallies its results and describes the attire of a typical male and female at each of the colleges. On a given day, all the teams distribute their reports to the other teams. Data and typical attire for each school is examined for replication in other team reports. The data may indicate clearly that each school develops its own norms.

Discussion

How do norms develop? What function do they serve? Are they the result of outside influences? How are they changed? Interviews may also be conducted with some of those being observed and used as a stimulus to further discussion.

Variations

Any number of variations are possible in gathering data on contrasting populations; for example, dress codes of students or teachers in
schools in different parts of a city or the city and suburban areas, the
dress of ministers or priests in different orders or denominations, the
dress of members of various civic organizations. Data relating to
other norms could also be observed after hypotheses are developed
for various groups. Dating behavior, conversation patterns in different
offices, or between classes, hall behavior in local high schools are a
few examples.

CATEGORIES OF DRESS
(Basis for tallies; separate sheets for each institution)

1. *Hair length*
   a. Females: Short—to nape of neck
      Average—to shoulders
      Long—beyond the shoulders
   b. Males: Short—no sideburns, well-trimmed at back and
         sides
      Average—sideburns, length not passing the collar
         in back, sides full but not over the ears
      Long—that which exceeds the previous description
      Clean-shaven
      Facial hair—moustache, beard
2. *Slacks*
   a. Females: Jeans
      Other pants
   b. Males: Dungarees
      Levis
      Pressed slacks
      Bell-bottoms
3. *Shirts*
   a. Males: Ivy league
      Button-down collar
      Pointed collar
      Tee-shirt
      Turtle neck or other casual shirt
4. *Blouses*
   a. Females: Shirts
      Jerseys (turtle neck, jewel neck)
5. *Skirts or dresses*

6. *Shoes*
   - a. Males:
     - Penny loafers
     - Laced dress shoes
     - Sneakers
     - Sandals
     - Boots
     - None
   - b. Females:
     - Flats or small heel
     - Loafers
     - Sandals
     - Moccasins
     - Boots
     - Sneakers
     - None
7. *Stockings/Socks*
   - a. Males:
     - Crew
     - Dark
     - Light
     - None
   - b. Females:
     - Nylons
     - Panty hose
     - Knee socks
     - Colored stockings (yellow, green etc.)
     - None
8. *Pocketbooks*
   - a. Females:
     - Shoulder
     - Handbag
     - None

Exercise 3
Toward Changing Group Norms

Objectives

To understand what is meant by group norms

To recognize the difficulty in changing norms

To offer an opportunity to examine and change norms at various levels

To develop insight into how norms can be changed in organizations

When appropriate, this exercise can be used after a group has been working together for some time. It can be a work team, a task group, an organization, a segment of a class group, or a seminar.

Action

Phase 1   The facilitator presents a small lecture on norms—what they are, their influence on a group, etc. The material in the first part of the chapter might be the basis for development of such a talk.
    (Approximately 10 min.)

Phase 2   The groups are asked to examine their norms. They list as many as possible (dates, times, seating arrangements, order of meeting or work, typical behaviors, etc.). These should be listed on paper.   (Approximately 20 min.)

Phase 3   The group is then asked to change some of its norms. The facilitator says, "Which norms can be changed?" He has the group change them and holds a brief session under the new conditions.
    Typically, groups change superficial norms: they will sit on the table instead of sitting in chairs; or will shout rather than talk to one another; or attempt to conduct the session nonverbally. This encourages laughter and a reduction in inhibitions—perhaps even a party atmosphere.   (Approximately 20 min.)
    (Usually a break is indicated here.)

Phase 4   The groups are asked to examine which norms they changed, and how relevant the changes were in helping accomplish their goals. What impeded changing norms? What norms need to be changed? The group then goes into its work session on this basis. (The ensuing discussion is very different from the party atmosphere of the first change; it raises difficult issues for the group and involves members in high-risk behaviors.) An observer might be assigned to watch for behavior that changes norms.

Phase 5   Later, perhaps the next day, the next week, or the next group meeting, a discussion of what norms were changed, which were difficult to change and why, should be conducted. Who was most influential in changing or proposing changes in norms? Who has highest status and role in group? What are the problems involved in changing norms to increase movement toward the group's stated goals?

REFERENCES

Alpert, B. and Smith, P. A. How participation works. *Journal of Social Issues,* 1949, *5*(1), 3–13.

American Heritage History of 20's and 30's. New York: American Heritage Inc., 1970, p. 166.

Asch, S. *Social psychology.* Englewood Cliffs, N.J.: Prentice-Hall, Inc., 1952.

Bennett, E. Discussion, decision, commitment and consensus in "group decision." *Human Relations,* 1955, *21,* 251–273.

Buchwald, A. The grown-up problem. In *Son of the great society.* New York: G. P. Putnam and Sons, 1966.

Bradford, L. P. and French, J. R. P., Jr. (Eds.). The dynamics of the discussion group. *Journal of Social Issues,* 1948, *4*(2).

Dean, J. P. and Rosen, A. A. *A manual of intergroup relations.* Chicago: Univ. of Chicago Press, 1955.

Dentler, R. A. and Erikson, K. T. The functions of deviance in groups. *Social Problems,* 1959, *7,* 98–107.

Festinger, L. Informal social communication. *Psychological Review,* 1950, *57,* 271–282. Reprinted in D. Cartwright and A. Zander (Eds.), *Group dynamics.* (2nd ed.) Evanston, Ill.: Row, Peterson, 1960. Chapter 16.

Festinger, L. A theory of social comparison processes. *Human Relations,* 1954, *7,* 117–140.

Festinger, L. and Thibaut, J. Interpersonal communication in small groups. *Journal of Abnormal and Social Psychology,* 1951, *16,* 92–99.

Galbraith, J. K. *Time,* March 30, 1970, 88.

Gardner, J. *Self-renewal: The individual and the innovative society.* New York: Harper and Row, 1963.

Gould, L. J. The two faces of alienation. *Journal of Social Issues,* 1969, *25*(2), 39–63.

Grinder, R. E. Distinctiveness and thrust in the American youth culture. *Journal of Social Issues,* 1969, *25*(2), 7–19.

Hall, J. Decisions, decisions, decisions. *Psychology Today,* 1971, *5*(6), 51–54, 86–88.

Hall, J. and Williams, M. Group dynamics training and improved decision-making. *Journal of Applied Behavioral Science,* 1970, *6*(1), 39–68.

Hollander, E. P. Competence and conformity in the acceptance of influence. *Journal of Abnormal and Social Psychology,* 1960, *61,* 365–370.

Homans, G. C. A conceptual scheme for the study of social organization. *American Sociological Review,* 1947, *12,* 13–26.

Homans, G. C. *The human group.* New York: Harcourt, Brace, 1950.

Janis, I. L. Group think. *Psychology Today*, 1971, *5*(6), 43–46, 74–76.

Jenkins, D. H. Feedback and group self-evaluation. *Journal of Social Issues*, 1949, *2*, 50–60.

Lewin, K. Frontiers in group dynamics. *Human Relations*, 1947, *1*, 5–42.

Lipsitt, P. D. and Steinbruner, M. An experiment in police-community relations; a small group approach. *Community Mental Health Journal*, 1969, *5*(2), 172–179.

McDavid, J. W. and Harari, H. *Social psychology*. New York: Harper and Row, 1968.

McGregor, D. *The professional manager*. New York: McGraw-Hill, 1967.

Mills, T. M. *The sociology of small groups*. Englewood Cliffs, N.J.: Prentice-Hall, 1967.

Parsons, T. and Shils, E. A. (Eds.) *Toward a general theory of action*. Cambridge, Mass.: Harvard University Press, 1951.

Rokeach, M. Long-range experimental modification of values, attitudes, and behavior. *American Psychologist*, 1971, *26*(5), 453–459.

Schachter, S. Deviation, rejection in communication. *Journal of Abnormal and Social Psychology*, 1951, *16*, 190–207. Reprinted in D. Cartwright and A. Zander (Eds.), *Group dynamics*. (2nd ed.) Evanston, Ill.: Row, Peterson, 260–285.

Schachter, S. *The psychology of affiliation*. Palo Alto, Calif.: Stanford University Press, 1959.

Stock, D., Whitman, R., and Lieberman, N. The deviant member in therapy groups. *Human Relations*, 1958, *11*, 341–371.

Schmuck, R. Helping teachers improve classroom group processes. *Journal of Applied Behavioral Science*, 1968, *4*(4), 401–436.

Schmuck, R., Runkel, P., and Langmeyer, D. Improving organizational problem solving in a school faculty. *Journal of Applied Behavioral Science*, 1969, *5*(4) 455–482.

Watson, G. (Ed.) *Change in school systems*. Washington, D.C.: National Training Laboratories, 1967.

Willis, R. H. and Hollander, E. P. An experimental study of three response modes in social influence situations. *Journal of Abnormal and Social Psychology*, 1964, *69*, 150–156.

Dennis Stock / Magnum

4 goals

One of the central concepts of small groups is the concept of goals. Goals guide a group toward an objective or desired location, or out of a difficulty or an undesired location. A goal can be conceived as a location where the group would like to be. Certainly one of the prime group goals is to "stay alive." Consider, for example, a redistricting plan set up in New York City.

Three community school districts were created on an experimental basis. Community efforts were mobilized with varying degrees of success and frustration to acquire more community involvement: in hiring of teachers, for a revised curriculum, for smaller classes. Power was limited, but the community leaders hoped it would be expanded. Instead, the courts ruled to abolish the community school districts and to integrate them into much larger ones. Try to imagine the reaction at a community school district executive committee meeting:

"The redistricting decision means that Complex 205 is to be absorbed, and we will no longer be a community controlled school district. Are we going to sit passively and watch our efforts, our beginnings at getting a decent education for our children, die? Let's have some ideas—what can we do?"

"Blow up City Hall." (Laughter)

"Blow up the school district." (More laughter)

"Explode the judge's house?"

"Let's get an injunction. They have no right to end this school program."

"Get a lawyer. We never got a fair hearing. The witnesses were plants. We never got a chance to call our witnesses."

"Get up a petition. We mothers have to show them we care about our children's education and the school."

"Insist on a meeting with the superintendent. I don't know where it will get us, but it will make me feel better to tell him what I think about his promises, and that hearing."

"We have to insist that the programs we started stay, and Lou Hill stays as our business manager."

The group is working on the very serious fundamental goal of remaining in existence and exploring some means of achieving that goal through a number of operational objectives. One objective is to have the court rescind its decision; another is to put strong pressure on the school district to show community dissatisfaction with loss of control; a third objective is to maintain, as a minimum, the benefits already gained. Goals are generally seen as the place the group would like to be (in existence and with power in the above illustration) or out of difficulty or out of a place they would not like to be (terminated, in the illustration). Objectives are the shorter term specific means of achieving the goal, although frequently the terms objectives and goals are used interchangeably.

Consider the illustration again at a personal level. What is the goal of the person who suggests "telling off" the superintendent? Is it to feel personally powerful, if only for a few minutes? What are the goals of the person who says that Lou Hill stays as our business manager? Is it that he sees Lou Hill as an excellent administrator whose skills are sorely needed, or is Lou Hill a friend whose job he would like to protect? Were the people who suggested blowing up the school district or the judge's house jesting, or were they seriously recommending that course of action as a desperate means to remain in existence? While a group is working toward a group goal, members are simultaneously also working toward individual goals.

Individual Goals—Group Goals

This difference between individual and group goals—once a source of raging controversy among psychologists—is no longer a prime issue (Allport, 1924; Lewin, 1939), but it is still a source of confusion (Quey, 1971). We can examine individual goals of members and hope to better understand their behaviors, or we can understand the group goals. Our perspective in viewing produces different understandings, which is not to say that one is more important than the other, simply that the data derived will be different. A direct illustration may make this clearer. Assume two players are engaged in a competitive game, tennis for example. Each player's goal is to win the match, but is the group goal to win the match? Is the group goal simply a summation of the individual goals? Obviously not. Each has an individual goal to win; the group cannot win; if one player wins, the other loses. If, then, the goals are individual, is there a group goal? It would seem that the group goal is to have a good game—to have imaginative play, to land and to return some "good shots," and to have superior play win. How does a player feel when his opponent defaults, or when the player is ill or tired? Why are there handicaps or rankings except to insure a good game?

The group goal occurs in the minds of the players as to a desirable outcome for the group (a good match, in the illustration). Consider two levels of goals: personal goals (referring to the individual participants) and group goals (referring to the occasion as a whole). In the illustration above, the individual goal is to win over an opponent; the group goal is to have a good game between the opponents.

How Are Goals Formed?

We recognize that we are motivated and we move with direction, but how is this formulated into a goal? The theory (Zeigarnik, 1927; Morrow, 1938) is that as a person sets a goal for himself, an inner tension system is aroused which continues to motivate the person until his goal has been reached. These tension systems exist until either the person's goal is actually achieved or there is a psychological closure for him. According to the theory, if a person were required to do a series of tasks and he were interrupted prior to completion on some tasks but permitted to complete the others, he would remember the incomplete tasks more frequently. This theory has been tested and verified with a wide range of subjects. An illustration of a tension system in action may be helpful here.

A student has a goal to do well in a course, and a subgoal to pass a subsequent examination. He reviews the texts, studies his notes and apprehensively submits himself to the ordeal of taking the examination. At the end of the test period, is the tension system reduced? Certainly not. He waits anxiously in the hall and queries others on their responses to difficult or ambiguous questions; he enters the next session of class eager to know if the papers are marked. Someone can be depended upon to ask almost routinely at the beginning or end of each session, "When will the papers be back?" The tension system subsides when the student has his paper returned, and he knows more about his progress toward his goal. He then can determine what his next goal will be—with its coordinated new tension system.

A tension system coordinated to a goal and its recall as an in-completed task weighs heavily on all of us. The tension system was in action when friends invited us to dinner, or to see a play, or to take a couple of hours off while we were writing this book. Immediately there was the almost routine tension of "the book will never get done that way"; "at the rate we're going this won't be a book but a lifetime project; better stay home and work on it." The authors can attest to the recognition of a tension system coordinated to an incomplete task, and the tension system which exists in an individual for completion of a task also exists at a group level (Horwitz, 1954). Members feel a closure when a task is completed whether they perform the final stages of a task or another member of their group actually does.

How Are Group Goals Formed?

How do goals change from individual goals for the person to goals for the group? In the transmittal, what are the problems, the implications?

Individuals Have Goals for the Group   Basically, individuals participate in a group because they believe they will derive more satisfaction than if they did not participate or belong.

Individual motives may be characterized as "person-oriented" or "group-oriented." Although the reasons are roughly classified in one category or the other, these motives should be viewed as a "mixed bag"—a percentage of each will motivate an individual's behavior. Person-oriented motives exist mainly to satisfy the personal goals of an individual. Recreational groups (tennis clubs, golf clubs, bowling teams); educational groups (classes in marine navigation; Great Books discussions; stock market clubs); therapeutic groups (group therapy; marriage counseling); "growth centers" (personal awareness groups, yoga-meditation groups, "games" groups)—all exist to serve primarily person-oriented motives. The individual seeks to meet his goals through the group activity.

Others belong to a group for what is termed a group-oriented motive, that is, they accept and conform to the group objective even though accomplishment promises no special benefit to them individually. The person, here, is satisfied by results favorable to the group as a unit. For example, a person may be active in his political party although he does not personally know the candidates, is not anticipating a job in government, and does not expect any direct rewards. He is motivated to act because he believes his party represents the better choices in the forthcoming elections; he will be satisfied if his party wins and especially pleased if his party "wins big."

Another illustration is the social agency board member who recognizes that facilities at the agency are inadequate and antiquated. He recommends the establishment of a committee to raise funds for a new center. He is fully aware that his children are grown and will not utilize the new center, that a building campaign will mean he has less time to spend on his business, and that it will cut into his already limited free time. It will entail the onerous task of asking people for money, and it will be a thankless job. Yet he votes for the establishment of the committee, knowing full well that if it is approved, he will become a member.

As previously stated, this classification is not to be viewed as a dichotomy. However, the distinction helps to understand individual motivations in conjunction with a group goal. An individual whose prime concern is the person-oriented motive is likely to consider a suggested group goal in terms of alternatives for himself. Which of the alternatives will be most satisfying? Which permits the greatest benefits at the least personal costs? The individual whose prime concern is the group-oriented motive will consider which goal, if attained, will be most beneficial to the group, even when the consequences may not be of benefit to him. In the person-oriented situation, he thinks, "If we agree on this goal, how will I look? How can I look best?" In the group-oriented situation, he thinks, "What chance do we have of making it, of accomplishing it? What would block us, how can we get around it and be successful?"

Although the terms used are person-oriented and group-oriented, the reader is aware of the similarity of these terms and the age-old distinctions between "selfish" and "altruistic" motivations, or "ego orientations" as opposed to "task orientations"—which still interest researchers (Cartwright and Zander, 1968; Lewis, 1944; Lewis and Franklin, 1944). Does it really make a difference for which reasons a person helps a group achieve its goals? Isn't the real issue that he be willing to accept the group's goal and move in that direction? It seems that it does make a difference (Fouriezos et al., 1950). Research has indicated that groups with more self-motivated behavior had longer meetings, yet covered fewer items on their agendas. Also, they reported being less satisfied with both the decision making and leadership in their meetings than those groups having more group-oriented members (Ricken and Homans, 1954).

Individual Goals Are Converted to Group Goals   There are certain limitations set on the determination of goals. First, there are the limits set in the purposes of the organization. A United Fund Committee does not determine what its goal will be, e.g., whether to raise money or not, but, rather, how much money. The organizational purposes determine the goal in this case, and it is the subgoal, how much money this year, which is discussed and agreed upon.

A second limitation concerns changes in the group or its environment that may necessitate a reevaluation of its goals. In the illustration of the community school district, the court ruling of the dissolution immediately changed the group goals from a continuance of previous projects to a sudden emphasis on survival. Within these limitations, groups develop goals based on the criteria of fairness or effectiveness, or some combination of the two.

There seems to be a sustaining myth that groups arrive at goals in a manner reminiscent of a New England town meeting. Each person speaks and makes his point of view known. The others listen, consider the information, and arrive at a decision that represents the most effective method for dealing with the situation, or at least, the best decision possible. The group decision arrived at is compatible with the individual interests of the majority. In reality, the picture is quite different. Although ideally each member should have an equal say in the determination of goals, it rarely happens. Some by their personalities are more verbal and forceful than others; some speak with interest on many subjects, while others only speak in an area in which they disagree; still others simply do not participate. On another level, some are excluded from even an opportunity to speak as decisions are made by the executive board or the planning committee. The criterion of fairness, i.e., full participation, in setting of goals is not met. Frequently the decision making or setting of goals by a select few or even one person is justified in terms of effectiveness. It is assumed that the head of a company knows best what a group can achieve; the expert is most knowledgeable in setting a goal for the whole group. The argument frequently goes, "If we had unlimited time, we could allow all members to participate, but it becomes such a long and frustrating procedure that it is a time-saver and more effective to have goals set by one person or a few people."

For some, an attempt at fairness means reduced efficiency; they believe time expended in arriving at goals could be better expended in progress on the goal. However, it is possible that the preceding two criteria may be compatible, i.e., it may be possible to widen member participation in setting goals and direction for the group (increasing the fairness criterion), and through this increased participation, there may be goals arrived at which are also most effective (based on discussion of alternatives, resources, interests of members). A problem-solving method of arriving at group goals involves discussing alternative choices, examining the resources of members for developing each of the alternatives, considering the time factor for accomplishment, and questioning the probability of success.

In terms of the previous discussion of person-oriented and task-oriented motives of participants in setting goals, some differences in behavior may be discernible (Kelley and Thibaut, 1954). If task-oriented motives are most dominant, members are more likely to arrive at group goals through problem-solving approaches, i.e., through exchange of information, opinions, and evaluations. If person-oriented motives are more dominant (Fouriezos, et al., 1950), goals are apt to be determined only after arguments, negotiations, bargaining, and forming of coalitions.

This section can be illustrated by Robert Kennedy's report on the 1962 Cuban missile crisis (Kennedy, 1968). Typically in meetings there were the usual fights, coalitions, tensions, and decisions by a special few.

> The late Senator Robert Kennedy described the tension and disagreement among the men meeting to recommend an action that might "affect the future of all mankind." After considerable talking, they divided into groups and wrote their recommendations. They submitted their recommendations to other groups for criticism, then reworked their original ideas. Gradually there developed the outline for definite plans.

> During all these deliberations, we all spoke as equals. There was no rank and, in fact, we did not even have a chairman. . . . As a result, the conversations were completely uninhibited and unrestricted. It was a tremendously advantageous procedure that does not frequently occur within the Executive Branch of the Government, where rank is so often important.

Goals were set with optimal opportunities for all to participate, with development of a plan based on consideration of alternatives, resources, time factors, and the probability of successful accomplishment.

Classification of Goals

Goals can be classified in a number of ways. They can be viewed as formal or informal, operational or nonoperational (March and Simon, 1958), and movement on goals can be derived from the "surface agenda" or the "hidden agenda" (Bradford, 1961). Perhaps these concepts can be explained through an example of a severely troubled community mental health board.

> Community mental health centers are required by law to establish community advisory committees made up of area representatives. Their function is to help the professional staff be more aware of community problems, be a liaison between the professional staff and members of the community, and act as an advisory board on development of priorities and policies. In one area there was an active community coordinating council that represented many long-time residents. They were active in planning for the mental health center and became the community advisory board.
>
> Shortly thereafter, professionals residing in the area but employed at other mental health centers began attending the board meetings. Individuals from less organized communities and newcomers who were black also began to attend. Some of those in the last two groups questioned policy by the staff, intimating that priorities seemed to include services only to the seriously ill or residents of the more affluent sections of the community. Some young staff members preferred a more activist role in shaping the community than fulfilling accepted social work roles. Then some ministers began to attend.
>
> The board meetings soon became the battlefield for warring camps. Resident professionals, perhaps frustrated with limited power in their own agencies, were critical of the professional staff, and said so on the open floor. Newer members and blacks questioned the honesty of the secretary of the board because they said they were not receiving meeting notices. Some noted that only the wealthy communities were officially represented on the board, with little representation from minorities or a range of neighborhoods. The junior staff began feeding information to newspapers, to the dismay of the senior staff who preferred that certain information be private. Some of the ministers were most vocal in pointing out the advantages of their churches as "Get Set" centers, of course omitting references to the fees that help support the financially troubled churches.

The difficulties and conflicts were reported by the newspapers; innumerable meetings were called; letters to the editor and to Washington were routine; there was considerable staff turnover—some by dismissal, some from frustration.

In the most recent phase, one segment of the community petitioned Washington to withdraw funds citing the community board as unrepresentative. One group of citizens claimed that they are the community board, since they are more representative than the officially designated board. Letters were sent to the city's Director of Mental Health condemning the professional staff for poor follow-up on clients, refusing clients, being repressive and authoritarian in their personnel policies, being unresponsive to expressed community needs, and having a poor relationship with the community board.

Formal—Informal Problems abound for this community board, as they do for many such boards, but a difference in goals becomes one method for developing understanding and increased ability to diagnose and resolve group difficulties. The formal goal of the professional staff in appointing a community board was to meet a requirement, without which the mental health center would not be funded. It was an easy task to appoint an already functioning portion of a community group as the community mental health board. The formal goal of the community council subcommittee that worked toward the establishment of the community mental health center was probably to help create a community mental health center in their area. The informal goal for the professional staff might have been to perpetuate a good working relationship—the committee was properly respectful to the staff and acquiescent to the staff's knowledge on priorities. The informal goal of the community subcommittee was to keep control of its mental health center. The formal stated goal was that there be a representative community advisory board; the informal goal was that the status quo be maintained. Movement on goals is understood in terms of the dynamics at the informal level.

Operational—Nonoperational Another aspect of goals has to do with their being operational or nonoperational. The community board was to advise the mental health center on short-term and long-range planning and in the establishment of priorities. These goals are broad, vague, and largely nonoperational. Any discussion about problems of various aged populations, relations with schools, drug education programs, or out-patient versus in-patient services could all be construed as work on the goal. How can movement on a nonoperational goal be measured? Within nonoperational goals, a group must determine operational goals which can be the basis for directed action. Thus, an operational goal would be to discuss and develop a plan for meeting the health needs for those over 65 in local centers manned 24 hours a day. Another operational goal might be to develop a series of programs to be presented at schools in the area on community relations. Each operational goal creates a group requiring different roles, norms, and leadership patterns. One of the obvious reasons for strife on the board was the lack of operational goals. There was such conflict and so little mutual trust that goals remained nonoperational. Operational goals, which would have required subcommittees and members gathering data and making recommendations, were not established. Actions were limited to nonoperational discussions at board meetings, and in "full view."

Explicit—Implicit   In addition to kinds of goals, movement on goals can also be understood at two levels. As mentioned earlier, there is the surface agenda and the hidden agenda. Ostensibly, at any given time, the group is working on its task, attempting to cover its open agenda—discussing services, outlining new procedures, reporting on activities. This is what the group is supposed to be doing, the agreed-upon reason the members are together. However, even the novice recognizes that what a group is supposed to be doing is often tangential at best to what seems to be happening. A report is made on activities for the month by the executive director, and one mental health worker from another agency begins a hostile attack. The remarks are so negative that one wonders whether he is attacking the executive director or releasing resentment over his not being appointed to the position. Other mental health workers join in the blast, and once more the question arises: Are they concerned with the activities, or are they feeling a bit of power and hurling back the kind of attack to which they are subjected in their work?

Then, a long-time resident and member of the board gives his reaction to the report on activities. It is inevitable that he will be countered by a new resident, who is not on the board and was not officially informed of the meeting. The new member will forcefully note that perhaps that's how it was 10 or 20 years ago, but that is not the situation today. The more radical members will speak out that the report represents "perpetuation of the establishment" and not new solutions to help the poor. This last outburst is such a regular occurrence that board members discount it and act as if nothing were said; the "radicals" are seen as using every opportunity to discuss their own private agendas regardless of the public agenda. Since private agendas occupy so much of the meeting time, movement on the public agenda is ground to a halt. This becomes apparent when one member asks that each person who speaks state his address and what group he represents. Each speaker is then interrogated as to the representativeness of his group, whether he was formally selected to represent the group, and whether the group agrees with his position. The chairman also has his private agendas. He is careful to call upon members of the officially constituted board to speak rather than members of the community; he is more sure of a favorable response from those who elected him. There is also a board private agenda. They must act as if they are working on the public agenda, and they ignore statements from all others; in addition, they must justify and defend the programs, services, and activities of the center.

All this leaves members expending a great deal of energy at meetings but seeing little of the agenda dealt with. Meetings are considered a waste of time; coalitions develop, and outsiders do not receive meeting notices; more of the services of the center are determined by the professional staff and not even brought before the board for discussion; communication between staff and board steadily diminishes. This community advisory board has, among its many difficulties, formal goals different from its informal goals; goals maintained at a nonoperational level; and conflicting motives, desires, aspirations, and emotional reactions that limit movement on the surface agenda or long-range goals.

From the viewpoint of members, goals are sometimes classified rather globally as being "clear" or "unclear." Where there are clear goals, each member, if polled, would respond with a statement of the goal and would know the steps for attainment of that goal. Clear goals might be viewed as operational goals; they are more likely to be stated formally and more apt to be surface agenda. Where there are unclear goals, as in the illustration, members would answer with a variety of responses depending upon their personal interests, and each would have his own ideas about how these goals could be attained.

Generally, a successful group has clear objectives, not vague ones, and members of a group have personal objectives which are identical or compatible with the group's objectives. The more time a group spends developing agreement on clear objectives, the less time it needs in achieving them, and the more likely that the members' contributions will converge toward a common solution.

Importance of Understanding Group Goals: Relations Between Group Goals and Group Activities

Group goals steer a group toward a given location, and movement toward that location greatly influences the activities and relationships of the group.

Content of Goal Affects the Group[1]   Let us assume that the goal of a correctional institution is the treatment of prisoners (Zald, 1962). Staff members might be given a great deal of autonomy to develop new methods, there might be staff teams to work with groups of prisoners, there might be a number of lectures to keep prisoners informed, and there might be periodic visiting privileges to maintain ties with the outside. Contrast these activities with another correctional institution whose goal is simply the custody of prisoners. In the latter case, there would be fewer professionals and more guards, authority would be very centralized, and rules plus penalties for infractions would be the basis for relationships. The difference in content of goals would result in a difference in relations among staff and prisoners as well as a difference in activities.

Difficulty of Goal Affects the Group: Aspiration Level   Suppose that out of a 12-game season, a football team won 8 games. What will be the team's goal for next season? Will it set a goal at winning 2 games? To win only 2 games would be regarded as a disaster; it would be too easy. Will it set a goal of winning all 12 games? This seems too difficult, and would seem to doom the team to failure.

Assuming none of the key players graduate or have sustained serious injuries, the group would set an aspiration level of probably 9 or 10 games. To win this number would be regarded as a successful season, a fine performance by the team.

The example is meant to illustrate the aspiration level of a group, i.e., when a group confronts a set of alternatives ranging from easy to difficult and selects one, this is referred to as the group's aspiration

[1] Korten, 1962.

level. Performance above this level will be considered successful; performance below this level as failure. The level of aspiration will influence members' self-evaluations, group activities, attractiveness of membership, and subsequent group cohesiveness.

Groups that are successful tend to be realistic about their aspirations (Atkinson and Feather, 1966). Recently, there has been interest in determining whether a group in setting its aspiration level is more conservative or takes greater risks than an individual. It seems that given a set of alternatives, a group after discussion typically selects a higher risk alternative than the individual (Bem et al., 1965; Lippitt, 1961; March and Simon, 1958). It may be that the riskier decision comes from fuller discussion of the alternatives, and a diffusion of responsibility for the decision making among the members.

Type of Goal Affects the Group: Competitive or Cooperative Goals
Whether the goals are competitive or cooperative greatly influences the activities toward the goal and the relations among members. The earlier illustration of the tennis match was an example of a competitive goal; one player can attain his goal only if the other does not. Baseball is another competitive game. If one team wins, the other loses; there is never a tie. However, baseball also has cooperative goals. Each member of the team can only attain his goal of winning if the entire group also attains its goal—the team must win as a unit. Members therefore attempt to cooperate with one another, coordinate their efforts, and use their resources jointly. Observers report significant differences between groups working under competitive conditions or cooperative conditions. Where there were competitive goals, members would seek to "one up" each other, withholding information, and displaying hostile feelings and criticism (Klein, 1956).

> In schools where grade-point competition is keen and colleges will accept only a limited number from one high school, competition is unbelievable. High-ranking students push to become presidents of obscure clubs thus gaining one more degree of status to edge out competition. It comes as no surprise that a student will remove the notice of a prospective visit from a prestigious college from the bulletin board, or remove information on scholarships to reduce competition. And the competitiveness induces hostility and criticism toward those who figured out the best "angles."

Cooperative groups, in a task requiring collaborative activity, were found to have greater coordination of effort, greater attentiveness to members, orientation to the goal, orderliness of procedure, a sense of obligation to other members, and a better quality product (Chapin, 1957; Deutsch, 1960).

> Some high schools have organized tours for students to visit a number of colleges in a given area. All students who are considering attending colleges, let us say, in the Massachusetts-Connecticut area, are asked to list them. An itinerary is then developed and posted, and students interested sign up for the weekend tour. The school makes arrangements with the admissions offices for those desiring interviews; students write to graduates of the high school for appointments to learn about how they see the schools. Following the trip, students meet to share their impressions of the schools and discuss who will be applying to which schools.

Group Goals Themselves Are Inducing Agents   Previously we discussed the tension systems coordinated to a goal. It seems that when a group accepts a goal, those who most strongly accepted the goal display a strong need to have the group achieve its goals. Acceptance of the goal is for them an inducing agent (Horwitz, 1954). However, if the group goal is not accepted by a significant section of the group, there is likely to be a high incidence of self-oriented behavior rather than group-oriented behavior, with activities being coordinated to personal rather than group goals.

The Relationship Between Group Goals and Group Productivity

A group goal represents a "desired location of the group"—a location where they would like to be, a "place" from which they reassess their movement and determine future goals. Did they accomplish their goals? Were they clear enough and operational enough to be measured? And at what costs? Are members disillusioned, relationships strained? Are they glad the project is over so that they can terminate associations? Some might question the validity of asking: "At what costs?" For others, the productivity question is the only one to be asked: "Did they accomplish the goal—raise the money, develop recommendations, reach the desired level of product manufacture?" That is productivity. However, it has become standard (Barnard, 1938) to describe the adequacy of group performance in terms of two concepts: "effectiveness," the extent to which the group is successful in attaining its task related objectives; and "efficiency," the extent to which a group satisfied the needs of its members. Certainly each factor can be viewed independently of the other, but it is possible to examine just the task accomplishment—in fact, it is frequently the only factor considered. It is possible to examine only the relations among members, although this is much less frequently considered. Yet, a group expends energy on both factors, and the effectiveness and efficiency of a group set upper limits on each other. Perhaps some illustrations will clarify this relationship.

How Does Cohesiveness Relate to Productivity? If members spend their time strictly with business—the surface agenda—and ignore interpersonal relationships and hidden agendas, misunderstandings can increase, and communication is limited; each does his job but is outwardly unconcerned about the others as people. On the other hand, what if members spend a great deal of time getting acquainted, building personal relationships, developing increased listening and influence among one another, but have little time to work on the task, to work on activities that lead to the task goal? High task involvement may mean high productivity but possible future difficulties in unresolved personal issues. High personal involvement may mean high morale, but little effort on task activity, and consequently low productivity. The dilemma of which is to be sacrificed, the productivity or member relations, is ever present.

However, there is evidence (Berkowitz, 1954; Thelen, 1954) that if the group spends more time initially in permitting members to discuss their personal goals and to get to know each other, they build a common frame of reference, a "set toward problem solving." They learn over time that some issues are to be avoided, while others can be dealt with. Members develop a clearer view of their roles and where they fit into the group. Frequently, more cohesive groups are more productive than less cohesive groups. There seems to be a general circular relationship between group solidarity and effectiveness. As members work together and see one another as more competent, they are drawn closer together, and this relationship increases the likelihood of successful performance. But, increased cohesiveness does not necessarily mean increased productivity. Increased cohesiveness means that members are able to influence one another more. If they desire to use this influence for increased productivity, potentially they can be very effective; however, increased cohesiveness could also mean that workers might band together to restrict production and thereby lower productivity.

When a group seems bogged down in movement on its goals, the reasons for lack of productivity could be understood by examining the relationships between tasks and maintenance behaviors, or to put it differently, studying the relationship between effectiveness and efficiency.

How Does Interpersonal Style Relate to Productivity?   The closeness-distance interpersonal dimension is a recurrent theme in groups. For some, it is the interpersonal friendships that are most important. Others are there to get a job done and discourage personal questions. Findings are that groups who prefer more formal relationships when working on a task were productive (Berkowitz, 1954) but that groups who prefer more informal and closer personal relationships were also productive (Schutz, 1958). That is, both groups of "likes" were more productive than "mixed" groups. The latter were characterized by personality clashes between those who wanted to be close to associates and those who did not. The result was lower productivity (Roethlisberger, Dickson, 1939).

These illustrations are by no means exhaustive (stress, a disinterested person, self-oriented behaviors might be other illustrations), but simply are indicative of the necessity for understanding productivity at both the task and the socioemotional levels.

Consequences of Group Productivity

As a group works together in determining its goals, in integrating personal goals into a group goal, in synchronizing a series of activities with specialized roles for members, in reevaluating the goals and perhaps modifying or changing them, what is happening? How is the group different after this process?

First, groups have increased knowledge of their resources. After a group has worked together, members have increased knowledge of one another: who never attends; who talks a good show but cannot be depended upon to stay with a responsibility; who really knows how to coordinate activities; who has resources in the community that are helpful; who rarely speaks but seems interested; who causes less friction if he works alone; who is highly committed to the group goal.

Second, they have increased experience in working as a group. They gain experience in how to determine a goal, how to get the information they need and what skills are required to perform a task, and there is increased confidence in the resources of the group. The initial floundering, indecision, lack of knowledge, inexperience become less so. Members may begin to move more freely and clearly.

Third, there may be an emergence of new standards. Working together develops a better insight into the problems to be overcome, the additional resources needed, the reality of the aspiration level. There may be new group norms for development of goals, new methods for evaluation of group activities, new criteria of success and failure.

Also, the emotional level of the group changes. The initial surface politeness is gone. Members know one another and may feel more friendly. There may be greater flexibility in role behaviors. It may mean less time is required to say what members really think, to respond more honestly and less guardedly. On the other hand, it may mean the opposite: there may be cliques, antagonism among members, reduced willingness to accept group goals.

Most successful groups, when compared with less successful ones, seem to make a fuller commitment to the group goal, communicate more openly, coordinate activities aimed more specifically toward the goal, and achieve better personal rapport. And the effect is a spiral one. Work on one task influences the next, and there is a greater likelihood of success in pursuing goals in each subsequent task.

How Can Goals Be Kept Current?

Goals in the broadest sense include a forward time perspective—a future different from the present (Bennis et al., 1969). Sometimes group goals are inappropriate and should be reexamined and changed, but goals, like norms, are difficult to change. However, there is a greater likelihood that there will be increased support for the change with concomitant implementation if there is active discussion to determine the new goals. If those involved in carrying out the new goals are also involved in setting them, it is more likely that they will be integrated into their personal goal structures. Setting goals through group discussion is more effective than separate instruction of individual members, external requests, or imposition of new practices by a superior authority. The paradox, though, is that while it is easier to change people as group members than as isolated individuals, it is difficult to change the group's goals because of the very support members receive from one another. A number of steps have been suggested (Lippitt, 1961) to help a group be more productive:

1. It must have a clear understanding of its purposes. It is important at the beginning of any group's life that it have a clear understanding of the goals it wants to reach.

2. It should become conscious of its own process. By improving the process the group can improve its problem-solving ability. The group should be encouraged to continuously diagnose its process and act accordingly. Time invested in building interpersonal effectiveness may lead to quicker and more effective task performance.

3. It should become aware of the skills, talents, and other resources within its membership. Over time there is a tendency for groups to lock persons into certain roles; a continuous flexibility to other roles based on resources should be encouraged.

4. It should develop group methods of evaluation, so that the group can have methods of improving its process. Data from evaluations help members become aware of the opinions and feelings of others.

5. It should create new jobs and committees as needed and terminate others as outdated when no longer compatible with the goals.

Summary

Initially a member acts in that group as he acted in others (Mills, 1967); there is for him an undifferentiated membership role. He looks to others for norms, expected behaviors, and actions consistent with the norms. As he becomes familiar with the norms, i.e., which behaviors are rewarded and which are deviant, he increases the boundaries for his behavior. He begins to operate at a higher level. He understands the group goal, accepts it, commits his personal resources to accomplishing it, and gives it higher priority than his own goals. He evaluates his performance and the performance of others in terms of movement on the goals. He is helping the group become more effective in accomplishing its goals. The centrality of goals as a group concept is such that some theorists define a group as a goal-seeking system (Deutsch, 1963; Parsons and Shils, 1951). Group goals influence all aspects of group behavior.

Exercise 1
A Series of Skill Exercises

Objective

To increase skills in goal areas[2]

Rationale

Goal setting seems obvious; participants often feel they have no difficulty setting goals, or agreeing on them. Frequently, any difficulties that arise are seen as "personality conflicts," which is another way of saying that nothing can be done. These exercises give participants an opportunity to check out their perceptions on goals and movement toward goals. There are also exercises that allow members to build skills in goal setting or statement of the problem. These focus on the group problem rather than inducing individual defensive behaviors. The following exercises should be used individually as appropriate.

1. *Setting up the Problem*

Usually when defining a problem we do so in a way which implicitly suggests a solution. This may cause some people to become defensive and work on their private or personal goals rather than the group goals. This exercise attempts to help participants overcome that difficulty.

Action

Participants are divided into groups of 6 to 10. The facilitator introduces the exercise by saying, "While all of us publicly state we want the group to make a decision, we behaviorally don't mean it even when we think we do. For example, we say the office secretaries use the phone too much and ask what we can do about it. But this question does not allow the group to make a decision based on determination of the situation. Rather, it puts the secretaries on the defensive. We do this all the time. How can we state the problem in such a way

[2] Also, see Chapter 6, exercises in problem solving, for additional exercises which may be used to understand goals.

that some people do not begin to feel guilty and in which there is no implied solution? This will be an exercise to practice these skills."

The facilitator may state one or several problems that have occurred in the life of the group (one is preferable). In each case, the facilitator asks each participant to assume the appropriate position for asking the question (in the illustration cited, he could be the office manager). Each person writes the problem so as not to make anyone feel guilty and so as not to imply a solution. Then each member reads his statement and the other critique for meeting the criteria. The group suggests improvements, and the next person is heard. As the analysis goes on, some general principles of stating the problem emerge. Each group reports its best statement of the problem and the general principles. As additional skill building, groups make up a problem and submit it to the next group. The same procedure as above is used, and there is a testing of the general principles. This exercise is cognitive, but members usually find the experience interesting in that they come to appreciate the difficulties of avoiding predetermined solutions as they refine their skills. Some problems for restatement, if the group does not create its own, would be as follows:

1. A bus driver reports that children in the buses are destroying property, using abusive language, and picking on younger children. The high school buses especially have this problem on the morning run at 7:00 A.M.

2. Shortly, we will be electing class officers. I believe that they should be truly representative of the class. In the past this has not been done.

3. Mr. Brown from the American Federation of Teachers came to visit me yesterday, and he urges us to affiliate. Last year Bill and John led the opposition, and we did not join.

2. Clarity of Goal Setting

Here the objective is to increase observer skills in goal setting and to increase awareness in various aspects of goal setting. The facilitator introduces a role-playing situation (the hidden agenda one in this chapter is appropriate, or another that involves a current group issue). Depending upon the facilitator's objectives, he may have one group role-play and all others observe, or he may divide the total membership into a number of role plays with two observers for each role-playing group. The first method builds common skills in observation and goal setting; the second develops an understanding of personal and group goals with observations.

Observers are instructed to note whether behaviors are person-oriented or group-oriented, which behaviors helped to clarify the problem, and which impeded movement on the problem. Sheets like the following are distributed to each observer:

Behavior	Tallies	Examples
Person – oriented behaviors		
Defends self		
Deflates others		
Off subject		
Provokes tension		
Group – oriented behaviors		
States problem		
Clarifies problem		
Develops alternative solutions		
Attempts to harmonize points of view		
Tests consequences		

The facilitator cuts the role playing when a decision is reached, or if it becomes evident that a decision will not be reached. Role players report back how they feel, especially with regard to movement toward a goal. How did their private agendas help them? Or did they impede them? What would have helped them become involved in the group goal? Was there a group goal? The observers report back. In the hidden agenda role play there are usually so many more individual behaviors it becomes obvious that a decision cannot be reached until these factors are in some way dealt with. Some might be brought out into the open, some consciously ignored.

After the exercise, members begin to understand both the problems and pervasiveness of work at several levels on goals. They also develop increased awareness of the behaviors needed to help the group center on group issues rather than personal goals.

3. *Diagnosis of Goal Clarity and Goal Movement*

If groups are to work efficiently at goals, at both task and maintenance levels, it is essential that they become aware of their own processes. It is important to gather data on the current state of the group and use this information for helping the group set its goals, clarify them, and learn the degree of involvement.

Simple Reporting   One method is to stop each session 10 minutes before the end. The members of the group discuss their answers to these two questions: How much progress do you feel we made on our goals today? What would help us?

This can be done in a workshop at the end of each session; it can be used effectively in ongoing work groups. Initially there is resistance to the concept as well as the process. If it is begun at a routine session or becomes part of an ongoing process, it loses much of its threat and becomes a simple, effective device for helping the group get feedback on its goal movement.

Individual–Group Reaction, Reporting   The design is similar to the one above. It is used about 20 minutes before the end of the session. Sheets with the following questions are distributed to each group member:

What did you think the explicit goals of the group were?

What do you think the group was really working on (implicit goals)?

What was helpful?

What hindered movement?

Each person replies to these questions privately and individually. Members then share their replies and consider actions based on data.

This method is also initially threatening to members, but if it becomes routine, it develops increased skills in diagnosing group problems on goals and allows for greater group productivity.

Feedback on Goals, Instrumented   Another method for achieving clarity of goals as well as movement on the goal is to use a chart which is distributed, scored, and the results fed back to the members. Because it has a more objective, statistical format, it sometimes encourages members to be more open to the findings and less defensive. It takes more time, and perhaps a half hour should be allowed. The group is rated on three dimensions, as illustrated below.

			Goals					
Poor	1	2	3	4	5	6	7	Good

(Confused)   (Clear)
(Conflicting)   (Shared)
(Couldn't care less)   (Involved)

			Participation					
Poor	1	2	3	4	5	6	7	Good

(Few dominate)   (All participate)
(Some passive)   (All listened to)
(Some not listened to)

			Feelings					
Poor	1	2	3	4	5	6	7	Good

(May not express feelings)   (Express responses honestly)

The sheets are collected. One member tabulates the data. A check is scored at its numerical value on the scale (a check between 3 and 4 is scored 3.5). The numbers are totaled for each question. The findings on each dimension are reported in terms of highest and lowest scores as well as average. The higher the score, the closer to the objectives of goal clarity, group participation, openness in response. Members then discuss the findings.

Although these problems may meet with some initial resistance (and therefore the simple open-ended discussion is the first recommended), each helps the group diagnose its own situation and hopefully modify its behaviors toward increased productivity.

Exercise 2
Setting Individual Goals and Reassessing Them

Objectives

To increase the understanding of what is meant by setting goals as an individual

To develop skill in stating goals clearly and specifically

To recognize that goal setting is an ongoing process

To periodically reevaluate goals and determine whether any changes or modifications are needed

To increase understanding and skill in giving and receiving help

Rationale

We participate in many group experiences with only vague ideas of what we expect to derive. This exercise is designed to help the participant formulate his goals specifically and realistically, and then reevaluate them at regular intervals. It is hoped that in the course of the experience he will not only develop skill in formulating his goals, but that once this has been brought into consciousness, he will be motivated to pursue these goals in his activities. As we move toward a goal, we have new insights, new obstacles, new understandings. Thus, as a result of increased understanding at time A, we can make revisions of goals and move into time B. At this time we again reassess goals for time C, and so on.

Timing

Phase I of the design should take place early in the program. It might be used after an initial "micro-lab" or "getting to know each other" opening session. It is appropriate for a workshop or course which will continue over a period of time. Phase II should occur about the middle of the program, and Phase III at the end. Each phase takes approximately an hour.

Action

The facilitator announces the exercise, and may informally state some of the objectives. The group is divided into trios. These trios become a support system for each individual, helping to redefine his goals as well as analyze the forces that help or hinder him. Each helps and receives help from the others. The facilitator reads and explains Phase I, Steps 1 and 2 (see below and on page 130). When completed, the facilitator suggests the group continue with Step 3. Discussion questions may be considered at this point.

Phase II is scheduled midway through the learning experience. The groups form into their original trios. The facilitator reads and explains Phase II (see page 130). The trios work. If there is time, a discussion similar to the one after Phase I occurs; however, the exchange will be very different from the first one. Trio members will be much more comfortable with one another; there will be much less anxiety and more willingness to share and to help. More time should be allowed.

Phase III should be scheduled at the end of the learning experience. It will be conducted similarly to Phase II, but there will be a marked change in atmosphere. Trio members will feel closer and will honestly discuss their feelings and reactions to the workshop. The prospect of continuing in a home setting produces mixed responses. There are those who "can't wait" to continue on the goals, and others who are apprehensive about whether their situations will permit even tentative movements in the directions they would like to go. However, Phase III cannot be eliminated. It must be continued in "real life" if developing skills in individual goals is to have any permanent value. A discussion following Phase III might allow participants to discuss the aids and hindrances they expect to encounter, and to show how they may find alternatives for dealing with these factors.

Goal-Setting Procedure

PHASE I   INITIAL GOAL SETTING

Step 1   Take five minutes to write one to three responses to the following question: *What do I want to learn most from this workshop* (or course or laboratory experience)?

Step 2 Take turns going through the following procedure: One person starts by reading one of his responses from Step 1. All discuss the response (goal). The following guideline questions may be helpful to clarify and amplify the goal under discussion:

Is the goal specific enough to permit direct planning and action, or is it too general or abstract?

Does the goal involve you personally, i.e., something you must change about yourself?

Is the goal realistic? Can it be accomplished (or at least progress made) during the period of this program?

Can others help you work on this goal?

Is this the real goal, or is it a "front" for a subtle or hidden goal?

During or following the discussion the person whose goal is being discussed revises his goal so that it is specific and realistic. This procedure is used for each goal listed. Allow about 20 minutes per person.

Step 3 Discuss in turn the barriers you anticipate in reaching your goal(s). Write them down as specifically as you can. Take a few minutes to list ways you individually, or with the help of others, can overcome these barriers. Discuss your lists with your trio.

PHASE II   REASSESSMENT

Earlier this week (day, month, session) you prepared your initial assessment of goals for this workshop. One purpose of this session is to reexamine your goals in light of your experience so far. Refer to your earlier responses. Look at the goals stated there. Also look at the helping and hindering factors you listed earlier.

Step 1—Goal Reassessment Within your trios take turns reassessing and discussing your goals. As you discuss them, one of the other members should enter your modified or reconfirmed goal in the goal column of the chart on page 125. These statements should be checked out to your satisfaction.

Step 2—Analysis of Helping and Hindering Factors After your goals have been reformulated or reconfirmed, discuss in turn your perception of the present helping and hindering forces—in yourself, in others, in the setting. List them on the chart.

PHASE III   REASSESSMENT

We are now in the concluding period of this workshop. Within your trios reexamine your goals as modified and the helping and hindering forces you listed. How much progress did you make? What still needs to be done?

Step 1—Evaluation of Progress on Goal Each person in turn discuss how much you feel you accomplished on your goals. What helped you most? What hindered you?

Step 2—Goal Setting for the Home Discuss how you could continue on your set goals at home. What forces will help? What will hinder? As you discuss these questions, another member of the trio should enter the new goals on the charts.

Discussion

For some people, revealing personal goals and inadequacies is extremely difficult. Attempting to verbalize expectations is a formidable task for others because they lack practice in doing it. Giving help or accepting help may also be new and difficult experiences. Some of the following questions give participants an opportunity to discuss their feelings in these areas, and thus reduce anxiety.

What problems did you encounter in first stating your goals? Why?

How did your goals change after discussion?

How do you feel about help on your goals?

Are these your real goals? How honest do you feel you were in stating them?

What is the relationship between your goals and the goals of this workshop?

Are they compatible? Where is there conflict?

REFERENCES

Allport, F. *Social psychology.* Boston: Houghton Mifflin, 1924.

Atkinson, J. W. and Feather, N. *A theory of achievement motivation.* New York: John Wiley and Sons, 1966.

Barnard, C. I. *The functions of the executive.* Cambridge, Mass.: Harvard Univ. Press, 1938.

Bem, D., Wallach, M., and Kogan, N. Group decision making under risk of aversive consequences. *Journal of Personality and Social Psychology,* 1965, *1,* 453–460.

Bennis, W. G., Benne, K. D., and Chin, R. *The planning of change.* (2nd ed.) New York: Holt, Rinehart, and Winston, 1969.

Berkowitz, L. Group standards, cohesiveness and productivity. *Human Relations,* 1954, 7, 509–519.

Bradford, L. Hidden agenda. In L. Bradford (Ed.), *Group development.* Washington, D.C.: National Training Laboratories, 1961, 60–72.

Cartwright, D. and Zander, A. *Group dynamics: research and theory.* (3rd ed.) New York: Harper and Row, 1968, 403–405.

Chapin, F. S. Social institutions and voluntary associations. In J. B. Gittler (Ed.), *Review of sociology: analysis of a decade.* New York: John Wiley and Sons, 1957, 273.

Deutsch, K. *The nerves of government.* Glencoe, Ill.: Free Press, 1963.

Deutsch, M. An experimental study of the effects of cooperation and competition upon group process. *Human Relations,* 1949, 2, 199–231. Reprinted in D. Cartwright and A. Zander (Eds.), *Group dynamics* (2nd ed.) New York: Harper and Row, 1960, 348–352.

Fouriezos, N. T., Hutt, M. L., and Guetzkow, H. Measurement of self-oriented needs in discussion groups. *Journal of Abnormal and Social Psychology,* 1950, 45, 682–690.

Horwitz, M. The recall of interrupted group tasks: an experimental study of individual motivation in relation to social groups. *Human Relations,* 1954, 7, 3–38.

Kelley, H. and Thibaut, J. Experimental studies of group problem-solving and process. In G. Lindzey (Ed.), *Handbook of social psychology,* Vol. II. Reading, Mass.: Addison-Wesley, 1954, 735–785.

Kennedy, R. F. The 13 days of crisis, *Washington Post,* November 3, 1968, B-1, B-3.

Klein, J. *The study of groups,* London: Routledge, 1956.

Korten, D. C. Situational determinants of leadership structure. *Journal of Conflict Resolution,* 1962, 6, 222–235.

Lewin, K. Field theory and experiment in social psychology: concepts and methods. *American Journal of Sociology,* 1939, 44, 868–897.

Lewis, H. B. An experimental study of the role of the ego in work. I. The role of the ego in cooperative work. *Journal of Experimental Psychology,* 1944, 34, 113–116.

Lewis, H. B. and Franklin, M. An experimental study of the role of ego in work. II. The significance of task orientation in work. *Journal of Experimental Psychology,* 1944, 34, 195–215.

Lippitt, G. How to get results from a group. In L. Bradford (Ed.), *Group development.* Washington, D.C.: National Training Laboratories, 1961, 34.

March, J. and Simon, H. A. *Organizations.* New York: John Wiley and Sons, 1958.

Mills, T. M. *The sociology of small groups.* Englewood Cliffs, N.J.: Prentice-Hall, 1967, pp. 81–82.

Morrow, A. J. Goal tension and recall. I and II. *Journal of General Psychology,* 1938, *19,* 3–35, 37–64.

Parsons, T. and Shils, E. A. (Eds.) *Working papers in the theory of action.* Cambridge, Mass.: Harvard Univ. Press, 1951.

Quey, R. L. Functions and dynamics of work groups. *American Psychologist,* 1971, *26*(10), 1077–1082.

Rappaport, A. *Fights, games, and debates.* Ann Arbor, Mich.: Univ. of Michigan Press, 1960.

Ricken, H. W. and Homans, G. C. Psychological aspects of social structure. In G. Lindzey (Ed.), *Handbook of social psychology,* Vol. II. Reading, Mass.: Addison-Wesley, 1954, 810.

Roethlisberger, F. J. and Dickson, W. J. *Management and the worker: technical vs. social organization in an industrial plan.* Cambridge, Mass.: Harvard Univ. Press, 1939.

Schutz, W. C. *FIRO: A three-dimensional theory of interpersonal behavior.* New York: Holt, Rinehart, and Winston, 1958.

Shepherd, C. *Small groups.* San Francisco, Calif.: Chandler, 1964.

Thelen, H. *Dynamics of groups at work.* Chicago, Ill.: Univ. of Chicago Press, 1954.

Wallach, M. and Kogan, N. The roles of information, discussion, and consensus in group risk taking. *Journal of Experimental Social Psychology,* 1965, *1,* 1–19.

Zald, M. Organization control structures in five correctional institutions. *American Journal of Sociology,* 1962, *38,* 305–345.

Zeigarnik, B. Über das behalten von erledigten und unerledigten handlunger. *Psychologische Forschung,* 1927, *9,* 1–85.

Dennis Stock / Magnum

5 leadership

If you were asked to name a great leader, what person would come to mind?

> I remember half-dozing over the late news on television as the day's events were recapped. A sleek Air France descended and swarms of reporters and cameramen zeroed in on the stairway slowly being lowered. Scurrying for positions, cameras set, they awaited his arrival. The cabin door opened and a stewardess emerged. Several dignified-looking men followed, obviously functionaries. More people. And then he emerged, looking not as if he came from another continent but rather from another planet. He was no longer young, nor even middle-aged. His hair was sparse, his stance not as erect as it had once been. But he carried himself with an undeniable grandeur, a sense of majesty, an imperious authority. A microphone was set before him, and he uttered a few words of joy at his arrival among compatriots. Surrounded by reporters, photographers, and officials, there was no doubt, even for an instant, who was the leader—he stood head and shoulders above all the others. He was the immediate focus when he spoke. Although the television cameras followed the moving mass of people, his height made it simple to ascertain his every movement, his gestures, his mannerisms. The others looked like pygmies. When he arrived in Canada, Charles DeGaulle stunned television viewers and witnesses alike with his physical impact as a leader.

It was not a matter of being impressed with the leader's policies, or being favorable to him, or even agreeing with him. It was rather the compelling vision of the man as a leader.

And similar visions loom in reading the *American Heritage History of the 20's and 30's* (1970). One in particular:

> His early life and times were the American dream come true, 1920's fashion. At 23, he was washing dishes in a Brooklyn cabaret, and when he could get it, a part time bartender there. At 28, half a dozen years removed from his dish-washing days, he was known throughout the nation. He was glamourized, viewed as a hero. And why not,

he was head of an organization grossing around a hundred million dollars a year. It was not always easy—hazards such as machine gun and pistol fire, for one thing, made it difficult to keep fully staffed— but what business does not have its problems? However, in a competitive nation, in a highly competitive business, where risks were daring and the stakes high, he was number one. Al Capone was not only a leader, he led a charmed life. More than once he was saved by the steel armor and bulletproof glass of his limousine. The real sign, however, occurred when one of his enemies ran eight full cars of gunmen past his headquarters, and riddled the building with shotgun and machine-gun fire; Capone emerged unharmed.

The leader appears as someone bigger than life, for whom the mundane problems of life seem nonexistent. Whether heroes, or antiheroes, they are viewed as singular, unique men of their times. There is a special aura about them; they are seen as "men apart." Each of us has a remembrance, our story of being somehow connected with a great leader. We recall the emotions his presence evoked in us— awe, respect, admiration, anger. We recall our seeming compulsion to talk about our experiences to others, to give our description of him— and how it varied from other accounts—and our judgment of him.

Leadership—As Traits

The concern with leadership has probably always existed, but it became a prime area for research by social scientists about the time of World War I. With our increased knowledge of testing and new statistical tools, there was a strong impetus to accumulate data and determine what traits were common to leaders. If these could be identified, perhaps those who had these traits could also be identified, and leaders could be selected quickly and efficiently. Therefore, the usual procedure in studies on leadership has been to select certain personality attributes and relate them to success or lack of success in certain leaders. Implicit in most of this research is the belief that the qualitative components which make for effective leadership are consistent. In other words, you have it or you don't. The leader might have been born with these traits (one theory) or he might have acquired them (another theory), but in either case he possesses the traits of leadership. The only problem, it would seem, is that personality traits are still poorly conceived and unreliably measured.

Results, however, of this approach, have been disappointing. The sorting out of leaders with various leadership traits from those without them, and then testing these abilities has been notoriously ineffective. One study (Bird, 1940) extensively reviewed relevant research and compiled a list of traits which seemed to differentiate leaders from nonleaders in one or more studies. However, only 5 percent of the traits listed appeared in four or more studies; many of the other traits were limited to a single study. Other researchers (Gibb, 1954; Gouldner, 1950) still search for the behavioral scientists' (if not the alchemists') gold, but report contradictory findings as to supposed leadership traits. There is some evidence (Berelson and Steiner, 1964) that leaders tend to be a bit taller, perhaps more intelligent than average, of higher socioeconomic status, more active, and have greater social participation than nonleaders. But these findings are vague, inconclusive, and hardly the basis for identifying or placing leaders. After an extensive survey of the literature from which he sought to identify leadership traits, one researcher (Stogdill, 1948) came to the weary conclusion that leadership is not the possession of some combination of traits. Rather, leadership seems to be based upon a working relationship among members of a group, in which the leader acquires his special status through active participation and demonstration of his ability to carry tasks through to completion.

And the search goes on (Geier, 1967). There are a variety of theories as to why the romantic conception of the leader with magic attributes persists. Some relate it to the common childhood experience of having a father, a prestige figure, magically endowed (Knickerbocker, 1961). Many find security in that figure. Since each of us continues to need security, perhaps we carry with us from childhood that symbol, the Leader. If such an assumption is accepted, it would be more readily understandable that the leader, or the man we conceptualize as the leader, should be larger, more intelligent, more cultured, more impressive than we. He represents the symbol, the ink blots onto which people project their desires for security, dependence, glamour, and power. It perhaps makes more understandable the persistent search for leaders who will arrive "full blown," without an abracadabra or seven-league boots, but by their presence can have difficulties vanish, obstacles overcome, and the goal attained. And yet most of us realize that this is fantasy. How familiar is the disappointment we fleetingly feel when we discover that the bigger-than-life hero is really very small, almost insignificant physically, but we in our own minds and with the aid of the media have blown him out of realistic proportion. We know from the avidly read "inside stories" by leaders' friends, assistants, even valets, that they are very human. To those who know them well, they can be infuriating or charming, opinionated or receptive, verbose or taciturn—in short, human beings working at their jobs. We know the leader is not the man for all seasons; great leaders have been repudiated at the polls, viewed as anachronisms—throwbacks to earlier eras who have lost symbolic favor with a fickle public. So far, research findings seem to indicate that leaders do not possess qualities which demarcate them from nonleaders; that who will be the leaders depends upon a complex of forces which do not permit prediction; and, finally, that leadership potential is widely diffused.

Leadership—As Position

Another type of response might be evoked by the question, "Who is a leader?" A leader is the President of the United States, chairman of a corporation, a superintendent of schools, or a general in the army. At another level, he is the mayor, the district manager, the school principal, the lieutenant. Yet at another level, he may be the foreman, the head of the English Department, the shop steward, the corporal. By now it is evident that in answering the question, we have responded with a series of titles representing positions. We call the person a leader if he holds a particular position in an organization (Jenkins, 1956). It's that circle (or dot) at the top of the organizational chart, or farther down the chart if it represents a lesser leader.

Leaders could have attained their positions in a variety of ways: by official choice of the organization, by appointment or selection by some higher authority, by succession, by seizing control. Regardless of how they got there, the position grants them authority or influence over people. Often, when we talk about leaders, we are talking about certain people who hold positions that carry authority. We say they can influence the group because of their position, or because they have control over the group. Think of the power of the chairmen of committees in Congress; as for example, the "Woman's Amendment" which "sat in committee" for 47 years before it was reported out by the chairman. Consider how important is the President's feeling on termination of the war, or the role of the press, or advocacy of civil rights. Or, think how we feel when the boss does not listen to our suggestions, or hear our side of an issue.

A position gives the occupant power to influence (Abrahamson and Smith, 1970). One theory of leadership states that leadership lies with the position rather than the person. Leadership is conceived as what the person in a position does; by definition of his position he is a leader. Thus the announcement of a new superintendent of schools (which is a rather usual occurrence) produces apprehension among the staff. They wonder what he will be like in a working relationship, what he will favor, which programs will be cut; the apprehension is directly related to the degree of power and control he has over them. The staff does not know the new superintendent as a person, nor do they know his style, but they are consciously aware of the power of his position and its implications for them. This anxiety recurs whenever a new supervisor or principal or "position above" is filled, in terms of what it will mean to those in "positions below." One source of concern is how the new appointee will use his authority and power, and for those below him, this is an area of central concern.

Moreover, the position may be a source of influence even for those not on the staff. We have expectations for how an occupant of a position should behave, and these expectations influence both our perception and our behavior to the position occupant. Imagine yourself with a bank president: his office, his appearance, his manner of dress, his education, his race, his sex, his religion, his style of speech, his manner in greeting a business executive. It seems quite simple to conjure up an image. The banker will of course be male, white, Anglo-Saxon, middle-aged, conservatively dressed, well-spoken, and lodged in a well-appointed office. Now imagine yourself with a marine captain. What is his appearance as compared with the bank president's? What is his manner of dress, his education, his style of speech? How would he speak to a recruit? Or, finally imagine a ward leader in an urban center. Consider his office as compared with the others, his physical appearance, his style of dress, his education, his manner of speech. How would he greet adults in his area? In each case, the naming of the position projects onto our personal screens a series of specific images of specific positions, and we respond to these positions in terms of our expectations. We speak formally and intellectually to the bank president, and our manner is subdued; his position seems to require it. We subconsciously straighten up our posture, tuck in our stomachs, and speak tersely with the marine captain. With the ward leader we are preoccupied, busy; he will be informal, ingratiating, laugh at our jokes.

Each position produces for us expectations of how the occupant of that position should act, and frequently we respond to our expectations for the role occupant rather than to the behavior of the individual. In fact, an area of considerable debate centers on whether position occupants are selected because they meet role expectations, i.e., because they have the attributes of the "part"; or whether they develop the behaviors expected in a certain role. For example, when we say someone is "school-teacherish," are we saying that this was her behavioral style before she became a teacher, or did she develop it from teaching over a period of time? The question has no clear answers and usually results in circular answers. Although the sequential pattern is not clear, it is abundantly evident that an individual's behavior is influenced by his position, and also how others define his position.

> There is a children's story of a good, kind king who lived modestly, was concerned for the welfare of his simple farmer subjects, and found time to hunt, fish, and enjoy his family. One day an ambassador from a distant kingdom came. He was shocked at what he saw—no palaces with turrets, no counting houses for storage of money and treasure, no army or soldiers—and worst of all the king in simple raiment. The ambassador clearly doubted that this man was really a king. Even fairy tale kings have identity crises. The king had never before wondered about whether he was real, or whether he performed his kingly duties properly. Obviously, he was not playing the king role as it should be played.
>
> Therefore, he set forth to levy taxes, raise armies, build counting houses, win wars. With each success, he added a new turret and a new flag pole to his palace, a new set of kingly raiment, and a new counting house from which to count and store his new wealth. He conquered and added, with no time left for his subjects, his family, his former interests. One day while counting riches, he slipped from the topmost turret and fell, hitting each flag pole until he reached the ground, broken, tattered, unrecognizable. He pleaded for help, but no one, except finally his daughter, even knew him or would bother with him. He did not look like the king; he was not acting like a king; thus he was not treated as a king.

Our expectations of how the occupant of a position should behave frequently influences our interaction with him as well as influencing his behavior in the position.

Let us return to the prime question. Is the person in the position of leadership automatically the leader?

If any behavior in a position is leadership behavior, we are in a clearly untenable position. History is replete with actions of kings of very limited intelligence who had tremendous influence and whose whims were law. Are we placed in a position of saying such behaviors are appropriate? We all know from our experience that there have been "position leaders" whom we saw as excellent or outstanding and others who were failures and about whom we raised questions concerning their "connections." Our work experience includes an array of relationships under a number of occupants of positions with a variety of leadership styles. We get into evaluations of "good leadership" when the leader is doing things that help the group, or when he does things we like, or "bad leadership" when the leader does things that hinder the group, or things that irritate us.

It is necessary to draw a distinction between leader and leadership (Holloman, 1968). A leader may be a person in a position of authority; he is given the right to make decisions for others—as a teacher is given the right to teach the class, or the foreman the authority to assign work for his crew. From his position, the leader may influence others who look to him for "clues" or seek to emulate him. However, from another perspective, it might be said that whoever influences the group is the leader; that is, any person who influences the group (whether in the position of leadership or not) exhibits leadership behavior. Leadership behavior is distinguished from the leader position; leadership behavior has to do with influence on the group regardless of the position. An illustration may be helpful as a means of clarification.

For example, after-school meetings are a chore; they are usually a tiresome extension of an already long day. Representatives of the faculty and an equal number of representatives from the student council were to meet to plan a workshop which was to explore possibilities for improving faculty-student relations and to redefine the duties of the student council. These were the explicit agenda items; many others were obviously present.

The room had the institutional pallor of a chamber impervious to changes in time, generation, or subject matter. The drab walls, nondescript flooring, and windows with shades precisely drawn on an invisible line were all reminiscent of school rooms built for the grandparents of the present school population. The participants sauntered in: the students wore bright colors, miniskirts, jeans, and long hair of varying lengths; the teachers were most somberly dressed, except for a few who regarded themselves as young. Some of the women wore brighter colors and shorter skirts, and some of the men had more informal attire and long sideburns. Student teachers had not yet declared their visual allegiance. Some dressed as students, and others identified with teachers.

The principal called the meeting to order in his most informal style. The small talk stopped; he was given attention. A teacher was asked to state the previous duties of the student council. Those sitting close to her listened; the others renewed their subconversations. One red-haired student talked about how "phony" everyone was since her election. They now see her as one of the most popular girls in the school, someone who has influence, someone they should get to know. She felt as if she was some kind of superstar; as if she now had obligations to be a certain kind of person in school—the perfect person. Other students responded with laughter; it was ridiculous. But they then got into a discussion of what is expected by students, by the school, by teachers, by leaders in the student council. Are these requirements fictional; does it influence their behavior; is it helpful or harmful?

A black faculty member, the only one, arrived and attempted to be inconspicuous by sitting in a chair closest to the door. Two black students quickly stood up, greeted him, and suggested that he sit in a chair by them. He did. More talk. One of the black students indicated that he could not come to the workshop. People looked at one another with silent messages. A tall student, very casually, asked why. The black student replied that he had a job on Saturday mornings, a new job, and he could not jeopardize it by not arriving the second week. There was an obvious sigh of relief among participants. One of the teachers suggested that he would be glad to call his employer and explain the situation. Someone suggested that the teacher do it then so that they could be assured of all attending.

The above illustration is a brief sample of a meeting, one not very different from many meetings. But, who was the leader? Was it the principal who opened the meeting? What were the issues the group was working on? Who influenced the discussion; how?

An effort to understand the meeting in terms of the leader or his position, in this illustration, would yield little in recognizing the issues or those who influenced the group. A study of leadership in terms of position is limiting, then, on several counts. It accepts any behavior by a person in a position as leadership behavior, which can result in terming contradictory behaviors in the same position (i.e., as principals) leadership behavior, thus escalating the confusion. Second, it loses the dynamics of what is happening in a group—who is influencing the members, how, and on what basis. If the positional leader says little, does that mean that by definition nothing is happening? Finally, there is the problem of the "leader behind the throne." We are aware of persons who occupy the position, but do not have the influence or power of the position. Well-documented accounts of boss rule in politics are generous in their details of mayors or governors who were handsome, mellifluous-voiced errand boys for the "boss," who himself held no official position. Each of us knows of occupants of positions who are given the name-on-the-door trappings of office; but in reality they must check almost everything with someone who may be in a higher position, or someone who has retired from office but who still must be consulted prior to any move. Study limited to occupants of positions obscures who influences the decision making, the processes in that group, how they develop, and with what consequences.

Leadership—As Situational

In addition to traits theory and position theory there are other theories of leadership (Barnard, 1938; Cattell, 1951). A situational theory states that leadership is a function of the situation at hand rather than the person or what he does. Here the type of leader needed depends primarily on the job. For example, Lincoln was an outstanding president, because he was the right person for the job to get us through the Civil War. Had it been another time, Lincoln might not have been elected, or at least would not have become a person of such profound influence. In other words, the situation creates an environment that produces leadership.

The difficulty with this theory is that the emphasis is weighted primarily on the environment and inadequately on the individual and what he does. While the captain of a football team may not have the vocabulary skills or coordinating skills needed to be a discussion group leader, are those the only skills needed? Isn't there more involved than finding out who has the most experience as a discussion group leader? Or who speaks best? Aren't there other factors such as whether one wants to be a discussion leader and to what extent? What competition is there? How familiar is he with the subject of discussion? What year in school is he? What year are the others in the group? What is the sexual composition of the group? What is expected of the leader? What status does the group have in its context? What would enhance that status? While the situation is a factor in who becomes the leader, the nature of leadership involves considerably more than knowledge on the situation.

Leadership—As Functional Roles of Members

Our understanding of leadership has changed dramatically over the last half century (Golembiewski, 1962). It is still changing and will continue to change as research and practical experience modify our present understanding of leadership. However, as we come to see leadership as behavior in a situation and as a dynamic relationship, the subject is viewed differently. The emphasis currently is focused on what actions are required by groups under various conditions if they are to achieve their goals, and how group members take part in these group actions. Leadership is viewed as the performance of those acts which help the group achieve its goals. When the question is recast so that leadership acts are performed by any member of the group who helps in setting group goals, or moving toward the goals, or improving the quality of the interactions among members, or making resources available to the group, it becomes evident that leadership acts can, at least in principle, be performed by almost any member of the group.

When the leadership question is reframed in terms of behavior that furthers the goals of the group, it is difficult to distinguish leadership from followership. There are some who feel that the word "leadership" impedes understandings of group processes and that the term would be better eliminated. Regardless of the term, many agree that the functional approach to both leadership and membership permits increased understanding of the processes and dynamics of groups. This approach recognizes the uniqueness of each group. Actions required by one group may be quite different from those of another, and subsequently the nature and traits of the persons having influence will be different in each group. In addition, a variety of factors affect leadership: the goals of the group, its structure, the attitudes or needs of the members, as well as expectations placed upon the group by an external environment (Bass, 1960; O'Brien, 1969).

For example, a pilot may be the acknowledged leader of his group while in the air. He may have the skills of coordinating his crew, knowledge of his mission, ability to cope with difficulties with which the crew is faced. What if the plane crashes and the crew is faced with the goal of surviving in the wilderness and finding its way back to safety? The skills needed are now very different. Who knows the terrain on the ground? Who knows about "survival training"? What plants are edible? Who can calm the members and reduce squabbling? Who can organize the group for utilizing their resources? The person who will be the crew leader on the ground may be very different from the leader in the air, and the functional approach recognizes that a variety of behaviors by any member may be helpful in the achievement of the group's purposes. The functional approach stresses behaviors that influence the group. If a group is threatened by conflicting subgroups, members who engage heavily in mediating functions may be expected to be influential. If, however, a group is faced with low prestige in the community and members are leaving, quite different behaviors will be required to be influential.

Types of Functional Roles

Leadership is basically the execution of a particular kind of role within an organized group, and this role is defined essentially in terms of power or the ability to influence others. Conceived as a role, leadership may be more or less specific to the particular structure of a particular group (McDavid and Harari, 1968). A leader in one group does not emerge as leader in another group. As membership changes, the leader may change, or if the purpose or activities change, the leader may change then too. Leadership implies followership. One person exerts influence or social power and others are influenced. Leadership is defined as the frequency with which an individual in a group may be identified as one who influences or directs the behaviors of others within the group.

Studies by Bales (Bales, 1950; Bales, 1970) and others (Benne and Sheats, 1948; Rieken and Homans, 1954) have identified three types of leader-member behaviors (hereafter referred to as member roles, since they can be performed by any member). They are:

Group Task Roles   Roles of members here are to help the group select and define the common goals and work toward solution of those goals.

Suppose representatives of school and community groups decided to work together to "do something about the drug problem." Members whose actions would be categorized in the task realm would "initiate" discussion of what could be done, or how the problem may be approached, or they may give new ideas for getting teenagers involved. Someone may offer "information" on what other groups in the city are doing and what official agencies are available for further help.

Another may offer his "opinions" on the subject. Others may "elaborate" from their experience or reading. With this variety of opinions and suggestions, some can "coordinate" or clarify the various suggestions in terms of which are appropriate for this group to work on and which are more appropriate within the province of other groups. One person may summarize what has happened, perhaps point out departures from the original goals, and raise questions as to whether the group can proceed as suggested or whether it lacks the resources needed. (He would be "orienting" the group.) There may be "critics" or "evaluators" who question the facts as presented, or the effectiveness of such a volunteer group. An "energizer" may prod the group to reconsider its potential and stimulate members to greater activity. There may be a "procedural technician," who knows where materials on drugs can be obtained inexpensively; he may have access to means of distribution of leaflets or a speaker who could help clarify some of the technical questions being raised. A "recorder" may be writing down the suggestions, or making a record of group decisions on what has been assigned for the next meeting.

These are functions that members undertake to help the group accomplish its task.

Group Maintenance Roles   While task roles focus on the intelligent problem-solving aspects of achieving movement toward a goal, equally important but at a different level are the roles that focus on the personal relations among members in a group. These are known as group maintenance roles.

At a meeting, members may sound as if they are giving information or opinions, or evaluating ideas; yet a newcomer may sense that an opinion is attacked before it is fully expressed. The group keeps getting bogged down with inconsequential points, members subtly attack one another on a personal level. A newcomer may feel that to present an idea means being open to attack, and he will therefore remain silent; there is such bickering that more must be going on than can be understood. Perhaps there are interpersonal rivalries or alignments being settled, and he should stay out of the crossfire; he may sense that who gets listened to depends on his outside status or position or education rather than his ideas, and he reevaluates his own status in terms of whether it is worthwhile to remain in the group. While it looks as if a group is working in the task area, since these are seen as legitimate roles, members are concurrently accumulating data on, "What kind of a group is it, how will I fit in, will I be accepted or rejected?" Members acquire personal data and formulate feelings that significantly influence their behavior.

Just as task roles are helpful in aiding a group to achieve its explicit goals, maintenance roles are helpful in aiding a group to work together and maintain itself so that members will contribute ideas and be willing to continue toward progress on the group task. Both kinds of roles are needed, and each complements the other. While the chapter on problem solving (Chapter 6) examines these relationships in greater detail, it can be briefly noted here that the relationship is not only complementary but induces forces which are spiraling.

To return to the illustration of the group studying the drug problem, as opinions are given, the "encourager" may ask for additional examples or ask if others have similar opinions. The "supporter" may agree with suggestions of others and offer commendations. The "harmonizer" may attempt to mediate differences between members or points of view, or relieve tension with a joke. Someone who previously felt that public health agencies and not citizens' groups should work on the drug problem may, after hearing the discussion, come around and agree to a compromise whereby the coordinating group sponsors a series of meetings in which public health officials describe their efforts in drug abatement. Someone, a "gatekeeper," may notice that the representatives from one community group have not spoken, and may ask if they have any ideas on the subject. These roles help a group maintain itself in order that work on its task can proceed without becoming immobilized by inappropriate social behaviors and so that individuals are brought effectively into the emotional sphere of the group's life.

Individual Roles   Another set of behaviors has been identified in which members act to meet individual needs that are irrelevant to the group task and not conducive to helping the group work as a unit.

In fact, this individual-centered behavior frequently induces like behaviors from others. An attack on one person leads to a response of personal defense, unrelated joke telling may escalate to "I-can-top-that" jokes, and blocking by one member may lead to retaliatory blocking. The goal and the group are forgotten, and the individual acts primarily to satisfy his personal needs.

To return to the representative citizens' group, the "aggressor" may question, with thinly veiled sarcasm, the competence and veracity of the person giving his opinion; or he may imply that the speaker does not have the foggiest notion of what he is talking about; or he may suggest that this "half-baked" committee would not know what to do about solving a serious problem; why not sponsor a day for the kids at the ball park and accomplish something? It might have been agreed that drug addicts would be referred to the local community mental health center; however, the "blocker" persists in stating that unless a center is opened especially for addicts, the committee is useless. He may turn every request for suggestions into a renewed attack on present plans or a renewal of advocacy for a treatment center. The "self-confessor" may use the audience to express personal problems and gain sympathy through catharsis. He may reveal the problems he is having with his son who flaunts authority, is disrespectful, shocks the neighbors with his late hours, and in general is a disgrace to him—a father who has worked hard all his life that his children may lead better lives than he did. In an emotional voice, he despairs that family relations and respect are not what they once were. The "recognition-seeker" may respond with his own personal advice and describe in glowing detail how it was successful in numerous other instances; or he may remind the group of the "paper" he has just delivered at the convention, or other important committees on which he has served. The "dominator" attempts to take over with an assortment of strategies by interrupting others, flattery, or asserting superior status.

I vividly recall one strategy for building status. A rather prestigious community committee had been appointed. The members were prominent businessmen: well-known lawyers, a sprinkling of university faculty, several executive directors of health and welfare agencies, and a few upper-middle-class community representatives. One woman, who came from a prominent family, had a college education, was the wife of a member of the state Supreme Court, and had decades of experience serving on community committees. Nevertheless, she felt inadequate and lacking in status in this committee. However, she did have strong feelings about the stand the committee should take and the direction of its work, and wanted to get her proposals properly listened to. Whether consciously or not, she prefixed each statement or opinion with, "Just the other day I was discussing this with my husband, the Justice, and he said . . ." or, "My husband, the Justice, feels. . . ." On the one hand, the members of the committee inwardly smiled, but, on the other hand, they were not quite sure of how influential she really was—so they listened.

There is the "playboy" (or girl) who jokes, keeps bringing up unrelated subjects, and is cynical about what meetings like this accomplish; or who may read a newspaper for part of the meeting in his conspicuous efforts to indicate his lack of involvement in the problem. There is the young man who states he "speaks for youth, and young people want . . ." or the parent who stands up "representing the concerned parents of the community, and we want. . . ." In both cases the "special-interest pleader" cloaks his wishes in "representative" terms. (Note that this is different from the delegate who represents a neighborhood youth group, or a specific businessmen's association.)

There are others. However, a high incidence of individual-centered as opposed to group-centered participation is an indication that the group will probably have a difficult time reaching its goal.

Both task and maintenance roles are needed by the group, but even though role functions may be identified, it is not always easy to separate them. Any member behavior may have significance for both goal achievement and maintenance. When a member offers information which the group sees as just what was needed (the missing piece in the puzzle) and now at last they can proceed, the information may not only have served a task function but also a maintenance one in that members feel encouraged and anticipate movement. In a similar way, group work on a difficult problem may increase solidarity, participant interest, and efficiency simultaneously.

In the functional approach to leadership, who is the leader? Is it the person who has the greatest variety of behaviors, the person who excels in the task areas, or the person who is the social-emotional, maintenance leader?

It seems that, much like in the traditional family in which the father is the task specialist and the mother the socioemotional specialist, differences appear in groups between the individuals who press for task accomplishment and those who satisfy the social and emotional needs of members. Over time, groups develop one or more leaders in each category, and when faced with a choice, most group leaders tend to give up the instrumental role in favor of popularity. Some researchers define the "hero" (Borgatta et al., 1955) as the leader who pushes the group to higher achievements, or tries to, at the cost of his own immediate popularity. One way to look at the "great men" (Borgatta et al., 1955) is to consider them both simultaneously and over some period of time as those satisfying the best-liked and the best-ideas requirements. The distinction between leader as a position and leadership as a functional role is an important one. The first session of a T-group (training group) illustrates this distinction.

> The room is a room. Participants enter as if arriving at any other class. They arrive with notebooks, pens, perhaps some reading material on sensitivity training which they hope will be impressive to others. They arrange themselves in the circle of institutional chairs, and wait. Some stare blankly; some appraise or stereotype the others by sex, age, or clothing clues. Some avoid any contact. Some make a fleeting contact by discussing the heat or offering a cigarette. They wait, with growing impatience and anxiety. Where is the "teacher"; did he forget, is he there? Who is the teacher, which one? In due time, the facilitator introduces himself, probably to the extent of his first name. In casual tones, he indicates that the participants will create their own learnings, that feelings are important, that participants can share their "here and now" experiences. This is followed by silence, long silence. Very anxious members are thinking, what kind of a leader is this; what happens now; isn't he going to do something? Others decide that he has probably never run a group before, and resent getting stuck with him. Still others may be thinking that this is some kind of game, that they are being tested.
>
> One rather confident male member begins cautiously by saying, "We're going to be spending the next couple of months together; we might as well begin by getting to know each other."
>
> "How shall we do that?"
>
> "Maybe we could go around the room and have each person introduce himself."
>
> "I have trouble remembering names, and besides that doesn't tell me anything about someone—who they are."
>
> More silence. Glances toward the facilitator. More silence.
>
> "How shall we proceed?"
>
> "Does anyone have any ideas about how we could get started?"

And so it goes, with the facilitator taking on a behavioral role. He is not acting in the directive, lecturing position students expect of a teacher. The distinction is especially clear as to the difference between position and the process. The facilitator's behavior indicates that an invitation to lead is open to all—to examine expectations and develop goals and means for implementing them. Acceptance by one member of a leadership function does not preclude others from participating, and it may even encourage others to begin to assume some responsibilities for the direction of the group. By his behavior, the facilitator indicates that leadership in the group is to be shared; he does not see himself as responsible for all of the functions of the group. In this group, any member regardless of his position can perform leadership functions.

Who Attempts To Lead?[1]

If any member can perform leadership functions, who attempts to lead? Who attempts to influence the group? In the illustration of the T-group, who is the person who first suggests an action; how is it that he ventures forth? Who are the others who offer suggestions and try to move the group in their direction?

There are two basic conditions for a member to take initiative: first, he must be aware of what function (i.e., information, opinion, encouragement) is needed; secondly, he must feel that he is able to do it and that it is safe to do it. Therefore, prior to action a member needs to have diagnosed the group situation and determined what behavior is needed to help the group move ahead; then, he must make the difficult appraisal of whether he has the skills, the influence, the resources to act; and finally he weighs the consequences or repercussions. Some members of the T-group might have felt that the facilitator was sitting it out, but they had no idea of what could be done. For them, it was the facilitator's responsibility to lead the way; if he did not, there was very little they felt they could do or knew how to do. There might have been others who knew it was up to the participants to start, but they were not quite clear about how to go about it, or on what topic. Others might have known what they would like to do, or how it might have started, but they would not be first. To be first means acting without clues, without knowing the "lay of the land." What if this attempted initial behavior revealed some inadequacy which would be better unrevealed? It is better to play it safe and keep quiet. These are the basics. A person must know what functions are needed, and have the skills to perform them.

[1] Hemphill, 1961; Pepinsky et al., 1968.

Our illustration has been a T-group with the characteristic ambivalence about the role of the facilitator and the role of members. However, to some degree, a predictable ambivalence about leadership is found in many non-T-groups. There is the conflict between a desire to be dependent and a need to be independent. On the one hand, we admire strong leaders who chart a definite course of action and give orders as to what needs to be done next; on the other hand, we resent taking orders; we value using our own initiative, developing our own plans. A nondirective leader may be viewed as weak and lacking in leadership abilities, and we may wish he were more directive; a directive leader may be viewed as authoritarian, and we wish he were often more open to suggestions from others. From childhood we are taught to be independent, to develop our own skills and resources; and yet as human beings we are frequently nurtured and dependent well beyond the time of physical maturity, and frequently this lasts well into the third decade of life. Is it any wonder that our ambivalence about leaders, our expectations of them, our conflicts between being dependent and being independent is a perennial source of stress in many groups?

But, it is important to return to the prime question of who attempts to lead. One series of experiments attempted to develop some tentative answers. The researchers found that while some people enjoy exerting influence at any and all occasions, this was not typical. Rather, they found that the most potent source for attempting an act of leadership was generated out of the situation (Gershenfeld, 1967; Hemphill, 1961). When someone found himself in a situation in which he had expert information required for the solution to the group's problem, he was strongly motivated to lead and influence the group in how to solve the problem. A statistician could readily determine the procedures needed for a survey problem and would try to influence the group on how to approach the problem.

Then, too, tasks have different requirements. In a discussion task, many people may give opinions, yet there may be few efforts to change the opinions of others or suggest a given course of action. In a discussion it may not be seen as appropriate to attempt to have others change their opinions. However, in a situation where a complicated product must be assembled, more leadership efforts will be made since suggestions for coordination of efforts are necessary for development of a constructive plan. In other words, the number of leadership attempts is influenced by the degree of coordinated effort required by the task. A finding of particular significance, and wide applicability, is one that we frequently feel but infrequently admit. Whether or not a person attempts to lead depends upon how his previous efforts were received (Gray et al., 1968). If a person offers a suggestion, and finds others nodding in agreement, he is likely to offer more suggestions. If, however, he offers a suggestion and gets disapproving glances or negative comments, he picks up the clues and desists from further leadership attempts. In one research study (Ring and Kelley, 1963) sets of four-member teams were assigned a task, and two members, by design, were cast in rejecting roles. Every time one of the members attempted to lead, a rejecting member expressed disapproval. There was a marked reduction in attempts to lead. However, when two confederates were assigned accepting roles, there were many more attempts to lead; participants who had rarely led before did so unhesitatingly.

Another factor that influenced motivation to lead was how important the task was to the person, and whether he was in a position to help the group solve the problem. Thus many of us may feel that certain goals are important, as for example, greater flexibility of curriculum in the high school. But as parents or "outsiders," we may feel our position to influence is extremely limited if not hopeless, and we will therefore not exert energy toward influencing the curriculum committee. However, if we are appointed to a Parents' Council committee to examine school curricula, we would feel that the task is important and that we are in a position of influence, and greater attempts to lead will be forthcoming. Frequently, those who perceive themselves in higher or more important positions are more likely to attempt to influence the group.

In summary, when leadership is conceived as a function that can be performed at least theoretically by any member, the question arises as to who attempts to lead. It would seem that this is dependent upon many factors: the degree of coordination required by the task, the ability to diagnose, the ability to perform the needed behavior, the importance of the task, the possibilities of action leading to success, the feelings of personal acceptance or rejection.

Whose Attempts to Lead Are Rewarded?

Leadership is defined as the frequency with which an individual may be identified as one who influences or directs the behavior of others within a group. A first step in this process involves an attempt to lead, but the crucial step is whether the group accepts the influence attempt. Why does a group do what one person suggests over what another suggests? Why are some suggestions listened to closely and considered, while others are dismissed without even a full hearing? How does the person whose suggestions are frequently accepted attain this influence? Why do members do what he advocates? Simply put, when one person does what another wants him to do, we would say that the influencer has power over the other. Leadership clearly involves power, i.e., the ability to influence other people by whatever means necessary (McDavid and Harari, 1968). A person may be very influential and have a great deal of power in one group, and he is considered the leader because the group frequently accepts his direction. In another group, he may have little power; his suggestions are infrequently accepted by the group, and he would not be identified as one of the leaders. It is not unusual in community groups that a person who is a clerk in a business may be a powerful board member in a Boy Scout Council. The reverse, although less usual, also occurs. The chairman of a university department, a high power in the department, may only be window-dressing (low power) in a community association. Power is not a universal; it is limited by the person being influenced. A powerful person only has power over those whom he can influence in the areas and within the limits defined by the person being influenced.

Power

Discussions of leadership sooner or later evolve into a discussion of power. The word itself evokes visions of manipulation, the omnipotent "big brother," and personal feelings of powerlessness. We think of Machiavelli's *The Prince* and his strategies of power; the dictum of Lord Acton, "Power corrupts, and absolute power corrupts absolutely" in relation to the centralization of power; and politics is defined as the ultimate power game. Perhaps we fantasize and begin to think of flower power, black power, and power to the people as also being power concepts. Power, then, is a multifaceted concept. What determines who has power? One conceptual scheme (French and Raven, 1960) distinguishes five different kinds of power.

1. *Referent Power* First, there is the kind of influence we do not even think of as power. We may emulate the clothes of someone we

consider fashionable, we may espouse an argument we first heard from a brilliant intellectual with whom we identify, we may buy a book because someone whose opinion we value commented favorably on it. These people have referent power over us; we identify with them in certain areas, and they influence us without our feeling manipulated. In smaller groups, we hear the suggestions of those whom we perceive as having good ideas, or as being "with it" quite differently from those whom we categorize as pedestrian and "out of it." We hear the member who speaks for us, who represents our point of view, who sounds as if he understands our position, and we are much more influenced to act in accord with his suggestions. We may be influenced by those of higher status, a position we regard as important, a personal style, or a charisma. In each situation, the powerful person has power because we accept his influence and do it voluntarily. Obviously, this power exists only as long as that person is a referent for us. Fathers are powerful referents for children until they are teenagers, and perhaps for a period become powerful negative referents, but later their referent power frequently diminishes.

2. *Legitimate Power*   A second kind of power is legitimate power. This is an authority relationship in which one person through his position is given the right to make certain decisions for others. It is the congressman who represents our voting preferences, the department chairman who represents us at the faculty executive committee, the foreman who supervises our work. It may also be the person we elect as president of an organization, the members of the committee we agree will make arrangements for a banquet, the observer we ask to process our behavior at today's session. The legitimacy may be derived from a number of sources. It may be from a higher level of the organization, it may be by law, it may emerge from the group. However, the recipients of influence see it as legitimate that the powerful person has a right to make decisions for them. (Goldman and Fraas, 1965; Julian, et al., 1969).

3. *Expert Power*   Frequently allied with legitimate power is expert power. Over time a person may become expert in an area, e.g., a congressman may point out to a citizen's group a strategy which will be carefully considered, because he will be seen as both an ally through his legitimate power and also an expert in terms of being knowledgeable on the machinations of Congress. Expert power may also exist independent of position. It is based on the person's special-

ized knowledge, information, or skills. When preparing a brochure, we call in a printer to give us an estimate, since from experience we know that our guessing will not be helpful in planning a budget. In the same way we seek the services of a plumber, a TV repairman, a counselor, a psychiatrist; they have power over us because we see them as experts. And, as with all classes of power, we determine who the experts are, for how long we will be influenced by them, and the area of their expertise. In each of the first three mentioned types of power, we are voluntarily influenced. Somehow, because they are voluntary actions, we hesitate to think of these influence situations as power. We are more likely to conceive of power in the emotional "kid glove" or "iron fist" dimension; we normally think of power as reward or coercion.

4. *Reward Power*   In the reward situation the powerful person gives carrots, promotions, gold stars, A's to the recipients for complying. It may be the "bribery" of a parent as he entreats a child to finish dinner with a reminder of ice cream for dessert, or the parent who tells his teenage son that if he makes the honor roll, he can have the car on weekends. Usually, reward power is situational, i.e., determined by position. The parent rewards obedience in children, the boss gives rewards to his workers. Often the recipients of the rewards feel controlled. It means compliance, running the rat race, playing the "company game," playing by the rules. We do, however, tend to accept reward power, because the reward is more pleasant than the unfavorableness of the task or the other alternatives; we go through the task in anticipation of the reward. We enjoy the nod of approval, the smile, the support for our suggestion, the increased responsibility, the fatter paycheck. However, when the reward is not one that we perceive as more favorable than the other alternatives, the person who can administer the rewards has no power over us. If the child does not like ice cream, the inducement to finish dinner is clearly lacking. The student who does not care about grades considers the rewards of more time with his friends and other alternatives more attractive. Reward power can only be exerted if the recipient values the offered rewards.

5. *Coercive Power*   If compliance does not occur with reward, those in authority frequently resort to coercion. The child who does not finish his dinner will be told he cannot leave the table until he does, or he is sent to his room. The teenager who does not bring up

his grades is threatened with having his allowance cut off or revocation of rights to the family car (Kahn and Katz, 1966). The student who continues to create a disturbance is coerced with threats of detention; the employee with dismissal; the committee member who does not perform on a high-status committee with threat of not being reappointed. Coercive power, however, is not just the opposite of reward power. Whereas with reward the individual does what the powerful person desires in hope of attaining the reward, in a coercive situation the individual usually will first attempt to escape the punishment. Coercive power invokes not only coercion but no way to escape what the powerful person wants.

These are the types of power. Acts of leadership, if they are to be effective, must rely on some basis of power. Referent power, where the person identifies with the other and respects him, often will have the broadest range of influence. With reward power, there is increased attraction because of the promise of reward and low resistance. Coercive power is likely to produce increased resistance, although the more legitimate the power, the less the resistance. At the right time, when it is functional, each type may be very powerful. In many situations the leader's influence is based on a combination of sources of power.

A student mechanically attends the first session of class in a required course. He carefully scrutinizes the teacher for clues as to how much reading will be required, how much work, how often examinations are given, how interesting the instructor or the course sounds. He also looks for clues on attendance requirements, and the possibilities for getting a good grade. Simultaneously, he acquires data on how expert the instructor seems to be, and over time determines how he feels about the instructor as a teacher, as a scholar, as a human being.

The university gives the instructor legitimate power to teach the course and administer rewards or coercions in the form of grades. The student also perceives the legitimacy of this power. The student, however, determines the degree of expertness he attributes to the instructor; the student determines the extent of his being influenced by the instructor as someone to emulate or relate to. How much influence the course will have on the student will to a large degree depend upon how much power the student attributes to the instructor. It may be only coercive power, and in a hostile environment the student "gets through." Or the course may have a profound influence; the student may relate to the instructor as a personal model at least in some aspects, consider him genuinely knowledgeable, and find the course personally rewarding in adding to insights or skills. Although legitimate power is the basis for influence of an instructor, and while some students even question this and drop the course, other bases for power develop and determine the extent of influence.

For some, legitimate power is enough. Many enjoy being in a position to make decisions for others, to wield power in the form of rewards or sanctions. Being liked is unimportant or at best secondary to having power. A position of being able to influence decision making is indeed powerful.

Styles of Leadership

Most of us concerned with leadership, however, face the dilemma of wanting to be liked but also of wanting to get the job done. We may think: I know it will make the staff feel good if they think they are making the decisions, but what if they make the wrong decisions? I should want their help, but I have been here longer and know the realities; they may go off on some idealistic notion that would not be practical. Sure, I want to be popular, but I also want my job, and ultimately I am responsible for the decision made. Leaders at every level—teachers in a classroom, presidents of voluntary organizations, supervisors in business, parents raising children—face these dilemmas and ask these basic questions phrased appropriately for their own individual situation.

Conceptions of Man Influence Leadership Style How a leader answers these questions and resolves the dilemmas rests on his assumptions about other people. The assumptions usually are not conscious or formally defined, but his conception of man has implications for his leadership style (McGregor, 1960; Schein, 1969; Maslow, 1954). There are two images or theories. In the first (theory X according to McGregor; rational-economic man to Schein), man is seen as having little ambition, a reluctance to work, and a desire to avoid responsibility. Man is motivated by economic competition, and conflict is inevitable. Without managerial effort, basically man would do nothing. The leader operating under these assumptions must motivate, organize, control, and coerce. He directs, people under him accept and even prefer it, because they have little ambition or desire for responsibility. The leader bears the responsibility and burden of his subordinates or followers' performance. This represents the traditional theory of management, especially business management. Another theory (theory Y for McGregor, self-actualizing man for Schein), holds that man is motivated by a hierarchy of needs. The assumptions in this theory are that as man's basic needs are met, his needs become motivating forces. Man has a desire to use his "potential," to have responsibility, "to actualize" himself. It assumes that man enjoys work as well as play or rest. This conception suggests that individuals will exercise self-direction and self-control toward the accomplishment of objectives they value. Furthermore, they can be creative and innovative. They will not only accept responsibility but also seek it. That potential for imagination, ingenuity, resourcefulness is widely distributed within the population but poorly utilized in modern society. In this theory the leader creates challenge and an opportunity for subordinates to use their abilities to a greater extent. There is no need to control or motivate men; the motivation is waiting to be unleashed. A leader's conception of man will greatly affect his style of supervision and the bases of power he will implement. The first theory is more likely to use money as a motivating reward and coercion to compel compliance. The second theory is likely to induce intrinsic rewards of self-satisfaction, pride in achievement, and coercion is used infrequently.

Does Leadership Style Make a Difference?   A classic research, the Lewin, Lippitt, and White studies (Lewin et al., 1939; White and Lippitt, 1968), investigated the following questions: What difference does style of leadership have on the group? Is the group more productive if the leader is autocratic, democratic, or laissez-faire? Does it make a difference in how members relate to one another? Is there a difference in the social climate? In each experimental situation three leadership types were established: the autocratic leader, the democratic leader, and the laissez-faire leader. Each leader had legitimate power as he worked with ten-year-old boys on basically similar craft projects. The findings were dramatic. The results indicated that demonstrably different group atmospheres developed. And further, in each experimental group, there were readily perceived differences in relations among members and ability to handle stress, as well as in relations with the leader. The findings were widely disseminated and showed beyond doubt, in that particular situation, that the best leader was the democratic leader. Yet, as the following will show, the implications for leadership are not that clear.

Which Leadership Style to Choose?   We label leaders, and the problem is: Which is the "best"? It all depends on how we perceive it. If a person is described as an autocratic leader, an image occurs in which he is allied with demagogues, dictators, and coercive administrative processes. Yet "autocratic" can also describe a person who is directive, who stands firm in his convictions, who accepts the responsibilities of supervision and ultimate responsibility for decisions—in short, one who has the necessary attributes of leadership. How can he be effective and also be viewed as democratic?

To be labeled a laissez-faire leader is to be viewed as in a fog, incompetent, lost at sea without a captain, shirking responsibilities. This is clearly an offensive label. Yet, on the other hand, "Creativity must be given free rein"; "he who rules least, rules best." Shall the leader supervise closely, or "trust his men"?

To be labeled a democratic leader usually suggests that the person is well-liked. As for his behavior, does it mean that he shares all decisions with others regardless of the consequences? Does it mean that the staff members are one big happy family, that they talk in terms of *we* rather than *I*, and that all relationships are collaborative rather than competitive? Do all decisions have to be group decisions; is giving up power the price of popularity? Is the "big happy family" the goal to strive for no matter what; is any aspect of competition to be avoided at all costs?

At one time this labeling was important as we sought to understand the continuum which went from the laissez-faire leader who was minimally involved to the autocratic leader who arbitrarily made decisions based solely on his own style. At that time, the democratic leader was in the middle, neither the "abdicrat" nor the autocrat, and there was a desire (especially in an era of World War II dictators and totalitarian governments) to reinforce our conviction that democracy is "best." The entire concept of experimentally inducing three different leadership styles, analogous perhaps to governments, was powerful, and the results generated increased understanding of the problems and limitations of each style. Today, the question of whether one is an autocratic, democratic, or laissez-faire leader is no longer meaningful. Nor do we view leaders as being in a box that can be labeled, whether by their detractors, or friends, or their own dilemmas. The question to be asked is: Which style or combination of styles will help the group arrive at its goals consistent with the values of that organization? The question is a difficult one (Margulies, 1969; Argyris, 1957).

Leadership Styles: A Continuum   Leaders can choose behavioral styles not only at the extremes of a continuum (laissez-faire versus autocratic); it is important to recognize that there are a number of in-between positions, and that the leader can choose different positions at different times (Tannenbaum and Schmidt, 1960). He can vary his behavior according to how one situation is diagnosed as different from another. The variety of behavior available to a leader can be charted on a continuum.

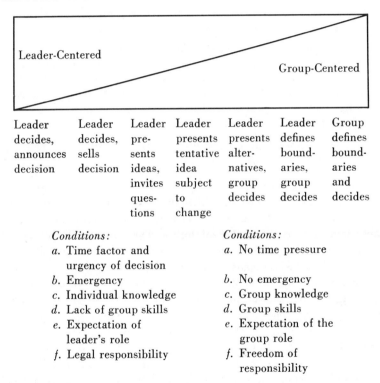

Leader decides, announces decision	Leader decides, sells decision	Leader presents ideas, invites questions	Leader presents tentative idea subject to change	Leader presents alternatives, group decides	Leader defines boundaries, group decides	Group defines boundaries and decides

Conditions:
a. Time factor and urgency of decision
b. Emergency
c. Individual knowledge
d. Lack of group skills
e. Expectation of leader's role
f. Legal responsibility

Conditions:
a. No time pressure
b. No emergency
c. Group knowledge
d. Group skills
e. Expectation of the group role
f. Freedom of responsibility

1. At one extreme, the leader decides; he can make the decision himself and announce it. Thus, "Everybody will take their vacation the first two weeks in July."

2. The leader announces his decision and "sells" it to group.

3. He can put out his ideas, and invite reactions and comments prior to making the decision, but retains power to determine the use of the comments. He would explain why he wants everybody to take their vacations the first two weeks in July—easier scheduling, less curtailment of production. Reactions may arise from someone getting

married in June who wants the last two weeks as a honeymoon; someone who likes skiing may want a winter vacation; some may point out that it really means a month off what with getting ready to go on vacation and getting reorganized upon return, etc. The leader listens and then announces his decision.

4. He can present the issue, but not present his ideas on it; instead, he invites ideas and alternatives from others. Based on these alternatives, he makes his decision.

5. He can present the group with several alternatives, and they can choose among the alternatives given.

6. He can state limits outside which the group cannot go, but he permits the group to decide (to choose) within these limits. ("Each person is entitled to his vacation time based on seniority and his position. Customers expect to be serviced every day of the year. What system could be worked out so that everyone can get his vacation and still allow us to remain open?")

7. The group sets both the boundaries and decides; the leader is a member of the group.

The continuum ranges from one in which the leader makes the decisions himself to one in which the group decides within outer limits. Where a leader chooses to behave on this continuum is probably influenced by a number of forces. There are the forces in the leader, the forces in the membership, and the forces in the situation (Dunno, 1968). The leader will select behaviors on the continuum consistent with his assumptions of human nature, the leadership style with which he is most comfortable, and his assessment of his own skills and competence as well as that of the membership.

There are forces in the membership that influence the leader (Bohleber, 1967). Individuals may be viewed as on a continuum ranging from those who are dependent to those who are independent, or individualistic. The dependent person is oriented toward formal structure, is outer-directed, good at taking orders, and geared for routine. The independent person prefers less direction and rebels against structure; he is informal, better in creative areas, inner-directed, and does not like routine. It is important for the leader to understand the types of members so that they can be most effective. For some, he should be more directive, supervise more closely; with others, he should take a different stance. The length of time the group has worked together is another factor. Are they ready to assume responsibility, or are they just beginning to work together? Their familiarity with the problem is yet another factor. How much knowledge and experience do they have with the problem?

Which leadership style is appropriate from a membership point of view is one of the sources of tension in every group. The question of whether the leader should be directive and the members dependent is raised regularly. If the leader is directive, individuals labeled counterdependents will tend to fight authority, block movement, and be aggressive toward the leader. If the leader is nondirective, the dependents will tend to be anxious until more structure is introduced. In many ways these tensions and anxieties are reflections of our own ambiguities. We are trained to be independent and yet nurtured for much of our childhood; we enjoy a dependent relationship for its comfort and security, and yet we yearn for independence.

Finally, there are the forces that influence the leader (Margulies, 1969). Factors to be considered are the type of organization, its values, traditions, size, geographic spread, frequency of meeting, etc. Then there is the nature of the problem in terms of its complexity or requirements for many kinds of experiences—and there is that great determinant of behavior: the pressure of time (Sadler, 1970).

Some Leadership Findings That Can Be Generalized

As is evident to the reader, there is probably no single right style of leadership. But there are findings that can be generalized in our efforts to understand the complexities of leadership. The following seem to hold true:

1. What at one time was the crux of a major theory—that leadership resulted from some personality trait, or was determined situationally, or was dependent upon culture, or arose from interaction of peculiar forces—today is seen as but one of many items considered in the complicated leadership equation.

2. Leadership is closely related to followership. An act of leadership involves acceptance of influence. Leadership can be understood in terms of the influence attempts that succeed in a group, and can be carried out theoretically by any member.

3. The kinds of assumptions a person has about people will determine how he will lead or supervise them. Becoming aware of one's

own assumptions is therefore an important factor in a personal leadership style.

4. An effective leader is one who can behave comfortably along the whole range of the leader continuum. He can adapt his behavior to the requirements of members, the problem at hand, and the factors in the situation. He is flexible enough so that his behavior helps the group move toward its goal.

5. There is generally frustration and confusion when a leader verbally states one position on the continuum and actually behaves at another point.

6. A leader has a number of choices about how tightly to centralize control and about how flexible he can be from one situation to the next. By diagnosing forces in himself, the group, and the situation, he can increase his flexibility and effectiveness.

Conclusions

Some questions with brief answers may be an effective way to summarize this chapter (Jenkins, 1961).

How Is Leadership to Be Judged?   Frequently a leader asks: How did others act? How do we generally solve this problem? What are the rules? However, to be effective, leadership is to be judged in terms of the goals and purposes of the group. The leader, or others in the group who would like to be influential, ask themselves the following questions: What is needed by this group at this time to move toward the goal? How can I help movement toward it? This is a difficult task because sometimes the goals are not clear; sometimes we are not sure of a diagnosis; frequently we question our skills and resources, or fear the consequences of attempting behavior that may have negative implications.

What Kind of Leadership Is Best?   There is no best kind. Groups working on different tasks need different kinds of leadership. Sometimes groups want a close personal relationship between members and the leader; at other times they prefer a more formal relationship. Some groups need to consider the alternatives and come to a decision themselves; others may need firm direction from the person in charge.

Groups need help in progressing on their tasks as well as remaining in healthy working condition. A leader must be sensitive to both aspects. Typically a leader is only concerned with the task role, but he also has to pay attention to increasing ways for members to communicate and work together.

How Is Success or Failure of the Group to Be Judged?   Success or failure, in most groups, cannot be attributed to the leadership. Usually the entire group is responsible for the success or failure of the group. Rarely can it all be blamed on the leader; nor can he be given all the credit. Leadership functions can be shared, and sometimes members abdicate their responsibilities.

However, leaders can impede efforts of members to be helpful to the group. The leader may not permit members to voice their suggestions and thus limit resources and information available to the group. He may limit too narrowly what he will permit members to do and thereby limit their potential contributions.

Groups can impede the effectiveness of their leadership. They may have antiquated norms that hamstring leadership. They may repeatedly reject leadership attempts and cause leaders to stop trying. On the other hand, encouragement and support are likely to produce increased leadership attempts.

Exercise 1
A Series of Nonverbal Experiences
in Leading and Being Led

The following exercises focus on our feelings of leading and being led, and provide data to examine both our behavior and attitudes in being a follower and being a leader. The exercises are appropriate as a beginning micro-lab in a longer workshop. They are also useful to members as a means of examining their typical roles and understanding areas in which modification or reevaluation may be needed.

The exercises lead to nonintellectualized discussions of leadership in terms of personal satisfactions or conflicts, areas of skill and ineptness, and enjoyment of authority or fear of responsibility. They also allow participants to see the complementary nature of leader-member relations in trust, openness, spontaneity, communication, and dependence-independence.

The exercises are of varying lengths and, depending on the purposes, can be expanded or reduced. They involve varying degrees of risk and should be used with an understanding of both the purpose of the exercise and the type of group involved. For some groups, any touching is beyond the bounds of propriety, and these exercises should be eliminated. Because touching is counter to the norms of the group, much tension is generated and effectiveness in examining leader-follower relationships is severely curtailed. Some groups who consider themselves serious and work-oriented may frown upon games that call for a childlike spontaneity; they may consider games as contrived and not a legitimate basis for learning. The values and resistances of the group should be seriously considered so that the exercises used will help members achieve their purposes.

The procedure is as follows: The exercise would be named, as illustrated below, and the facilitator would give instructions so that the reader has both a feel of the exercise and how it is to be carried out.

1. *Connectedness by Rubber Bands*

The facilitator begins by saying: "Pick someone. Put your hands out in front of you. Almost touch the hands of your partner. Pretend now that your hands and his are connected by rubber bands. Move—feel what happens."   (5 min.) "Pretend your feet are also connected by rubber bands."   (5 min.) "Talk about what happened." (10 min.)

The objectives of the exercise are to increase awareness among pairs of participants as to their own boundaries and those of others; a body awareness; control of self, control of another person. It also presents a situation of leadership-followership. Did one person lead all the time? Did they reverse roles? When? At what signals? Which role was more comfortable: leading or following? Did one partner see the other as being more comfortable leading or following? Did it make a difference whether it was the hands or feet that were connected?

Not all of these questions are asked. A few may be suggested, depending on what clues the facilitator observes. He may mention a few as basis for discussion, but it is important not to spend too much time in discussion; rather, participants should express their response to this experience and let their impressions build with subsequent exercises.

2. Communication by Clapping

With this approach, the facilitator gives the following instructions: "Pick someone who has not been your partner previously. Clap a message. Then let the other person respond." (The facilitator should select a member of the audience and demonstrate. The two stand facing each other, and the facilitator claps the phrase "How are you?" The other person claps back, "fine," or "angry," or whatever.) "You see how it is done. Remember that it involves restructuring meaning from familiar sounds. Now try having a conversation through clapping." (10 min.) "Between you, discuss what happened. What was expressed?" (5 min.) Then the entire group discusses what they experienced. (5 min.)

At one level, this exercise allows participants to experience expression through tactile and auditory senses, to create and hear rhythm and sound as expressive of emotion and sequence. At another level, communication is seen as a process requiring a sender and a receiver; one side is insufficient for communication. At yet another level, it is essential to recognize who initiated the "conversation," who "talked more," who led, who followed, who was frustrated and withdrew. The exercise can also be used to examine functional roles of members.

3. Leader-Follower Trust Walk

The facilitator begins: "This exercise focuses on being a leader or a follower. Half of you will be blindfolded. Those who are not blindfolded will select a partner. This is a nonverbal exercise, so you may not speak to your partner to tell him who you are. Let's begin by counting off to two." (Participants count off "1, 2, 1, 2," etc.) "Will all of the ones come to this side of the room? Here are handkerchiefs to use as blindfolds. Put them on and adjust them so that you cannot see." (The ones arrange their blindfolds and wait.)

Now, the facilitator talks to the twos quietly so that the others cannot hear. "Each of you will select a partner from the group of ones. Stand beside the partner you choose so that we can determine who still needs a partner. Remember, you and your partner may not speak, but by all means try to develop a nonverbal language between you. You will be the leader. How can you help your partner experience his world? Can you enlarge his world? Be aware of how you see your role; is it to protect him, to get him through safely? Is it to be with a minimum of effort on your part? Is it to be serious; is it to be fun? [Pause] Now select your partner.

"Explore your world, nonverbally, of course. I will see you back here in 15 minutes." (If this occurs in a building, 15 minutes is adequate time. If it is outdoors and time permits, allow up to an hour. It is frequently a moving experience to see the partners develop their own signals, an increased sensitivity to each other, a trusting relationship.)

The facilitator alerts the group two minutes before time is up. If the setting is outdoors, he simply hopes that they will straggle back reasonably on time.

When they return, he has the "blind" remove their eye covers to see who their partner is. (This produces tension, anxiety, even fumbling, as the "leader" wonders if his follower will be disappointed when identities are revealed. There is also the anxiety of returning to the "real world," which does not encourage the closeness and trust some of the partners felt. Now the mood changes; the "uncovering" produces laughter, squeals of recognition or surprise.)

The facilitator proceeds: "Would you share your feelings in the experience? What did you find out about yourself that was new? What did you find typical of yourself? How did you feel about your role—as a leader, or a follower?"   (15 min.)

"I am sure each of you wants to experience the other role. Will all of the twos come to this side of the room? Now, it is your turn for the blindfolds. You know what to do."

He then talks to the ones as he did previously to the other group. Although they have been through the experience and know what they want their partner to experience, nevertheless it seems helpful to remind them, through the questions, of a variety of possible relations they may have with their partner in the leader role. Once more, those not blindfolded select a partner and stand beside him. Frequently, the choosing partner will select his former partner so that he may "repay" him for his felt interest. For a variety of reasons, a person may prefer to select a new partner. After selections are made, the exercise continues as in the first pairing. The groups return, see each other, share their feelings.

Sometimes the participants feel their reactions are significant and relatively private; they may only want to share with their partners. Sometimes participants are quite eager to share their new understanding of themselves with the whole group. If there is a group sharing, one of the questions the facilitator should ask is how it felt to be a leader and how it felt to be a follower. What was learned?

This exercise has usually been considered primarily an experience of trust; however, it is striking how often members report on their relations with authority. Students frequently note that it helps them understand their parents or gives them understanding on what kind of parent they would like to be. Men and women discuss their societal sex roles in which a man is expected to be the leader, and their feelings when leadership roles are reversed. Some who usually see themselves as leaders are surprised at their reactions to being followers and gain a different perspective of the relationship; those who are usually followers give similar reports. Participants will also talk about clues they pick up from each other—being tired, bored, excited —which greatly influence the other person and the relationship; new insights are reported on complementary relationships.

As an aside, if a supply of handkerchiefs is difficult to attain, paper towels as they come from a dispenser and masking tape are equally effective as blindfolds.

4. *Follow the Leader—A Musical Variation on the Children's Game*

An instrumental record with a diversity of moods, tempos, and sounds is selected (Vivaldi's *Four Seasons,* for example). Participants are divided into groups of 8 to 10 and stand in a circle facing each other; in some groups participants take off their shoes to enhance a feeling of movement.

Then the facilitator says, "I'm going to play a record. Listen to it, get a feel for the mood. If it reminds you of something, or if you want to express what you feel, come into the center of the circle and do it. Those of us who can feel it with you will follow you in our places. When the mood of the music changes, return to your place. Someone else, who is feeling something he would like to share, will go into the center. O.K.?"   (10–15 min.)

"How was it? How did you feel about what happened?"   (10 min.)

One of the questions to be raised is, Who initiates leadership? It is someone who knows what is needed, feels he has the skills or resources to do it, and feels it is safe to try. Discussion will relate to all these issues. Some will say they cannot even think in terms of what that music could mean in a public place; their minds went blank immediately. Others had a mental image of what the music evoked but did not seem to have the skill or resources to transfer that image into body movement. Still others hesitated to come into the center for fear of appearing clumsy, or childish, or not very original. Another area for brief discussion is: How did the situation change? When did you start to feel comfortable, or enjoy it? What happened?

5. *Building a Group by Music*

This exercise is done with an instrumental record which has an easily discerned tempo, rhythm, and mood; ethnic folk dances are especially suitable (African dances, or Irish, or Israeli folk dance records work well).

1. *Pair*   The facilitator gives the following instructions: "Select a partner. When the music starts, one of you move to the music, as you feel it. The other person will be your mirror image; he will do what you do. If it helps to be more realistic, pretend each of you is touching the mirror with the palms of your hands. The person who is the mirror will try to follow facial expressions as well as body movements. Change who is mirroring when you want to." The record begins.   (About 3 min.)

2. *Quartet*   "Add a pair to your group. Continue to move to the music but do it as a group."   (About 3 min.)

3. *Octet*   "Add a quartet to your group. Continue to move to the music as a group of eight."   (About 3 min.)

4. *One More Time* (*A Group of 16*)   "You're right. Add an octet to your group. Stay with the music. Move to the music as a group."

(About 3 min., preferably to the end of the record so that there is a natural feeling of closure.) This produces exhilaration but also a good supply of creaking joints, and a surge of business for the water fountain. There should be no discussion for at least 15 minutes.

The objectives of this exercise are to examine leadership-membership relations in varying group sizes. Who follows, who leads? Is it easier to lead in a small group than a large one? Do some leadership patterns remain? Why? How is leadership determined? What role do members have? Do they have inputs which are listened to? Who was the leader (or leaders) at the end? How did he get his influence? On what was it based? The facilitator asks how some of the members felt in this experience. He expands on some of the answers given to the above questions or raises a few new ones. Once more, the discussion should be brief and informal.

Conclusion

The facilitator in closing might summarize by reminding the group that they have been through a battery of nonverbal experiences that explore leadership-membership relations. They may consider what new understanding they have about themselves, for example, how they acted when they were asked to pick a partner. Did they choose, or more typically wait to be chosen. Why? What new insight do they have on the subject of leaders, members, followers?

Participants may be asked to write a log, a self-report, verbalizing what they have learned. They can be divided into small groups to discuss some of their experiences. A large group discussion leaves too many as listeners without an opportunity to participate; at best it might be used briefly to begin the discussion.

The facilitator should be particularly sensitive to norms of the group with whom he is working. These exercises should only be used where appropriate. As noted earlier, they should not be used with groups who consider touching inappropriate, nor should they be used unless the goals of the training will be enhanced by these exercises.

Exercise 2
What Is My Role in a Group?

Objectives

To learn who is perceived as leader of the group

To understand the many roles in a group

To develop data on what contributes to being the leader in a particular group

To increase data to participants on their perceived roles

To increase data to participants as to relationships between their perceptions of their roles and others' perceptions of their roles

Materials

Copies of the Behavioral Description Questionnaire (see pages 173–174) are needed; also newsprint to record the data. If it is a large group that has been working in smaller units, data can be recorded within each unit. If there are 10 members, each person requires 10 questionnaires.

Rationale

This exercise is appropriate after members of a group have been working together and know one another. It provides information to members on their roles as others perceive them, and as they themselves perceive their roles. This information may be congruent, or at great variance. It is a valuable feedback to the member on his influence in the group. It also permits data on who is seen as the leader and with what dimension leadership in this group is allied. Data are also available on the degree of commonly shared perceptions. Do many see the same person as the leader, or are several people seen as leaders?

Action

A questionnaire is distributed listing 15 statements. Under each is a 5-point scale. Each member is given enough questionnaires to fill one in for every member of the group. The facilitator may begin by briefly stating that each group develops in a unique manner depending upon the composition of the group, its task, its situation. He continues, "Each of us takes on a unique role within a group. Sometimes it is our typical role, sometimes a blend of roles from many experiences. Sometimes we see ourselves taking one role, and others see us quite differently. Perhaps by developing and sharing this data, we can learn more about ourselves and our group." It is important that the facilitator explain this rather seriously. Sometimes groups are apprehensive about getting or giving feedback and need support from the leader that such data are both legitimate and helpful.

Each person lists the name of the person he is describing at the top and then proceeds to indicate how typical that behavior is of that person.   (30 min.)

An easy way to collect data is to give one person all the sheets for another person (not his own). He then charts the data on a blank questionnaire. Finally he totals points on each question (a rating of 3 is 3 points).   (15 min.)

The facilitator asks for a report from each person on the behaviors seen as most typical for the person he tallied; or he asks for the highest points on each question. The person who scores the highest points on question 9—who is the real leader of the group—is the leader. In what other areas did the people who score highest on that question also score high? What are the behaviors required for leadership in this group?

Following discussion, all the papers are given to the person whose name is on top. The person then has all the reported data on himself. He can examine its congruence or variance with his own perceptions.   (15 min.)

BEHAVIORAL DESCRIPTION QUESTIONNAIRE[2]

Indicate how well each statement describes each group member (including yourself) on a 5-point scale running from "very true of him" (5) to "not true of him" (1).

1. He prodded the group to complete the task.

| 1 | 2 | 3 | 4 | 5 |
Not true of him   Very true of him

2. He was the real "idea man" in the group, suggesting new ways of handling the group's problems.

| 1 | 2 | 3 | 4 | 5 |
Not true of him   Very true of him

3. He is a creative person.

| 1 | 2 | 3 | 4 | 5 |
Not true of him   Very true of him

4. He was concerned only with his own ideas and viewpoint.

| 1 | 2 | 3 | 4 | 5 |
Not true of him   Very true of him

5. He influenced the opinions of others.

| 1 | 2 | 3 | 4 | 5 |
Not true of him   Very true of him

[2] Morris, C. G. and Hackman, J. R. Behavioral correlates of perceived leadership. *Journal of Personality and Social Psychology*, 1969, *13*, 350–361. Copyright 1969 by the American Psychological Association, and reproduced by permission.

6. He interrupted others when they were speaking.

1	2	3	4	5

Not true of him   Very true of him

7. He criticized those with whom he disagreed.

1	2	3	4	5

Not true of him   Very true of him

8. He was an aloof sort of person.

1	2	3	4	5

Not true of him   Very true of him

9. He was the real leader of the group.

1	2	3	4	5

Not true of him   Very true of him

10. He worked well with others in the group.

1	2	3	4	5

Not true of him   Very true of him

11. He was disruptive to the group.

1	2	3	4	5

Not true of him   Very true of him

12. He was in the forefront of the group's discussion.

1	2	3	4	5

Not true of him   Very true of him

13. He kept the group from straying too far from the topic.

1	2	3	4	5

Not true of him   Very true of him

14. His attitudes hurt the group's chances of success.

1	2	3	4	5

Not true of him   Very true of him

15. He seemed to be a tense, nervous person.

1	2	3	4	5

Not true of him   Very true of him

Scoring. For each person, the scores which he gave himself and those he received from other members are summed to provide an overall indication of how characteristic each of the 15 statements was of his behavior.

Discussion

The data gathered and presented are the basis for discussion. Any issues considered appropriate should be developed.

Who are the most influential members of this group? Why? What behaviors are valued?

What behavioral roles seem to be missing? How does this affect your group?

What difference was there between your perceptions of your role and how others see you? How do you feel about that?

Exercise 3
The Power Game

The following exercise[3] helps to develop insights on the machinations in politics: conflict, negotiation, and collaboration.

Objectives

To sharpen understanding of what it feels like to be a "have" (powerful) or a "have not" (powerless)

To analyze the feelings of participants in a power experience

To learn more about why groups act the way they do in situations involving power

To learn more about our own ideas on power and sources of power

To learn more about the factors that lead to success or failure in negotiations and coalitions

To learn more about the effects of leadership, pressure, and power

To be able to form power coalitions and use either conflict or collaborative strategies, whichever is more appropriate

Rationale

Simulation games have proved increasingly popular as a means to help participants identify with a situation and also feel enveloped in that situation. In this simulation the traps, the frustrations, the futility

---

[3] The Power Game was developed by George Peabody, Pres., G. Peabody, Organizational Development Consultants, New York, N.Y.

of being powerless are experienced, as well as the advantages, the manipulations, the controls of being powerful. The game quickly becomes emotional, and the typically intellectual discussions of power are avoided. The game generates new understanding of one's own ideas about the uses of power as well as the sources of power.

The game has been used effectively with students, faculty, and administrators who wanted to examine aspects of power at a large university. It has been used with minority groups in a community to increase their understanding of political power. It has also been used in workshops that examined "ins" versus "outs," city residents versus suburbanites; blacks versus whites; males versus females. A word of caution. The game permits participants to experience power—which means that some get hurt, frustrated, or angry. Some are angry with themselves, some enjoy the feeling of being the manipulator, some like power no matter at whose expense, nor at what costs. The game is not bland; it will evoke emotion. It is of utmost importance that enough time be allotted for discussion after the game.

Materials

A set of Rules, one for each player (see below)

A visible clock

A score form, which should be placed where it can be seen by all the participants. It might be a board, newsprint, or a chalkboard

A sample score form is shown below

Play Number	Team I (20)	Team II (20)	Team III (20)	Team IV (20)	Team V (20)
1					
2					
3					
4 (double points)					
5					
Total					

Action

The group is divided into five teams and each team is given a name or designation. Each team has 20 points to commit toward its various deals. The game is played in rounds or time periods. In a given round, teams attempt to form coalitions to attain their objectives. At the end of each round teams report to a judge the number of points they commit and their deals, if any. The coalition with the largest number of points at the end of the round picks up all the points committed. Each team has to decide for itself what it wants in the game.

Rules

1. The game is played in time periods. A judge will announce the length of the time period, announce its beginning, give a warning 30 seconds before the end, and announce the end of the time period or round.

2. The first play will occur at the end of 20 minutes. Each play thereafter will be at the end of 15 minutes.

3. If a team has not submitted its commitment at the end of the time period, there is a penalty of two points paid to each team that does commit on time. For example, if one team is late and two teams submit their commitments on time, the late team is fined two points, which are divided among the winners. (Odd points are confiscated in any division, a half, a third, etc.)

4. Each team must commit at least 5 points at the time of play, or lose 5 points.

5. At the end of the period the judge will announce the commitments. The coalition with the highest number of points picks up all the points committed. These points are divided among the coalition according to any deals the coalition has made. If no deals have been made, the points are divided equally.

6. On the fourth play scores are doubled, i.e., points each team has and can commit.

7. No score is officially made until the judge announces the commitments at the end of the play. If the judge is not present or can be invalidated, the announcements cannot be made.

Design

For an overview of the game, the reader should consult the rules. It would also be helpful to refer to these as the game is explained in detail.

Players

There should be a large enough number of participants to permit the group to be divided into five teams. If this cannot be done, any number of odd teams can be used. Five teams are suggested since this provides opportunities of a number of possible coalitions; a smaller number limits this aspect. Each team should have a designation. This can be a number, a geometric symbol, a colored sash, etc.

The participants are divided into teams, and each team has its "home territory," which may be a table where the members gather, or a separate room. This is designed to heighten the common bond among members of a group and also to clearly separate them from others. The designation is analogous to a population (Puerto Ricans, blacks, females, suburbanites, to name a few), each with its own area.

The Judge

A judge is appointed. He in a sense represents the reporting of the legislative, executive, or judicial process. He counts the decisions and announces who the winners are—who becomes more powerful or less powerful, or even "out of it." The judge should have a visible clock, since he announces the periods of play. He should also be in full view so that all can give him their decisions, but he should be separated from the teams, since he is not a part of any team. He could be in a different room, or at a separate table.

A Brief "Run-through" of the Game

After the five teams have been assigned and have studied the rules, the judge will announce the length of the first time period (20 min.). During this time each team must make a commitment of a minimum of 5 points and a maximum of 20 points. It makes this commitment in writing to the judge, who must have it in his hands when the time period ends. At the end of the time period, he writes the coalitions and the points committed on the scoreboard. The winning coalition gets all the points of the losers, and divides them among the winning coalition. For example, suppose Teams 1, 2, and 3 decided to form a coalition, each committing 15 points, for a total of 45. Even if the other two teams form a coalition and commit their full 20 points, for a total of 40 points, they lose. The coalition which has 45 points divides the losers' committed points (in this case 40) among them and continues the game. The two losing teams in this case are out of the game. This example is extreme—a team would not be likely to commit all its points.

After the dividing of points, which the judge places on the scoreboard, the game enters time period 2, a 15-minute time period, and members make new coalitions or continue old ones. The game continues usually for five rounds. The number of rounds should be agreed upon in advance.

At the beginning of each time period, emissaries from each team go to other teams to see what can be developed in the way of a coalition. These may be secretive or open; they may be based on cooperation or collaboration. Each team has to decide for itself what it is they want. Note that the first time period is longer than the others. This is done so that teams have time to develop strategies. For example, will the team play for long-term advantage or will it play for an immediate win on the first round?

The five rounds of the game are played. Following the game, there is a discussion. A number of possible discussion designs are suggested, depending on the total design for the program.

Discussion

There are a number of alternatives as to how the game can be handled most appropriately. The game can be used as part of a two-session training design, with the game being played at the first session and the processing of data from the game at the second session. Data may be gathered in the course of playing the game on the various deals made, and there may be a discussion of the implications of these deals at a later time. There can be several observers appointed to be especially aware of the processes of negotiation, leadership behaviors, degree of member participation and involvement; and there can be discussion at the next session. A number of designs are suggested for the feedback session after the game:

1. A fishbowl of "haves" and "have nots" at the end of the game.

2. Sociometric instruments distributed at the end of play to members of each team to focus on interteam dynamics. Examples: Who are the three people who helped our team most? Who do you think had the most influence on us? Team members can fill in questionnaires, give feedback results, and discuss findings.

3. Feedback of observers' reports to entire group. This allows participants to understand the processes of each group and the membership roles.

4. Discussion based on questions from training objectives of the game.

5. Discussion of trust in relation to negotiations, collaborations.

6. Nonverbally team members line themselves up in terms of influence the members felt they had on their teams; most influential at the head of the line, least influential at the end. Discussion follows.

Variations

1. Teams can be heterogeneous or homogeneous, i.e., teams can be selected randomly or made up of particular populations (for example, teams of men and teams of women). However, it is extremely risky to have homogeneous ethnic groups.

2. The first time period in the game is of 20 minutes' duration; this extended period is to permit each team to build group cohesion. Each team is instructed to formulate:

    a. What is our target (what are we trying to do)?

    b. What are our strategies?

    c. What are our resources or sources of power? How do we use them?

    d. What are our tactics?

    e. What is our timing?

At the end of the time period, each group gives a 45-second statement of its position: this statement can be true or it can be "image building." Each group gives itself a name and announces it.

3. Each team can put in a certain amount of money, perhaps 50¢ each, to be used instead of points in the playing of the game.

4. Each team designation can be worn by participants for instant identification (a colored hat, a band, a neckerchief, etc.).

5. There can be an official document on which commitments are made. Each team is given one official commitment document for each round of play. The team submits it to the judge at the end of each round, and no other documents may be submitted.

REFERENCES

Abrahamson, M. and Smith, J. Norms, deviance and spatial location. *Journal of Social Psychology*, 1970, *80*(1), 95–101.

Argyris, C. *Personality and organization*. New York: Harper & Row, 1957.

Bales, R. *Personality and interpersonal behavior*. New York: Holt, Rinehart, and Winston, 1970.

Bales, R. *Interaction process analysis*, Reading, Mass.: Addison-Wesley, 1950.

Barnard, C. I. *Functions of the executive*. Cambridge, Mass.: Harvard University Press, 1938.

Bass, B. *Leadership, psychology, and organizational behavior*. New York: Harper and Row, 1960.

Bass, B. M. Some observations about a general theory of leadership and interpersonal behavior. In L. Petrullo and B. Bass (Eds.), *Leadership and interpersonal behavior*. New York: Holt, Rinehart and Winston, 1961, 3–9.

Benne, K. D. and Sheats, P. Functional roles of group members. *Journal of Social Issues*, 1948, *2*, 42–47.

Berelson, B. and Steiner, G. A. *Human behavior*, New York: Harcourt, Brace and World, 1964.

Bird, C. *Social psychology*. New York: Appleton-Century, 1940.

Blake, R. and Mouton, J. S. *Building a dynamic corporation through grid organization development*. Reading, Mass.: Addison-Wesley, 1969.

Bohleber, M. E. Conditions influencing the relationships between leadership style and group structural and population characteristics. Dissertation Abstracts, 28 No. 2A: 766–777. Unpublished dissertation, University of Wisconsin, 1967.

Borgatta, E. F., Couch, A. S., and Bales, R. F. Some findings relevant to the great man theory of leadership. In A. Paul Hare et al. (Eds.), *Small groups: studies in social interaction*. New York: Alfred Knopf, 1955, 568–574.

Carter, L. F., Haythorn, W., Meriowitz, B., and Lanzetta, J. W. The relations of categorizations and ratings in the observation of group behavior. *Human Relations*, 1951, *4*, 239–254.

Cattell, R. New concepts for measuring leadership, in terms of group syntality. *Human Relations*, 1951, *4*, 161–184.

Dunno, P. Group congruency patterns and leadership characteristics. *Personnel Psychology*, 1968, *21*(3), 335–344.

Elder, G. H. Group congruency patterns and leadership character. Parental power legitimation and its effect on the adolescent. *Sociometry*, 1963, *26*, 50–65.

French, J. R. P., Jr. and Raven, B. The bases of social power. In D. Cartwright and A. Zander (Eds.), *Group Dynamics*. (2nd ed.). Evanston, Ill.: Row, Peterson, 1960, 607–623.

Geier, J. G. A trait approach to the study of leadership in small groups. *Journal of Communication*, 1967, *17*(4), 316–323.

Gershenfeld, M. K. Responsible behavior under conditions of threat and non-threat. Unpublished doctoral dissertation, Temple University, 1967.

Gibb, C. A. Leadership. In G. Lindzey (Ed.), *Handbook of social psychology*, Vol. II. Reading, Mass.: Addison-Wesley, 1954, 877–920.

Goldman, M. and Fraas, L. A. The effects of leader selection on group performance. *Sociometry*, 1965, *28*(1), 82–88.

Golembiewski, R. T. *The small group*. Chicago, Ill.: Univ. of Chicago Press, 1962.

Gouldner, A. (Ed.) *Studies in leadership*. New York: Harper and Row, 1950.

Gray, L. N., Richardson, J. T., and Mayhew, R. H. Jr. Influence attempts and effective power: a reexamination of an unsubstantiated hypothesis. *Sociometry*, 1968, *31*(1), 245–258.

Hemphill, J. K. Why people attempt to lead. In L. Petrullo and B. Bass (Eds.), *Leadership and interpersonal behavior*. New York: Holt, Rinehart and Winston, 1961, 201–215.

Holloman, C. R. Leadership and headship: there is a difference. *Personnel Administration*, 1968, *31*(4), 38–44.

Jenkins, D. H. New light on leadership. *Adult Leadership*, June 1956.

Jenkins, D. H. New questions for old. In *Leadership in action*. Washington, D.C.: National Training Laboratories, 1961, 23–25.

Julian, J. W., Hollander, E. P., and Regula, C. R. Endorsement of the group spokesman as a function of his source of authority, competence, and success. *Journal of Personality and Social Psychology*, 1969, *11*(1), 42–49.

Kahn, R. and Katz, D. *The social psychology of organizations*. New York: John Wiley and Sons, 1966.

Knickerbocker, I. Leadership: a conception and some implications. In *Leadership in action*, Washington, D.C., National Training Laboratories, 1961, 69.

Lewin, K., Lippitt, R., and White, R. K. Patterns of aggressive behavior in experimentally created social climates. *Journal of Social Psychology*, 1939, *10*, 271–299.

Maslow, A. H. *Motivation and personality*. New York: Harper & Row, 1954.

McDavid, J. W. and Harari, H. *Social psychology*. New York: Harper and Row, 1968.

McGregor, D. *The human side of enterprise*. New York: McGraw-Hill, 1960.

Margulies, N. Organizational culture and psychological growth. *Journal of Applied Behavioral Science*, 1969, *5*(4), 491–508.

O'Brien, G. Effects of organizational structure, leadership style, and members compatibility upon small group creativity. *Proceedings of 76th Annual Convention*. Washington, D.C.: American Psychological Association, 1969.

Pepinsky, P., Hemphill, J. H., and Shevitz, R. Attempts to lead, group productivity and morale under conditions of acceptance and rejection. *Journal of Abnormal and Social Psychology*, 1968, 57, 47–54.

Petrullo, L. and Bass, B. M. (Eds.) *Leadership and interpersonal behavior.* New York: Holt, Rinehart and Winston, 1961.

Raven, B. H. and French, J. R. P., Jr. Group support, legitimate power, and social influence. *Journal of Personality*, 1958, 26, 400–409.

Rieken, H. W. and Homans, G. C. Psychological aspects of social structure. In G. Lindzey (Ed.), *Handbook of social psychology*, Vol. II. Reading, Mass.: Addison-Wesley, 1954, 786–832.

Ring, K. and Kelley, H. H. A comparison of augmentation and reduction in modes of influence. *Journal of Abnormal and Social Psychology*, 1963, 66, 95–102.

Sadler, P. J. Leadership style, confidence in management, and job satisfaction. *Journal of Applied Behavioral Science*, 1970, 6(1), 3–20.

Schein, E. H. *Process consultation.* Reading, Mass.: Addison-Wesley, 1969.

Schutz, W. C. *FIRO: a three-dimensional theory of interpersonal behavior.* New York: Holt, Rinehart and Winston, 1958.

Stogdill, R. M. Personal factors associated with leadership: a survey of the literature. *Journal of Psychology*, 1948, 25, 35–71.

Tannenbaum, R. and Schmidt, W. H. How to choose a leadership pattern. *Harvard Business Review*, 1960, 36, 95–101.

White, R. and Lippitt, R. Leader behavior and member reaction in three social climates. In D. Cartwright and A. Zander (Eds.), *Group dynamics* (3rd ed.). New York: Harper and Row, 1968.

Burk Uzzle / Magnum

6 group problem solving and decision making

For many years men and the groups they composed were looked upon and studied from a classical viewpoint. That is, when experimentalists became interested in problem-solving groups, they assumed a certain rationality of man and attempted to control all extraneous variables. Conditions were established which reduced the range of emotional and behavioral responses that would be elicited. The behavior of the experimental subjects was quantified and analyzed, and statistical probabilities were determined so that the information could be generalized for other groups. There is no doubt that such investigations raised an enormous number of highly relevant questions and, in some cases, answers for both theorists and practitioners. However, the approach of the experimentalist is a fragmentary approach to the problems of working groups. It is a view that tends to separate the technical-mechanical aspects of the process from the human-emotional factors. The trends and generalities developed about men and their groups may well provide diagnostic clues for understanding the group as it works on a task. But, it is only by beginning to understand the complex weave of both these sets of factors that one will begin to appreciate the uniqueness of each group, its needs, and the possibilities available for facilitating its work efforts. It is the purpose of this chapter to raise some of the experimental questions and answers for the reader and to present the information in a manner that will broaden his perspective of the problem-solving process (Edwards, 1967; Kelley and Thibaut, 1969).

The Nature of Man in a Problem-solving Group

A person entering a group is an individual with a past, a present, and a projected future. He responds to persons, objects, and relationships. His fantasies, stereotypes, biases, personal needs blend together to form a net of psychological factors impinging upon him at a given time and influencing his behavior. Even his simplest behavior represents a complex merging of what to him are the realities of a group, threats and possible rewards, doubts and expectations. How often have we been called to a meeting with six or seven others with the aim of solving a number of rather clearly stated problems in a time period of perhaps 2 hours? Starting with all good intentions and in a climate of apparent good humor, the meeting degenerates as tensions inexplicably rise and productivity declines. Three hours later the weary participants wonder how so much energy could possibly be expended over such trivial issues, and most members are at a loss to understand how it happened. Most disconcerting is the feeling that many of the resistances which appeared as the meeting progressed seemed to be directed more at personalities than at the topical issues under discussion.

What happened in this and thousands of groups like it can be explored from two perspectives. First, one may look at the more mechanical aspects of the group's functioning: the general arrangement of the room and its physical environment, how the agenda was developed and presented, the mechanisms used in the problem-solving process, and the methods used for arriving at a final decision. The second perspective is the shadowy, less easily defined dimension of group process in which the focus is on behavior as it is influenced by personal needs and stimulated by the conduct of others.

The Decision-making Process:
Sources of Tension and Conflict

Who knows a perfectly relaxed man? Simply fulfilling our basic life needs provides us with a never ending source of tension and the constant demand to make decisions. For every potential decision there are two potential sources of tension and conflict. First, whenever the decision involves a choice between alternatives, there is a loss-and-gain factor(s) that must be weighed. To eat roast beef means no chicken, to have another drink means feeling less alive in the morning, to buy six shares of IBM means foregoing a down payment on a piece of property, or to offer a suggestion means possible rejection. Similarly, just being in a group poses new tensions and decisions for an individual. What must I do to be accepted here? Should I relax and just be myself? They say they want my opinion, but should I risk having it rejected? I really don't like the way things are going. I wonder if things will be any better if I say something? These and hundreds of other personal decisions add an enormous reservoir of tension to any group even before its task has begun. Then when the group does begin its own process of decision making, there is further potential conflict as a result of disagreement among individual participants, as well as from the implications any decision will have upon the group as a whole (Lewin, 1948; Lewin, 1951; Adams and Adams, 1967).

A second source of natural tension and conflict is created after the individual or group makes a decision. This stems from being faced with having to live with the decision that has just been made and thus having to continually justify it in the mind of the group (or individual) and in the minds of others (Festinger, 1957).

It appears natural, therefore, that tension and points of conflict should exist within decision-making groups. The question becomes one of whether or not the sources of tension are clearly recognized and dealt with in the most constructive manner possible. All too often the greatest sources of tension and conflict are completely avoided (denied or ignored). If the actual sources of tension are not uncovered and dealt with, it is highly likely that they will be diffused into other areas of the group's experience. Here is a case in point:

A number of years ago all the principals of a large urban school system were urged by the administration to leave the city and attend an intensive 14-day human relations workshop. The workshop was aimed at increasing leadership skills and providing an opportunity for the group to work through a number of pressing problems that they all shared. Extreme tension developed to a point that the participants were practically immobilized. On the one hand, it was clear that the opportunity to get away from the pressures on the job, reappraise their own skills, look at their own shared problems, and build a supportive network among themselves would probably not come again. On the other hand, the members felt that they were not there of their own free will and that the request to attend had been a scarcely cloaked demand. Thus, feeling manipulated, the entire group was faced with the uncomfortable question of their own potency.

Second, there was an underlying fear that it was one thing to gather answers to problems in a "mountain haven" and quite another to apply them back in the "jungle." To develop new answers and new personal skills and then not be able to implement them successfully would be worse than to continue to struggle on with no new ideas. It is one thing to blame an unworkable system, but it is quite another thing to be faced with one's own inadequacies.

Both these sources of tension had to be surfaced before the real work of the group could even begin. The issue of coercion was dealt with by raising it for the group to discuss. By allowing them to legitimately vent their anger and by helping them to see there were few feasible alternative approaches given the shortness of time, the issue died. But, the very process of becoming angry as a group helped them recapture some of their lost sense of potency. The second issue was resolved by developing a training period of one week back in the city (cutting short the time away) where the skills learned in the workshop could be tested on groups of students and community members at a time when the principal group was still together and able to share in the success or failure of the programs they designed.

In this case, the group had to decide whether to acquiesce and accept the program or to resist (in some cases by overt action and in others by withdrawing). The tension was relieved once the issues of conflict were uncovered and dealt with, but this took nearly 2 days of the group's time and energy.

Tensions within a problem-solving group can arise so subtly that the participants find it almost impossible to extricate the real issue. For example, in a certain factory, the division manager was constantly being pushed to give more responsibilities in decision making to subordinate members of staff. At one point, it was decided to give more of the administrative decisions over to the workers themselves. The reaction to the decision was immediately favorable, and a representative group of eight men was elected to iron out the new administrative details to be presented later to the rest of the factory for a referendum vote. From the beginning, sources of tension were apparent among the working group, but no one could put his finger on the source of difficulty. After 3 weeks of virtually no progress, a pattern of behavior in the group had developed which seemed to lead to the following conclusion. Apparently, although the men had intellectually liked the idea of more influence, a greater awareness of necessary time investment and accountability for outcomes had dampened any original enthusiasm. It became increasingly evident that the group was in conflict over the fact that they had won an argument (more influence) but were going to lose in the sense of having to expend considerably more time and energy as a result. This is the kind of issue that is extremely difficult to dredge out of a group, but, without doing so, compromises and alternative administrative patterns could not even be raised.

Also, what does a person do in a case where someone wants to spend some time looking at the problem of openness and trust within the group? The idea may be supported by other members because who can argue against such hallowed virtues as trust, openness, and authenticity? Again, individuals are more willing to talk about an ideal condition rather than work at developing it. Even those who initiate the discussion may begin to feel the growing tension between self-exposure and job evaluation, between authenticity and ascribed role, between honesty and different levels of power in the group.

Even a choice that must be made between two positive alternatives may create tensions that show themselves through increasing interpersonal conflict. Often such a choice is put off, and the anxiety of the group is taken out in the discussion of other issues.

The point to be made is that groups, like individuals, are constantly being forced into making decisions. The problem is that the process often breaks down over personal issues that are not easily raised to the surface, but which leave a residual of tension that may debilitate the entire problem-solving process. Often the issues causing conflict are personal and emotional while those being dealt with are intellectual. By asking himself what it is that is causing the group to avoid the possible alternative and what are the real underlying issues of tension, a person standing apart may be able to move the group to another stage in its problem solving. Thus, if a person is really concerned with understanding why a group is functioning as it is, it may help to know the stated goals and bylaws of the group. Of even more value would be to observe the group as an objective observer, sorting out various behaviors in relation to possible causal factors. Most important would be developing an awareness of how the individual members personally feel about the group itself, their role in it, and their feeling about the issue being discussed. Too often we remain at a technical level when the sources of conflict are occurring at an emotional one (Lewin, 1936).

Sources of Resistance in Decision-making Groups[1]

Much of the frustration that often accompanies working with a decision-making group results from an inability to understand and accept as perfectly natural many of the resistances that develop during the

[1] Much of this discussion is drawn from Watson, 1967.

problem-solving process. This in itself can reduce some of the strain. Further, some of the points of resistance readily suggest procedural approaches that might result in a reduction of tensions and potential conflict.

Most people tend to organize their lives in a manner that reduces the amount of stress they must face. There are, of course, those individuals who create stress and crisis in their lives to satisfy other needs. Yet most individuals build a pattern of existence that is familiar and comfortable, a pattern in which habit, ritual, and precedent play a relatively large part. In a sense, the individual attempts to bring his life into a state of equilibrium where he is able to predict events and reduce conflict. To change this relatively stable, steady state results in a need to change accustomed patterns of behavior and creates, at least temporarily, discomfort and tension. Problem solving and eventual decision making often lead to innovation, alternative courses of action, and a disruption of a group's or individual's state of equilibrium. This is one reason we resist new ideas. It is why we sit in the same seats, tell the same tried-and-true jokes, maintain the same prejudices, and continue the same work habits. This is the safe and comfortable way; it requires little effort and helps us to feel secure and confident in what we do. A particular solution, even though it appears acceptable and useful, may, nevertheless, be met with the most subtle and resourceful resistances.

When people work with the familiar and within a framework of accustomed behavior, they build a relationship to authority and power that is based upon relatively clear expectations. When one changes his relationship to power, when he takes on new responsibilities, he immediately becomes more vulnerable and less sure of his own position. Thus, secure dependency relations are altered and personal security lessened. Again, this may occur within a particular group member or for the group as a whole if it is required to adjust to new lines of authority and new prospects of accountability. When decisions alter such relationships, one may anticipate conflicts and tension, which are likely to be expressed in overt or covert resistance to the proposal being considered.

As suggested in one of the previous examples, people fear being perceived as inadequate or impotent. It is one thing to feel inadequate and impotent; we somehow adjust ourselves to this. But to have someone else suggest we are less than competent, less than able to do what is expected, is intolerable. It is often an illusion of impotence that reduces the desire to risk, to try a new approach. This is a primary force behind the "Oh, what's the use?" or the "That's been tried before" syndrome. It is based upon experience, unfulfilled dreams, and real feelings of inability to alter one's conditions. The attitude a group has toward its role as decision maker will be greatly influenced by the combined measure of its own potency and sense of adequacy to carry out decisions. But, again, we find ourselves in the murky realm of the unmeasurable. (At a later point, the discussion will be directed at ways of reducing this and other resistances that may hinder the problem-solving process.)

Groups, as individuals, build security by establishing standards and rules of behavior. They tend to value the traditional. They withdraw from tests of their own potency and rebel against outside intrusions that may throw their own stable and tranquil world into disequilibrium. These and other resistances are generated from the emotional dimension of group life and may have little to do with the actual "goodness of fit" of the intellectual idea being considered. It is by beginning to look within the labyrinth of emotions upon which any group is built that a person will find the keys to real movement and progress. The first step is to discover what state prevails within the group at a given time and to attempt to seek validation of these perceptions. By its nature this requires looking beyond the rational scope of the problem and into the rational and irrational perspectives of both the individual participants and the group as a whole (Heider, 1958).

It is evident that unless individuals feel personally secure and relatively unthreatened within the problem-solving group, they will tend to respond with their own characteristic patterns of defense. These behaviors can themselves be important sources of diagnostic information. The obvious withdrawal of individuals from participation, signs of passive or active aggression, subgrouping, or an excessive amount of dependency or resistance to authority will often suggest emotional issues that reduce effectiveness. As mentioned previously, the conflicts and resulting tensions synonymous with these behaviors can usually be traced back to one of four areas of concern. First, there are conflicts arising from personal goals and needs that are at variance with those of the group. Second, there are problems of personal identity and acceptance (membership issues). Third, there are problems generated from the distribution of power and influence. And, finally, there is the question of intimacy which encompasses issues of trust and personal openness. Virtually all the examples explored to this point could be incorporated within these basic categories.

As long as such issues exist, much of the group's energy will be directed toward self-oriented behaviors, and the accomplishment of the task will be disrupted. Naturally, it is impossible to remove all sources of personal tension (nor would it be desirable), but the more such problems can be raised and dealt with, the more attention can be given to the substantive issues.

Additional Sources of Tension

Decisions by their very nature suggest alternatives, argument, and conflict. Basically, a decision represents the termination of a controversy with a particular course of action. However, the conflict and tension do not end with the decision. How the individual or group copes with the doubts, suspicions, and skepticism generated during the discussion has important implications (Festinger, 1957; Festinger and Aronson, 1968). It is reasoned that the longer and stronger the discussion, the more ambivalence will be created (whether or not this is overtly recognized is another question) leading to a state of "cognitive dissonance." This dissonance is a continuous source of tension, and the individual or group attempts to reduce it in a number of ways. For example, once the decision is made there is a tendency to begin valuing it even more than before (Brehm, 1956). As with a religious convert, many of the old questions and doubts are forgotten and the decision is constantly reinforced.

The trouble is that the decision may become overvalued, and an intransigent attitude develops which closes the door on future discussion of alternatives or even a fair evaluation of the decision at a later date. A subtle process of rationalization and justification may develop. This is particularly true if the decision turns sour and must still be lived with (a leader is chosen who proves inept; a tax is imposed to curtail inflation and unemployment increases, a surplus is guaranteed and a deficit is incurred). Similarly, people are prone to make the best of a bad thing when the decision is out of their control. Thus, even though it can be proved that most school grades lack objectivity and validity, students and parents alike will still defend them. Outwardly they may go through a long and involved defense of the system noting the value of the grading process, while inwardly the push for keeping the system lies in the more clouded area of, "I've suffered and so should you." This rationalization has nothing to do with the questions surrounding the legitimacy of grades. Still, such internal justifications tend to reduce dissonance and forge the major source of support for maintaining the status quo. Therefore, one needs to justify his expenditure of time, energy, and hope in a decision which is a matter more of image than principle and which will shape future behaviors and accompanying decisions (Festinger and Aronson, 1968; Festinger and Carlsmith, 1959).

A final source of tension and frustration may follow a particular type of group decision born more out of guilt than conviction. In this case the group makes a decision to remove the problem from view, reduce the pressure, and placate the antagonists.

The executives of a small plant were confronted by a group of militants and presented with evidence that this particular organization, although located within an urban ghetto, had systematically discriminated against hiring minority workers from the surrounding community. After considerable arguing, denial, and hostility against the outside intruders, the executives accepted the social realities. They reported that sweeping changes in their hiring policies would occur and that a fixed percentage of employees in certain job categories would be drawn from the community. The only stipulation was that the hiring would remain in the hands of the department heads and be contingent on the current demands of the plant. The militants left with the taste of victory, and the executives breathed a sigh of relief as the pressure underlying a potentially explosive issue was removed.

The executives had shown "great cooperation" once they were able to accept their own guilt in the issue. However, they also knew the potential internal conflicts that could result from a rapid integration of a minority group. In their decision, they intentionally left a number of loopholes which would not show up until later. Thus, the department heads reorganized their hiring procedures, created a "temporary" pool of workers and proceeded to hire the community members only on a temporary basis. This created a new hierarchical level among the plant workers and separated the community workers in terms of status, pay, job responsibilities, and possible advancement. The executives' decision was, in reality, a holding decision used to reduce pressures while the company completed plans to move to the suburbs.

What Causes Problems in a Group

During the last 15 to 20 years there has been an enormous proliferation of research in the area of group problem solving. Slowly a picture of ambivalent conditions has emerged, some facilitative, some disruptive of this process. One needs to ask such questions as:

1. What is the best mix of people to solve the problem when one considers such things as status, expertise, and organizational skills?
2. What size should the decision-making group be, and is there an optimal size and structure which leads to greatest productivity?
3. How important is goal clarity in accomplishing the task?
4. Can time pressure be used as a factor in increasing the productivity of a working group?
5. How important is it to develop trust and open communication in the problem-solving process?
6. What behaviors create competition and which kinds insure the development of more constructive interdependent behaviors? Also, are debating and other devices used to stimulate argument during the problem solving useful?
7. How does power and authority influence problem solving and eventual decision making?

The remainder of this chapter will focus upon these and a variety of other questions which seem to play an important part in creating an effective problem-solving atmosphere.

While it is often dangerous to attempt generalizations from one group to the next, it is helpful to know trends. For example, evidence indicates that shared decision making is usually considered a better means of developing commitment to goals and participant involvement than highly authoritative and directive decisions from a dominant leader. On the other hand, under certain situations (crisis, limited time, no future involvement), a controlled, authoritative approach may prove to be most effective and desirable. Following is a brief case study which will be used to stimulate discussion of many of these issues. Of course, it is always easier to sit in the bleachers after the game and conjecture about what should have been done. Nevertheless, it is from such processing that we learn and alter our approach the next time around.

THE COMMUNITY–UNIVERSITY CHARRETTE[2]

This situation has been reenacted many times throughout the country by many institutions—hospitals, shopping centers, factories, universities. In this instance the villain is a large urban university. Yet, in some ways, it is the victim as well because of the times, circumstances, and its own insensitivity to its neighbors. The university had grown dramatically from what was primarily a narrowly conceived evening school servicing a few thousand students to a thriving, expanding giant of an institution with nearly 40,000 students, four campuses, and a full complement of day, evening, graduate, and undergraduate programs. It fulfilled a great need for the education-starved, middle-class whites who poured into the confines of the city campus. The university was squeezed into a small area of land in the middle of a black community of more than a quarter of a million people. While this community might be classified as a ghetto, the majority of the residents have lived there for many years. True, the community has shown signs of deterioration in recent years, but it is home to many.

As its need for space grew, the university used its financial, legal, and civic resources to acquire new land. Hundreds of homes were systematically removed and replaced in the name of reclamation and learning. As the spread of the university continued, home values dropped, insurance became almost impossible to get, and the stereotype of the ghetto became even more pervasive. Also, black community resentment of the white university (1 percent black) rose as increasing numbers of friends and neighbors were displaced at great financial and emotional cost.

At this point in time, a small group of student activists and community members staged a protest which resulted in a much-publicized moratorium on new building prior to agreements on future land use between the black community and the university. In an effort to break the deadlock, the university proposed a charrette—a plan for community groups and university people to come together and resolve their differences. The plan was presented by the university in good faith, and they invested more than $50,000 in its organization and development. But, good intentions, money, and organization were not

[2] The term "charrette" has come to mean problem-solving meetings on a particular issue in a condition of crisis. It is derived historically from a time when architecture students at L'Ecole des Beaux-Arts would travel to school in special two-wheeled carts (charrettes) and often use the trip to study "en charrette" as they worked through last-minute problems before a test or class discussion. The connotation of limited time and urgency has been carried through to this day.

enough to overcome the limitations inherent in the plan. After more than 2 weeks of tense negotiations, the two groups reached an impasse, and the process ground to a halt a full day before the sessions were scheduled to close. During the following month a small group of university-community and high-level state officials (appointed by the governor) finally managed to come to an agreement which placed a large portion of undeveloped university land (56 percent) under the control of the community. The moratorium ended.

Following is an analysis of the limitations inherent in the problem-solving process and the implications such limitations have for other problem-solving groups. Again, one is not sure, given the tense conditions that existed, that any orientation to problem solving between the two parties could have been successful.

Value of the Charrette   Even though the charrette was an ineffective mechanism for problem solving, it proved useful on a number of other counts. These in themselves might have been enough to have warranted its existence. In the first place, it brought together a cross-section of people from both the community and the university for the first time. The "ivory tower" image of the university had been quite true, and many of the university administrators and faculty involved in the charrette had never met with a community group over any issue. In fact, it had been a white, suburban university that happened to be in a black urban community. Second, the format of the charrette provided a much-needed confrontation and legitimized the releasing of pent-up hostility and aggression, particularly by the black community. Third, the period of catharsis provided university representatives with an indication of the depth of resentment and feelings and a perspective of the issues which extended far beyond the use of land. Finally, the charrette gave the participants of each group an opportunity to familiarize themselves with the people behind the issues—an opportunity to humanize the conflict and break down stereotypes. All these factors suggested an important first step in any future negotiations and were important and necessary spade work. But, even with the issues and feelings out, even with the value of the "educational process," the structure of the charrette proved inadequate and self-defeating.

Factors Influencing the Problem-solving Process

The Impact of Size and Status Differences   For any planner of a problem-solving group a question of critical importance involves the representation of the participants: Who should be present, how many, and in what proportions? The planners of the charrette found themselves caught between several pressures. The university was constantly being accused of not seeking representative community opinion. They also were criticized for sending only token representation to many meetings involving the community. Thus there was great pressure to make certain that important voices within each group were not overlooked and that the real power was clearly represented. However, the greater the social stratification in a group, the greater are the perceived differences in power and the less effective is communication. It is more difficult to reach agreement (Hurwitz et al., 1960; Katz and Benjamin, 1960) as the number of participants increases; and the more tensions develop, the more effective communication is reduced. In the charrette, the community was represented by many different factions. There were men and women, young and old, militants and moderates, lower class and middle class, those with support of various groups and those who stood alone. From the university there were administrators with power and those seeking it, faculty of different rank and influence, and students of various ideological backgrounds. And, finally, there were representatives of the state and local governments, business groups, and consulting firms. It was an impressive array of people, a group which might have been ideal in diagnosing problems and getting them into the open, but the lines of conflict had been drawn, and the problems were on the table. Such a heterogeneous group would have great trouble coming to agreement (Kelley, 1951; Festinger, 1950).

Taking only size as a factor, certain things occur. As numbers increase, individual ideas are lost; there is less participation and involvement; people feel less potent, and communication is more difficult. Because it is difficult to feel influential and identify with a large group, there is a tendency to seek support and identity with smaller subgroups and stake one's position firmly behind a particular issue. Issues tend to become overvalued and polarized. Feeling less in touch with the actual decision making, sniping and criticism of procedures may become an outlet for feelings of frustration and inadequacy. This is particularly true if, as in the case of the charrette, issues are polarized to begin with and suspicion and distrust underlie the negotiations (Gibb, 1951; Hackman and Vidman, 1970; Idnik, 1955). Beyond about seven people, groups tend to be dominated by strong personalities, and increasing numbers of individuals find it is difficult to voice their ideas. A period of hearing the same voices and feeling personally blocked can make even the most pleasant person irritable and resistant.

If one adds clearly defined levels of status to the variable of size, other sources of tension will likely develop. For example, it has been shown that people of low status in a group tend to identify with those of higher status levels, seek acceptance by them, participate less than they do, and, generally, direct their communication to them. Similarly, those with recognized high status tend to feel and act more accepted, direct their communication to high-status peers, and dominate the discussion (Hurwitz et al., 1960; Katz and Benjamin, 1960; Kelley, 1951). In recent years, however, this pattern seems to be changing somewhat as minority groups with traditionally low status demand to be heard and, if anything, speak out forcefully in the face of the status-oriented "power structure." In the charrette a few community members were ascribed high status by both sides and accepted intellectually, if not emotionally, as equals in the negotiation sessions. Nevertheless, there is still reason to believe that the personal needs of many participants dictated their behaviors and that this inhibited and restricted the two groups (Fouriezos et al., 1950). Aside from finding viable solutions that both groups could live by, it was important to present a certain image of oneself (Goffman, 1959). With each side dancing to its own tune, concessions were most difficult to come by. Further, when low-status community people waved the flag of guilt and projected open hostility to those traditionally in a position of respect, one would anticipate at least covert denial and antipathy. Thus with so many diverse participants all seeking the limelight of the charrette, and with power addressing itself to power, increased tensions and minimal productivity were predictable.

The Need for Clear Goals   It has been suggested previously (Chapter 4) that a lack of clear goals can reduce the attraction of the group for its members and result in conflict and disunity. When two groups enter a problem-solving session with different views of the problem at hand and different views of the specific goals, other issues are bound to arise. For the university administration, the task was narrowly defined and to stray from the property issues would not be to their benefit. For the community, the land issue opened a never ending list of questions developed through the years, and the charrette provided the stage upon which these could be presented. To other members of the university team, there was a general lack of knowledge about the issues, a lack of involvement in strategy sessions, and considerable difference of opinion about the desired outcomes of the charrette. The lack of clear goals and agreed-upon strategies precipitated a number of power struggles among the university representatives.

The difference in perceived goals by the university and community groups resulted in hours of time spent in irrelevant tasks (according to one group) and in hours of avoiding significant issues (according to the other).

Mistrust and Lack of Credibility: An Inadequate Basis for Coopera- *tion* Whenever those participating in problem solving believe the other side wishes to reduce their power, it is likely that a competitive and hostile climate will result (Deutsch, 1969). In the case of the charrette, each side viewed the other from this perspective. The university perceived itself as protecting that which was rightly its own, felt unfairly pushed by unjust and irrational tactics (demonstrations, sit-ins), and saw the community as a potential threat to its autonomy and independence as an educational institution. On the other hand, the community felt that they were being dispossessed of their land by the use of sheer power, and that they were the victims of exploitation by the white power structure. To them this confrontation represented a test of will and power as much as anything. Furthermore, they viewed the university as coming to the charrette, not in a desire to remedy an unjust situation, but in an effort to redefine lines of power in their own favor. There is no doubt that there was some truth in both of these perspectives. The point to be made is that the prospects for agreement within any problem-solving group are limited by the degree of mistrust and suspicion that are present (Moscovici and Zavalloni, 1969).

Although the charrette represents an extreme example of communication breakdown, suspicion, and mistrust, the same elements are found, to some degree, in most problem-solving groups. For example, in recent years as a result of experimentation in the area of competitive group games, it has been shown that even when interdependence and cooperation are a distinct possibility, there is a tendency to mistrust the motives of the other party and to maximize one's position of strength at the expense of the other. Thus, since a cooperative strategy is not anticipated by either side, both sides project a win-lose approach and attempt to maximize their possible gains while minimizing potential losses (Deutsch, 1949; Crombag, 1966; Hammond and Goldman, 1961). Even in games when cooperation will maximize both parties' gains (but there is a risk of losing if the other side does not cooperate), the tendency will be to develop the more independent and defensive strategy (Von Neumann and Morgenstern, 1947; Edwards, 1967a; Luce and Raiffa, 1957). This predisposition for viewing a situation competitively (even combatively) can quickly turn a potentially constructive problem-solving climate—one based on mutual interdependence—into a circumstance in which secrecy, mistrust, and control take over. Under such conditions, to be vulnerable is not acceptable; to present the strong face is important, and raw power rather than equity and compromise are valued (Scodel et al., 1959; McClintock and McNeil, 1966).

An issue of critical importance for the group facilitator or planner is how to maximize a climate of interdependence, enhance a feeling of mutual power, and cultivate a responsiveness to the needs and position of each member (Deutsch, 1969; Guetzkow and Gyr, 1954). In the case of the charrette, the self-defeating strategy created from initial doubt and suspicion on both sides acted to further polarize the two groups. What began theoretically as an issue of land rights quickly became an issue that involved the personal integrity of the participants. The debating format, often seen as a democratic part of problem solving, only solidified positions and decreased the willingness of participants to seek alternative approaches. In fact, there is considerable evidence that debates seldom change positions. Those involved assimilate the messages that fit into their own pattern of accepted beliefs and screen out information that conflicts with their self-interests. Furthermore, rather than reducing intergroup rivalries and a competitive atmosphere, debating encourages groups to actually overvalue their positions and results in the development of greater "in-group"–"out-group" conditions (Sherif and Sherif, 1956; Ferguson and Kelley, 1964). The charrette focused on differences rather than mutual concerns, built inflexibility into roles and positions, and created an approach that was defensive and keyed toward self-preservation.

Power and Control: Realities Often Ignored

It has been suggested previously that individuals and groups are nearly always aware of how they are being controlled and who has the power to shape their destinies. Subordinates respond defensively in the presence of their superiors, adolescents with adults, parishioners with priests, students with teachers, and community people with white university officials. In some groups there is a tendency to respond to power by building dependency relations with those who hold the keys to reward and punishment. For others the effort is directed at countering the power and control, assuming a posture of independence, and, if possible, reducing the control of others.

It is between these two poles that most people fall, and it is from the push and pull at the two extremes that many tensions are created. As suggested in the discussion of status (Chapter 1), power seeks power, and it is not long before those with the real ability to influence decision making are discovered. The idea of shared decision making and distribution of power can be a good one, if it is based upon some experience and trust. But to have a large group involved in a decision-making process when, in fact, only a few individuals have the power to control what actually happens can lead to disillusionment and resistance among those who detect their own impotence. Credibility will become even more strained if those with power are perceived as being inflexible and using the elaborate problem-solving procedures to help them look as if they are open to new ideas. If there is no accountability and responsibility built into the group, if real decisions are made behind the scenes, then the work sessions of the larger group will be reduced to a climate of relative indifferences over the major issues, and energy will be channeled into secondary issues with less powerful individuals attempting to assert themselves.

In the charrette the power relationships were readily perceived by the black community. One reason secondary issues took so much time was that it became apparent that the university was, in fact, accountable to another power source, the state. It was discovered that because of some political realities and organizational ties, the state officials who were present in the role of observers were the ones who would have the greatest influence in making the final decision. Once the university team was perceived in light of its actual potency in terms of the primary land issue, the community leaders bided their time until the state finally stepped in and took a direct hand in the negotiations. The charrette then became an avenue for many other related community problems while the real negotiations took place between the recognized sources of power among the university, community and state representatives.

What the charrette accomplished in terms of opening new lines of communication, raising issues, and educating the university-community cannot be measured. But, as a problem-solving group, it was ill-conceived in terms of the specific problem. In the long run, it is doubtful whether the process helped reduce the credibility gap that existed between the university and the black community. The total process points to several factors that seem to have important implications for a wide variety of problem-solving groups.

1. Effective group problem solving assumes working groups that are small enough to insure involvement of as many resource people as are able to contribute effectively to the process. Each of these work groups must feel their own potency (see the next section) and have direct access to sources of power and influence.

2. If working groups recognize their own efforts as perfunctory and outside the lines of decision-making influence, they will direct their frustrations at the process itself (inhibiting work efforts) or by raising secondary issues that they do have the power to solve.

3. Similarly, lines of real power must be made clear to the participants and hidden interests (agendas) surfaced.

4. Goals for the working sessions must be clearly perceived and agreed upon by the participants. This assumes a process of joint diagnosing and planning prior to the problem-solving meeting. Even the format of the work sessions should be agreed upon. This preliminary planning can help establish a climate for cooperation and reduce any existing credibility gap. (In the case of the charrette the format of the meeting was perceived as "the university's" which would probably work to their ultimate advantage. Good intentions aside, it was perceived by many as another imposition upon the community.)

5. The introduction of a debating format tends to increase competition rather than cooperative interdependence. Thus, issues become clouded in a win-lose mentality with little room for compromise.

6. Similarly, the introduction of an extremely heterogeneous group of participants tends to draw a great many personal needs into the meetings, not the least of which is an internal source of competition. Such heterogeneity may prove to be particularly useful during a diagnostic phase of the problem solving when the widest possible range of feelings and opinions are sought. But, without a rather carefully organized and structured mechanism for solving the problem (see the next section), personalities may dominate, and the

result may be a poor use of group resources and a solution of questionable value.

7. While it is important to recognize and deal with the personal-emotional issues that can immobilize a group, it is often too easy for the problem-solving session (particularly in crisis conditions) to become a platform for a wide range of grievances extending clearly beyond anything the meeting can hope to accomplish. In one sense this may be a diversion from anxiety. Whatever the cause, it should not be allowed to divert the group from its purpose.

8. People tend to use available time either in problem solving or in pushing their own ideas. Given 2 weeks, the majority of time will probably be spent on issues outside those that need to be solved. Often a great deal more can be accomplished in a highly intensified, shorter period of time, in which motivation and work output can be maintained at a high level and where time itself can be used as a source of productive tension.

Overview:
The Difficulties of Problem Solving in a Group

For the most part, the steps one moves through in solving a problem are quite simple. First, there is the identification and clarification of the issue, a developing of alternatives, a selection of one or more of these, and, finally, an implementation phase followed by an evaluation of the outcomes. It is a wonder, then, that a process so straightforward and so lacking in complexity can result in so many problems and pitfalls. The issue, of course, is that people initiate the process and set their own traps and barriers. Groups are no less susceptible to these problems than are individuals, and it would seem profitable to spend some time looking at them. (See the exercises at the end of this chapter for examples of how to implement these six stages of problem solving.)

Stage 1: Problem Identification   The recognition that a problem exists can happen either by chance or as a result of systematic inquiry. More often than not it seems that problems arise naturally and announce their presence through increasing tension and conflict or, perhaps, inefficiency. Conditions will worsen if the presence of such tensions is not confronted, or if they are denied or covered over so that accompanying frustrations become a breeding ground for other problems. This is too often the case in groups where a little internal festering is somehow preferred to dealing directly with the issues as they arise. In some cases, there is simply no mechanism available to help bring the problems into the open. Something as simple as a suggestion box (if there is evidence that it is being used) can be a direct line to sources of individual, group, or organizational problems. Once recognized, it is then important to discover the degree to which they are shared by others, as well as the level of urgency. Occasional questionnaires or small group discussions can be helpful in drawing problems into the open before they become destructive. Such problem sensing of both task and emotional issues can help keep communication channels open. Other problems will arise, however, if the group or individuals are encouraged to identify specific problems which are then avoided or minimized by those in positions of influence.

Stage 2: The Diagnostic Phase   Once the symptoms have been recognized and brought to the attention of others, several steps seem to follow quite naturally. First, the problem must be clarified and relationships identified. Too often the symptoms are little more than a generalized recognition of discomfort or stress and tell little of the underlying factors creating the disturbance. At this point it must be discovered how much the problem is shared by others as well as its degree of urgency. A second step in the diagnostic process is to gather supporting evidence as to the nature of the problem. Third, with this new information, the problem should be restated in terms of a "condition" that exists and which, to some extent, needs to be changed.

Quite often problems are stated simplistically in relation to an "either-or" situation or in terms of "good" or "bad," which immediately polarizes the potential problem solvers into win-or-lose camps. If a condition can be shown to exist that is less than optimal, then the problem of the eventual decision-making group becomes one of identifying the factors that keep the condition from being optimal. Energy can then be directed toward isolating specific causal factors, such as a single person dominating the discussion, lack of time, or the need for clear goals. Thus, arguments become limited to the relative strength of such factors and not to whether they exist. This approach encourages compromise and multiple solutions. Finally, having gathered as much data as possible concerning the problem, stated it as a condition to be changed, and isolated the various causal factors, a determination must be made regarding how capable the group is to solve the problem. This involves looking squarely at the group's own power to influence the prevailing condition, what kinds of resources are going to be necessary, and how much impact their efforts will have on others. Nothing is more frustrating and deflating than for a group to design a clever scheme for solving a problem only to realize that it lacks the resources to carry out the plan. Therefore, before developing solutions, the group must test its own reality situation. The most important finding may be that because of certain limits (time, money, personnel, access to power) the problem should be stated more realistically, others should be drawn into the problem-solving process, or the issue should be directed to another group that does have the potential for solving the problem.

One final point should be made concerning this early stage of problem solving. For change to occur, those involved must see the problem as "their own." It cannot be imposed upon them. Thus, the diagnostic process is vital for involving those who will eventually be responsible for implementing the solutions. This has important implications concerning who takes part in the diagnostic process and which people are kept closely informed as to what is happening. Developing solutions will prove to be nothing more than an academic exercise if those to be affected have not even come to the point of admitting that a problem exists. It does little good for a doctor to prescribe specific therapeutic treatment for a patient if the patient believes himself to be well. It is crucial that an individual or a group comes to accept the fact that there is a problem. This suggests implicitly a process in which the determination is not imposed, but evolves among all concerned.

Stage 3: Generating Alternatives   Groups and individuals seek quick and easy solutions. It is one reason why the problem-solving process so often breaks down. There is a tendency to combine two distinct phases that can have important implications for the quality of the potential decision. Once a problem is identified, the usual reaction is to jump toward a logical solution. As we fasten onto what we perceive as a logical and ultimately resourceful solution, we automatically screen out numerous other possibilities, some of which may (difficult as it is for us to believe) be more appropriate. We commit ourselves to one idea and are then compelled to defend it. This may be particularly true in a group where some of us have a need to convince others of our wisdom and skill. Formulating solutions before ideas have been thoroughly explored not only reduces the potential quality of the eventual solution but also tends to inhibit open communication. It has the same effect as stating a problem in either-or terms. It forces individuals into a premature position of evaluation and places all members in defensive postures. Thus it is a major pitfall to evaluate solutions at a time when the intent should be merely to explore every potential solution that is possible. Done effectively, this process can reduce the tendency for groups to polarize around answers that are "comfortable," and it may also help them to look toward new approaches.

After the ideas have been generated and explored in relation to specific causal factors (isolated during the diagnostic stage), then there should be a general screening process to integrate and synthesize the solutions into a smaller number. Again, the effort here is not to select a "best" solution, since the problem is likely to be multifaceted with a number of possible alternatives. Before any final decision is reached, a period of weighing and testing of the alternatives should be initiated. If time and resources allow, an effort should be made to gather data about the various solutions reached up to that point. This could range from establishing a pilot study to seeking the opinions of other individuals, such as experts.

Stage 4: Selecting Solutions   With the new data and time to think about the alternatives, it is ideal to consider the consequences of each alternative in relation to the problem condition. Many times a group, anxious to get under way, will fail to explore the unanticipated consequences and focus only on the obvious benefits to be gained. Thus, it is at this stage that each potential solution should be carefully evaluated in terms of its possible limitations as well as strengths. The discussion should lead to decision by consensus, in which all members are willing to support a particular plan. While this does not assume complete agreement on the part of all participants involved, it suggests at least a temporary accord during a period when the decision can be fairly evaluated. There are, of course, times when decision by consensus is impossible, but when effective implementation of the decision is based partly upon support of those involved, consensus has important advantages.

Stage 5: Implementation   Many participants of decision-making groups, after being successful in developing a useful decision, have watched helplessly as the ideas so carefully designed and agreed upon are never implemented. Part of the problem often can be traced to the early stage of the process and the failure to involve or at least keep informed: (*a*) those with power to kill the idea and (*b*) those who would eventually be influenced by the final decision. Equally important is the failure to build accountability into the action or implementation phase. Too often interest is not developed in the decision-making group. Accountability must be carefully cultivated so that individuals feel responsible for the outcome and are answerable to the others involved.

Stage 6: Evaluation and Adjustment   One reason people are resistant to new ideas is that they believe that once change occurs, it will be just as impervious to change as was the previous idea. By building in a mechanism of evaluation as well as the flexibility to make adjustments once the data are analyzed, the entire problem-solving process remains flexible and open to new alternatives. Most important, it gives those who are being influenced by the decision the recourse to alternative procedures and a feeling of some potency in the process. Also, the notion of accountability is tied directly into the evaluation-adjustment procedure. Thus evaluation becomes more than a superficial exercise and tends to be used as an integral part of an ongoing problem-solving process.

Maximizing the Effectiveness of a Problem-Solving Group

It appears that although problem-solving models themselves are relatively simple, there are countless procedural and emotional factors that together make smooth group problem solving rare. As suggested earlier, certain approaches yield more success than others. There are a number of questions often asked about group problem solving and decision making. In responding to them it must be remembered that each group is uniquely different both in terms of its task and its human composition and that none of the replies can be transferred indiscriminately from group to group. Even when considering the problem-solving model described in the previous pages, one is aware of speaking in terms of the ideal. Thus, there are occasions when decisions must be made immediately, without a thorough diagnosis, without reaching consensus, and without building effective evaluation procedures.

Questions Frequently Asked on Group Problem Solving and Decision Making

Question 1: Do groups appear more effective in problem solving than individuals, especially considering man hours invested?

There are good reasons for using groups in some problem-solving endeavors. However, few of these reasons involve efficiency. Increasingly, research is pointing toward the conclusion that individuals and nominal groups are equal to or more effective than natural groups (assuming no training) when undertaking problem-solving activities (Campbell, 1968; Rotter and Portergal, 1969). A nominal group is one in which the ideas of members working independently are then pooled. A natural group is where members would work cooperatively at the same task. Some working groups are slowed down and reduced to a level of performance equal to the slowest member (McCurdy and Lambert, 1952), while others become polarized as a result of the group discussions (Moscovici and Zavalloni, 1969). Furthermore, even in groups designed to facilitate the open sharing of ideas, differences in status and perceived authority can inhibit productivity (Vroom et al., 1969; Voytas, 1967; Collaros and Anderson, 1969). Yet it is true that in a number of rather specific instances it does seem that a group effort can be justified over that of nominal groups or individuals. For example, when a task involves the integrating of a number of perceptual and intellectual skills, it has been found that group members tend to supplement one another as resources (Napier, 1967). Also, when a major goal of the group is to create commitment to certain goals or to actually influence opinions, the involvement of individuals appears essential (Kelley and Thibaut, 1969; Lewin, 1948). However, when it comes to simply producing ideas in quantity or even quality, the evidence (although in some cases mixed) does not support the faith shown in recent years for working in groups.

Question 2: Are brainstorming groups more productive than individuals working alone, since their purpose is to allow individuals to build upon each other's ideas in a nonevaluative atmosphere?

Ideally this is true. Brainstorming is a tool designed to help individuals share their ideas without the interruption of discussion.[3] By allowing the participants to associate freely and present any idea that comes to mind, it is believed that more ideas will be generated and that their quality will be better than if the same individuals worked independently. However, the climate previously established is not altered just by setting a few rules, i.e., no evaluation or no discussion. For many people, brainstorming is a strange sort of experience, and it can create an initial sense of discomfort (Hammond and Goldman, 1961; Vroom et al., 1969; Collaros and Anderson, 1969).

Some time ago, a specialist in small-group behavior was asked to discuss brainstorming as a technique to approximately 100 army officers at a college for career officers seeking promotions. He was met at the door of the auditorium by a colonel who informed him that he would feel right at home since things at the college were conducted in a very informal and casual atmosphere. The consultant wondered what he meant by that. The colonel said, "Oh, everyone here is on a first-name basis, ties aren't required, and we really have some wide open discussions." The ultramodern lecture hall was arranged in three tiers. On the ground level were the students (mostly majors and colonels on the way up). A second tier held visiting dignitaries, nonpermanent staff, and those holding the rank of general. Finally, a third level contained the permanent college staff who passed judgment on the merits of the various students. It was in this "casual" and "informal" atmosphere that the lecture took place.

At one point the consultant wanted to loosen the group up a bit and involve them in the brainstorming process. He gave the officers the same warm-up example that he had given groups of high school and college students, sisters and priests, and a variety of other groups. The officers were asked to think of as many unusual uses as they could for a certain ladies' undergarment. They were given one minute to generate as many answers as possible—the wilder the idea, the better. When they were told to begin, all you could hear was a restless shuffling of feet by those on the ground level. Finally, one tough-looking major, risking his potential two-star rank, shouted, "basketball knee guards." The immediate laughter (and subsequent release of

---

[3] The reader may wish to refer to the first exercise at the end of this chapter, Brainstorming: An Important Tool in Group Problem Solving, which clarifies the rationale for brainstorming as well as the procedures for its implementation.

tension) was enormous, and slowly but surely the group squeezed out its self-conscious replies. At the end of a minute, which seemed like a year, there were 11 replies—not very many for an informal group accustomed to some "wide open discussions." It should be noted that not a single idea was offered by the upper two tiers as they peered down at the students. Things, however, did loosen up a bit when the group was told that the record of 35 responses was held by a group of nuns for whom "promotion" was no real problem.

Thus, to a relaxed group familiar with the process, brainstorming may be a stimulating and useful approach to generating ideas. To a restricted, self-conscious group, however, it could actually prove a hindrance, since it forces members into new patterns of behavior and breaks certain norms that usually protect the participants (Bouchard, 1969; Bergum and Lehr, 1963). Conversely, the use of brainstorming can break open a stuffy and inhibited group, if used at the "right" time. Much depends on the facilitator's ability to read the behavioral cues of the group effectively.

Question 3: What are the benefits of working in groups and using brainstorming and other procedures in problem solving?

First, we are living in a time when people are demanding to be heard and involved. It is hardly a question of whether or not a group is the most productive means of solving a problem. People are using group decision-making procedures for an ever widening variety of problems. The question becomes, How is it possible to facilitate the work of these groups? Brainstorming, given the proper exposure and a relatively nonjudgmental climate, has much to offer a decision-making group, particularly during the diagnostic and the generating-of-alternatives stages of problem solving. For example:

1. It reduces dependency upon a single authority figure.

2. It encourages an open sharing of ideas.

3. It stimulates greater participation among the group.

4. It increases individual safety in a highly competitive group.

5. It provides for a maximum of output in a short period of time.

6. It helps to insure a nonevaluative climate at least in the ideation phase of the meeting.

7. It provides the participants with immediate visibility for the ideas that are generated (assuming they are posted).

8. It develops some degree of accountability for the ideas among the group since they have been generated internally and not imposed from outside.

9. It tends to be enjoyable and self-stimulating.

Thus, the process is self-reinforcing; it draws the participants into new avenues of thought and into a new pattern of communication. How efficient the method is—and it can be efficient—is a factor of secondary importance to its potential for facilitating shared problem solving.

Question 4: Does training help the problem-solving capabilities of a group?

Work groups have existed as long as there have been problems, and there seems to be a rather casual assumption that the process is natural and even simple. But, as previously shown, using group resources effectively requires great skill on the part of the facilitator as well as skill and understanding on the part of the members. One reason why problem-solving groups tend to fare poorly when compared to the work output of individuals or nominal groups is that they are invariably untrained and, to make matters worse, they are usually "stranger" groups. The result is that the group members not only have to coordinate their work efforts, but also they are caught in the midst of tensions common to any developing group (see The Stages of Group Development, Chapter 8). Virtually no research exists in which the quantitative and qualitative products of trained and well-practiced groups are compared with those of individuals or nominal groups. There is evidence, however, that laboratory training sessions, in which individuals are given the opportunity to learn group skills through the systematic observation of their own performance on a variety of tasks, have impressive transfer value to other group situations (Hall and Williams, 1970; Stuls, 1969; Tolela, 1967).

In one interesting experiment, requiring the solution of a specific task-oriented problem, groups were involved in an interdependent, multistage problem-solving process. Trained groups revealed greater improvement, had higher quality products, and used the knowledge of members more effectively than untrained groups. In fact, it was shown that groups of institutionalized, neuropsychiatric patients scored significantly better than untrained managerial groups which were assumed to have greater knowledge of procedures and problem-solving operations (Hall and Williams, 1970). While such research is limited because of the type of training undertaken and because of the problems involved, the implications are clear. Effective training can maximize the benefits that are possible to achieve within the framework of problem-solving groups.

Question 5: What are the strengths and limitations of the democratic approach to decision making in groups?

For most working groups it seems that the key to decision making is found in a rather loose concept of the democratic process and the rule of the majority. It provides governing "by the people," reduces the threat of tyranny from within the group, and insures that at least half the members will be in support of a particular issue. Nevertheless, this approach to decision making has a number of severe limitations when applied to a group that must live by its own decisions. For example:

1. Under the pressure of a vote, individual decisions are often made for the wrong reasons. This is partly the result of different levels of knowledge and understanding present in the group and partly because of extraneous pressures (friendships, propaganda, payment of past favors, etc.). Thus, issues are often lost sight of in favor of other variables such as voting for "the man."

2. During the discussions leading to a vote, it is assumed that people will have an opportunity to express their opinions and to influence the group, but this is seldom the case. Many individuals simply do not have the skills to influence their own destinies in groups. It is the rare group where silence is not taken as consent, where the shy person is drawn into the discussion, and where the intent is to consider all ideas and not just to project one's own. Therefore, the basis upon which a vote is taken is often faulty or, at least, premature.

3. The will of the majority can be used effectively as a means of reducing tension (strong differences of opinion) and the time needed to discuss a problem. A vote can be a means of getting on to other business. This, of course, fails to take into consideration whether or

not the support for the decision is enough to insure effective implementation.

4. There is also the problem of power and despotism in a demo-
cratically run group. How often is the dissenting minority perceived
as a disrupting influence? How often is the minority opinion seen as
a threat to the cohesion of the group? And how often are such pressures used to coerce the dissenters back in line? If the vote is used to
override the opinion of this minority faction, the vote itself stands to
further polarize the group and magnify the divisive lines upon which
the vote is taken.

5. Similarly, rather than providing a solution, the vote may actually create more problems. Instead of resolving differences, the
minority may spend its time proving the vote wrong and reasserting
itself in the eyes of the group. Or, labeled as radicals or discontents,
it may try to live up to the image and really become a disruptive
force.

6. Finally, by encouraging a move toward quick decisions, there
is a tendency to simplify problems in terms of either-or dichotomies,
and there is a resulting failure to explore all the issues influencing
the problem condition. A quick vote based on an inadequate exploration of issues will inevitably create difficulties. Members may have
second thoughts and fail to support the vote in terms of behavior or
rationalize their vote and become intransigent.

Therefore, when weighing these kinds of problems often linked with
a simplistic notion of the democratic process, it might seem worthwhile to study other alternatives. The fact is that a democratic group
in the real sense of the word requires enormous patience, understanding, and cooperation. It also is very time-consuming. Few groups
are willing to face these realities and thus reduce the process to one
of convenience rather than effectiveness.

Question 6: How useful is Robert's Rules as a procedure within which
to make decisions?

Robert's Rules is based upon an assumption valuing the notion of
debate (Robert, 1943). It is a complicated procedural method keyed
to the majority vote and democratic process. It probably can be
stated fairly that nearly everyone who has worked within a variety
of groups has at one time or another been frustrated by the limita-

tions of this system. Those who understand the complexities of the process can easily control the meeting, but few people know the rules for a quorum, tabling a motion, adjourning, or even amending a motion.

On the one hand, the moderator of a meeting can be in a position of considerable power. On the other hand, since chairmen are not chosen necessarily by their understanding of Robert's Rules, it is fairly easy for them to lose control of the meeting to a few individuals who know the finer points. Another problem is that because the system is based on debate, there is a constant tendency toward polarization. True, the amending process does allow compromise, but usually these are political compromises, and the real issue can be pulled to pieces as factions based on broader ideological issues use the problem at hand to solidify their political position rather than seeking the best solution. Furthermore, it is relatively easy for the majority to stifle discussion by pushing for an early vote or using some other defensive measure to change the focus of discussion. Finally, because the system is not based on a cooperative and interdependent approach to problem solving, there tends to be a great deal of politicking, bargaining, and bidding for power outside the meeting itself. In relatively small groups (under 25 or 30), the method reduces open communication and the amount of participation. In larger groups, if the participants understand the system, it can prove useful in organizing discussion and stabilizing work procedures. Again, large numbers of participants present a limiting factor in the decision-making process, and accepting Robert's Rules must be done with the view that while it is gaining order, it is at the price of interdependence and, to some degree, cooperation.

Question 7: Is decision by consensus a viable method for small-group decision making?

Reaching a decision through consensus represents the ideal in terms of group participation, but it is by no means the most efficient or least tension-producing approach to decision making. It assumes that a decision will not be made without the approval of every member, but it does not mean that each member must agree totally with what is going to happen. It simply indicates that each member is willing to go along with the decision, at least for the time being. The process provides for full group participation and a willingness to compromise.

Immature groups that lack skill in processing their own interpersonal behavior may find this a painful approach to problem solving. Unlike a system based on majority vote (basically a tension-reducing system), decision by consensus seeks out alternative viewpoints and then struggles to find a solution at the expense of no particular group or person. The value, of course, in using this sometimes slow and belabored process is that by the time a decision is reached, it does represent a group decision and therein lies an important component of support. At times a provisional straw vote is used to test sources of differing opinion so that the full dimension of the problem can be explored. If it becomes coercive, the process breaks down. Usually, it requires time, familiarity within the group, and trust in the process before consensus becomes effective. Once this occurs, however, decisions can be made rapidly because there is a willingness to get to the core of the issue quickly, analyze the alternatives, and then compromise in finding the solution.

Question 8: Why do institutional committees become so ineffective?

Most committees are part of an inefficient hierarchical system which has developed over time with little built-in flexibility for change. Procedures become routine, more complex, and the interest of those participating wanes. Within the committees themselves, there are other barriers. For example:

1. Decision-making procedures are usually imposed and based on tradition rather than what is most useful.

2. People are often appointed to committees, and, even if they volunteer, they may be there for a variety of reasons (from interest in meeting important people to helping out a friend who is chairman).

3. Often committees lack the power to implement the decisions they make and thus feel their own impotence.

4. Committees seldom see processing their own interpersonal behaviors as part of the job, especially if the group only meets once every 3 or 4 weeks.

5. The committee is not necessarily composed of the people best equipped to discuss the issues confronting the group.

The above-mentioned factors do not mean that most committees are not designed with a functional purpose in mind or that their participants are not well intentioned. They merely suggest that such groups often become self-defeating because of their membership, their decision-making procedures, and their lack of potency within the larger organization.

Question 9: Are there useful alternatives to the committee system?

One possible alternative is the use of a task force. Ideally, when a special problem arises within an organization, instead of pushing it off to an already overburdened committee, a task force is appointed or elected. This group is composed of representative individuals (or, in some cases, individuals with special skills) who are given the job of solving the problem. It is assumed that their recommendations will be taken most seriously and, in essence, they are given the power of the large group. Unlike a committee:

1. They often have more power.

2. Appointments are for a short term.

3. A definite measurable outcome will be the result.

4. The members may develop working procedures that best fit the nature of the task and are not limited by tradition or previous groups.

5. They must work through all phases of the problem-solving process including the diagnosis, actual implementation, and follow-up.

6. Because of the immediacy of the problem, there should be high motivation and involvement, especially since the product will be its own reward.

One potential problem with a task force is that given support and some feeling of potency, these groups generate recommendations which are much less conservative than might have been expected and which are much more thoroughly documented than usual. Unhappy is the executive who turns an issue over to a task force and then, instead of the problem losing importance and momentum, which often happens when problems are referred to committees, the task force provides the organization with clear methods for altering the situation. These methods may unveil other problems.

It is often true that task forces are also used for political purposes. Instead of expecting solutions, the aim is to look as if something is being done while, in reality, the objective is to mark time. An example of this situation occurs when prestigious people are appointed to the task force and, because of other commitments, find it impossible to do the kind of job necessary. The final product is a watered-down and poorly conceived attempt to look competent with a minimum commitment to action.

Question 10: In summary, what conditions are ideally present in a problem-solving group?

1. The goals of the group are clearly understood by the participants.

2. Mechanisms that insure the active participation of the minority are established for making decisions.

3. A concerted effort is made to discover resource people within the group.

4. Ideas are explored in a nonevaluative climate.

5. Participation is shared, and control is not in the hands of one or two dominant members.

6. Member roles are differentiated according to group needs and specific skills.

7. Problems are stated as conditions and explored in terms of the factors causing the particular condition to exist.

8. The group is aware of its own potency to affect change and somehow involves the support of necessary individuals in both the diagnostic and solution phases of problem solving.

9. Communication channels are kept open by using process observers and making efforts to look at both the task and emotional dimensions of the group's work together.

10. Size and physical arrangement are deemed appropriate to the task.

11. Participants are considered in terms of status and power, and the composition of the group is such that ideas or solutions are maximized.

12. Time is long enough for the necessary problem-solving phases but short enough to be a motivational factor.

13. Solutions are (as much as possible) testable, and the impact of the decision is evaluated.

14. The group is held accountable for its own decisions.

Conclusion

Groups may be positive forces in the problem-solving process, but, in themselves, they offer no magic solutions. Without the proper training, without the time to work through the mechanical and human errors that evolve, they can be less effective than an individual working on the same problem and, at times, destructive to the problem-solving efforts. However, if individuals are not involved to some degree, if their concerns and ideas are not heard, if they are made to feel impotent within an organization, their influence can still be powerful indeed. After all, it is the individuals who actually determine the effectiveness of decisions handed down to them. They have the power to actively support a plan or to passively resist it. Today involvement is expected—demanded—by members of virtually every type of group. Thus, even though the "art" and the "science" of problem-solving groups are just beginning to be successfully understood and integrated, it is imperative that what we do know be applied as skillfully as possible.

In the exercises which follow, a number of methods are outlined that are designed to facilitate the group in the actual process of decision making. The exercises to this point have been directed at helping participants become more aware of the many factors that can limit productivity. Implicit in the information resulting from many of these activities were alternative approaches to problem solving that would advance the group effort. The activities presented here are by no means the keys to problem solving. They are merely tools that may help the process. They may increase participation and involvement, restrict personal dominance, and help to uncover many issues that have previously gone unnoticed. But they probably will do little to improve internal conflicts that can be so destructive in a working group. These problems, which develop out of membership, leadership, and normative problems at a personal level, are only partly ameliorated by structural interventions (such as brainstorming) and require other procedures.

Exercise 1
Brainstorming:
An Important Tool in Group Problem Solving

Rationale

Brainstorming is a method used to facilitate one phase of the problem-solving process. It is a means of generating ideas in quantity (often called ideation session) with the intent of maximizing the participation of group members. In essence it represents a period of time in which all evaluation is suspended and ideas are allowed to flow freely on a particular issue—a time for a free association of ideas and for opening new avenues of thought. It is keyed to removing participants from a self-orientation and a concern for the socially acceptable. Brainstorming is designed to reduce feelings of inadequacy and impotency. It is *not* a means for making decisions. It does not necessarily result in a better product than might have been developed by one or two people systematically attacking the problem from another perspective. It is a procedure to assist group members in many ways, some of which are listed below:

1. To reduce dependency upon authority figures in the group (the need to look for the "right" answer from a few)

2. To increase participant involvement and participation

3. To increase the safety of individuals in a highly competitive group where personal threat and evaluation is particularly high

4. To provide a maximum output of ideas in a relatively short period of time

5. To enable individual ideas to gain visibility (in itself a source of positive reinforcement for members)

6. To improve the level of social facilitation in the group—to develop a greater feeling of "groupness"

7. To make the session more fun, interesting, and stimulating

8. To develop a more informal atmosphere

9. To reduce the possibility of negative subgrouping during the critical period of idea building

Setting

Brainstorming can be used effectively with almost any number from one to fifty or more. Of course, the larger the number the more adjustments that will have to be made to insure that everyone is able to participate. In smaller groups of five to eight members, it is important that some diversity of opinion and background be present. Newsprint should be available so that ideas are retained and can be moved among various working groups. For new groups unfamiliar with brainstorming, it is important that a warm-up session of 10 or 15 minutes be held in which the rationale is discussed. Members may be asked to list those factors in a group that limit its production of ideas on a particular question. At this point the notion of brainstorming is introduced, followed by an explanation of the rules and a practice session.

Rules

Participants should be familiar with a number of ground rules to insure the success of the brainstorming session.

1. Criticism or evaluation of an idea is not allowed. The idea is suggested and simply placed before the group.
2. The session is to be "free wheeling," open to any ideas. The wilder and more fantastic the idea, the more chance there is for developing approaches to the problem.
3. Quantity is very important; thus, all ideas should be expressed and not screened by the individual—this will come later.
4. Everyone should be free to build onto ideas and to make interesting combinations from the various suggestions.
5. Individuals should be limited to one idea at a time to make sure that less dominating individuals get their ideas heard.

Warm-up Exercise

As with anything new, members may need encouragement to avoid being self-evaluative and thereby reduce their potential level of productivity. The following story may give a group unfamiliar with brainstorming an opportunity to practice it before tackling an issue of importance.

A small wholesaler in the hinterlands of Mexico had called his buyer in Vera Cruz and asked him to obtain an order of pipe cleaners from the United States. Señor Gonzales, the buyer, agreed. He also agreed to advance Señor Gomez (the wholesaler) 5,000 pesos to finance the deal. A month later, just as the ship was arriving in Vera Cruz, Señor Gonzales received a disastrous phone call from Señor Gomez. Apparently the warehouse and outlet store had burned down and there simply was no more business. Gonzales was suddenly faced with somehow selling 20,000 pipe cleaners.

The group should have one minute to generate as many responses as possible (with a recorder counting the number of different ideas) for getting rid of 20,000 pipe cleaners.

It is important that the facilitator help get the group moving and even add a few ideas himself (any idea is a good idea). He may wish to give the participants an extra half minute. An open and relatively spontaneous group will create approximately 25 responses in a little more than a minute. If a group responds with 15 ideas or less, it is advisable to give them another warm-up example since many have apparently taken a hands-in-the-pocket attitude. This can be done with some humor. It might also be that the group is anxious to get down to business and, if so, moving right into the actual problem would be the best approach.

It is also very important that the problem be well defined and specific in nature. It must be a problem that the group has the power to do something about. If possible, the participants should be notified in advance about the issue to be explored so that they will have given some thought to the problem. Even the most casual consideration beforehand may trigger useful ideas.

Action

In this example, the directions are to be given to a group of 24 participants. Many alternative formats could easily be designed, but the following one has proven successful: After the problem has been stated clearly (hopefully it is an issue of relevance and concern to members), three large sheets of newsprint are placed next to each other in front of the group. Three participants are chosen as recorders, given markers, and asked to stand in front of one of the newsprints. The group is instructed that it will have between 3 and 5 minutes to list all the possible causes for this particular problem (on another occasion they might brainstorm solutions). The first recorder posts the first cause, the second recorder the second, and so on. After approximately 3 minutes, the result should be three sheets with an equal number of responses.

The large group of 24 is then broken down into 3 groups of 8, each taking a sheet with causes for the particular problem. Their task in a period of about 30 minutes is:

1. To clarify and expand any of the statements.

2. To integrate similar statements and to delete any that are irrelevant.

3. To develop from the items a list of causes that are most important to deal with immediately and which are within the power of the group (basic priorities).

4. This high-priority list of perhaps three causes is presented to the total group of 24. In all, nine high-priority causal factors will have been identified. Some of these will be very nearly the same so that the real list will be about five items.

If the group agrees that something must be done with these five causal factors, it may prove useful to halve the groups of eight and have each group of four design specific action solutions to two of the problems. It is suggested that within 45 minutes or an hour the groups of four reconvene with their original group of eight and present their ideas to the other four for a critique. This will take another 20 or 30 minutes. Again, if the possibility for integrating the ideas (solutions) exists, it should be done.

Finally, the crystallized ideas of the three groups are presented to the entire group. There should be about nine separate ideas presented. It is very important that the facilitator stress the need to minimize the time of the various presentations (no more than 5 minutes). The main purpose of this session is to give visibility to the various ideas and to bring some closure to the problem-solving process. The total time for this session will be between 2½ and 3 hours. It is an exhausting process and may not result in final decisions. What often helps is to have a representative of each of the groups of four act as a steering committee and, at a later time, report back specific recommendations that incorporate the various solutions offered.

Discussion of the Problem-solving Sequence

There seem to be a number of practices in this sequence that could be used under a variety of circumstances and with different kinds of problems.

1. It is important that the ideas being explored are the result of the group's effort. This is the first step in building accountability for the eventual solutions.

2. If the ideas are developed in a nonevaluative atmosphere, there will be less of the vested interests that tend to be present in any group and that surround any problem of importance.

3. The process forces a look at a variety of alternative approaches *after* important causal factors have been isolated. This builds a norm into the group for exploring new ideas and stimulates interest and involvement in the process itself.

4. The participants are held under strict time limits during their various work sessions. By being held accountable to other groups at the end of brief work periods, a continuous flow of ideas is assured and withdrawal because of disinterest or boredom is almost impossible. It seems to be very true that people will use the time made available to them.

5. Each product is a product of a number of people's ideas, and this reduces the possibility of one or two vociferous individuals taking over the group. Even in the presentation, it is important that the presenting groups do not try to sell their ideas, but simply reveal them.

6. By having a representative body make recommendations to the entire group based on *all* of their efforts, consensus is much more easily used as a final decision-making device. By this time the group should be ready to stand accountable for its own product. And, of course, the decision is only as good as the group's willingness to implement it.

Exercise 2
Phillips 66:
Discussion and Decisions in a Large Group

Objectives

To involve large numbers of people in discussion of topics relevant to them

To maximize the use of time as a factor in reducing argument

To insure greater accountability in large groups, which often tend to be impersonal

General Description

D. J. Phillips (1948) at first saw this method as a means of involving large numbers of people in the discussion of a particular issue. For example, after a presentation, debate, panel etc., he would have the large group break into groups of six and develop a question that the group could agree was important to them in a period of about 6 minutes. The relatively small groups would have their interest focused, many individuals would have an opportunity to interact, and they could have some impact on the total group's discussion. It was impossible for a few people to dominate the discussion, and it assured a high rate of interest.

More recently, the method has been adapted to meet the needs of many groups. Members are given 6 minutes (it could just as easily be 10 or 15) to develop an agenda for the meeting. With all groups reporting, certain items are immediately perceived as having interest to many in the group. Or in other sessions, members are asked to offer a solution for a particular issue. Usually 6 minutes is long enough to define and clarify the issue, but it has been shown that in a relatively short period of time, an enormous number of good ideas can be generated and then refined at a later time. Brief reports on these findings can be an important stimulating factor in the large group.

Others, including Maier (1963), have used adaptations of this method for larger groups with as many as two or three hundred people. Groups of six are given a problem to solve or an issue to discuss, and then these groups are polled by the facilitator in terms of certain logical categories. Immediately the group gains a picture of how others feel and the range of ideas that exist in the group.

Of great importance in using this method is to make sure that the topics used for discussion are specific enough to allow an almost immediate discussion to get under way. Questions that are moralistic in tone will only frustrate people since there is no hope for any kind of resolution in a limited period of time. Similarly, when looking at a particular problem, the participants should not be limited to an either-or type of response. The enjoyment lies in the opportunity to be creative and to look beyond the commonplace response. The great value of having many people together doing the same thing is that one is assured of wide-ranging responses that may not develop in the more traditional committee work group, which is partly controlled by past experience and behavior.

Exercise 3
Force Field Analysis:[4]
From Diagnosis to Action

Objectives

To provide participants in the decision-making process a means of thoroughly diagnosing the factors causing the particular problem

To help those involved to look beyond the obvious and into new responses to the problem condition

To focus upon the possible repercussions of any decisions

Rationale

It is assumed that in most of the decisions we make we fail to have access to or, if available, to use all the information relating to a particular problem.

Basically, we fail on three counts in the problem-solving process. First, we often enter problem situations with some preconceived notion of what we would like the outcome to be. Thus, we fail to do a very thorough diagnosis of all the causal factors that created the tensions, and it is seldom that all the relevant data reach us. (It takes time and energy, and may lead to conclusions not desired.) Second, for similar reasons, we often limit our perception of all the possible alternatives for changing the existing condition. Finally, when making particular decisions, it is seldom that we look beyond immediate reactions and explore all the possible repercussions that could result.

The primary aim of this exercise is to give the participant access to more data and alternatives and a greater awareness of their possible implications in terms of later consequences.

[4] This design is drawn from Lewin, 1948; 1951.

Setting

Groups of about six or seven are ideal for this exercise, but the method can be effectively used by individuals or large groups in general problem-solving sessions. Often the method is quickly presented and the group fails to understand the reason behind the approach. Superficially it may appear to be nothing more than listing positive and negative forces that influence a decision. However, it represents a way of thinking about a problem and the changes that any decision resulting from the problem analysis will create (intentional or unintentional). Enough time must be allowed for the process to develop, although it is difficult to suggest how long since this depends on the nature of the problem, the motivation of the group, and the actual time available. Some designs have allowed 2 days for the analysis and development of specific solutions. Less than 2 or 3 hours on organizational problems or those of a small group may prove to be sufficient. Newsprint, markers, and tape should be available so that the ideas developed can be easily seen and recorded as the group moves through various phases of the exercise toward solution.

Action

A group using the Force Field Analysis should be involved in a brief theory and practice session. For example, the facilitator may point out that groups, when looking at a problem that needs to be solved, tend to: (a) move too rapidly toward a solution, (b) begin to argue and polarize, and (c) fail to look at all the causal factors behind the problem.

The following method helps to get out the data and explore them in a rational, nonjudgmental fashion. The first step is to view the problem as a condition that needs to be changed, and success will be determined by just how much this condition is altered. For example, smoking is a condition that exists to a certain degree in some people. If a person smokes a pack of cigarettes a day and thinks he should stop, then the problem becomes altering the particular condition (one pack a day). One reason individuals who attempt to stop smoking find it so difficult is they make it an all-or-nothing proposition, and it becomes a test of personal will. As in many other problem conditions, the person fails to look at the multitude of factors that are causing him to smoke. The self-will issue is only one and by no means the most important. Unless all the restraining forces inducing him to smoke are understood, a strategy for altering the condition will tend to be limited in its impact. The strategy must attack many of these factors. Following are some of these factors.

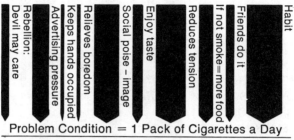

Problem Condition = 1 Pack of Cigarettes a Day

In the mind of the individual, each of these factors has a different weight and importance in restraining him from reducing the amount of cigarettes. Also, these restraining forces may change in weight and in character. For example, a mother-in-law visiting the house may add another source of tension, another force that may actually increase the number of cigarettes smoked. Thus, with more weight pushing downward, the problem condition changes, and more cigarettes are smoked.

However, we have looked at only half the picture. There are also existing in this individual's life a multitude of forces driving or pushing him to give up smoking: health advertisements, family pressure, sore throat, his own test of will, cost, etc. Each of these forces also has its own weight and is pushing against the restraining forces. They too can change in their importance (weight), as, for example, when the individual is visited by a relative who has had a lung removed because of lung cancer and it is discovered that he smoked two packs a day before the operation. For a while, anyway, this may add enough of a push to actually reduce his smoking output for a few days. It is the point at which the restraining forces and the driving forces impose the same theoretical amount of pressure that the level of smoking is determined. With more pressure from below (cancer reports, sick relative, etc.) the problem conditions will change to less smoking. More tension at work, a visiting mother-in-law, fear of weight gain may alter the balance of forces and increase the amount of smoking.

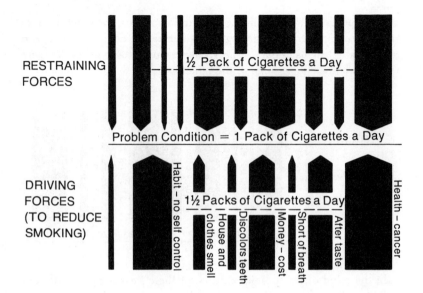

RESTRAINING FORCES

½ Pack of Cigarettes a Day

Problem Condition = 1 Pack of Cigarettes a Day

DRIVING FORCES (TO REDUCE SMOKING)

Habit – no self control

1½ Packs of Cigarettes a Day

House and clothes smell

Discolors teeth

Money – cost

Short of breath

After taste

Health – cancer

In one sense, the one-pack-a-day level represents a point of temporary equilibrium between the two competing forces. If a person is really interested in altering this level, or problem condition, then he may work at reducing the number of restraining forces, or he may work at increasing the number of driving forces which will then push the point of equilibrium (amount of smoking) to a new level representing fewer cigarettes a day. (Note: During the process of this brief theory session, it is helpful to have the participants add the forces in this example while the facilitator sketches them on newsprint or a blackboard. It is important that they grasp the feeling of weight or forces that are acting upon the person.)

At this point, the facilitator may wish to ask which (if there is to be a choice) appears more useful: to try to remove the restraining forces, or to add driving forces in order to reduce the level of smoking. The majority of individuals will tend to feel that adding to the driving forces would be easiest and most appropriate. Given more time to think and discuss the question, there will be a movement to a position of removing the restraining forces. The fact is that for most people change is the result of force or coercion. The problem is that it seems to hold true in the social sciences almost as much as in the physical sciences: for every action there is a reaction. People, whether individually or in groups, react to force or pressure. They build defenses to offset such driving forces. For example, "If you keep smoking, you're going to cut five years off your life" (coercion, threat). A frequent response may be, "Well, I would rather die sooner and be happy than cut out all the little pleasures of life" (rationalization, compensation). The response by cigarette companies to the surgeon general's famous cancer report was to increase cigarette advertising to a point that 6 months later total consumption had actually risen (by now, however, significant declines have taken place). The point is that none of these compensating reactions occurs when effort is directed at reducing the restraining forces, particularly those with the greatest force.

The use of driving forces can be an important factor in any movement toward change. The problems arise when unanticipated reactions create more problems than the newly introduced driving force is worth. It is from the driving forces, however, that creative new ideas tend to be generated. Thus, it may be anticipated that a new manager will bring many problems as people adjust to his new style and expectations, but, hopefully, these will be anticipated and offset with orientation sessions, social hours, personal discussions, and employee involvement in some of the accompanying changes.

Problem-solving Sequence Using Force Field Analysis

Having introduced the group briefly to some of the theoretical notions (it may be useful to take a few minutes to help the group work through an issue more relevant to them from a group perspective on the board), they are then given the opportunity to use the approach systematically in exploring a problem and developing specific solutions. Taking 3 hours as an example in this case, a possible problem-solving sequence might look like this:

10 min.	*Step 1* The problem is defined as a condition that exists with forces impinging upon it. The issue must be specific and one in which the group has an interest and some power to change. (Again, how the problem is arrived at is a very important step for the facilitator to consider.)
20 to 30 min.	*Step 2* The driving and restraining forces impinging upon this particular condition are brainstormed. It is best not to qualify or evaluate any responses during this phase, but simply list them

on a large sheet of newsprint (the restraining forces are placed on the left of the sheet going down the paper and the driving forces on the right).

30 to 40 min.

Step 3 The groups now concentrate their efforts on the restraining forces (particularly if time is limited). They do this by ordering the list they have brainstormed into priorities. Thus, they are, in a sense, weighting the forces and can more easily see those with which the group must come to grips. This process of establishing priorities is also a diagnostic process for the working group. It is best if the priorities can be agreed upon through consensus and if individuals try to be relatively flexible since a variety of solutions will probably be forthcoming.

10 to 15 min.

Step 4 Having arrived at agreement on priorities and defined the restraining forces more clearly, it should be possible for the group to eliminate some because they simply do not have time, money, resources, or the power to do anything about them. This is an important period of reality testing since the group can now focus its energies on those restraining forces that they have the power to change.

40 to 60 min.

Step 5 Having established those restraining forces that can be worked with by the group, the participants attempt to establish specific ways of reducing these restraining forces in a manner that will minimize possible offsetting reactions. It might be best to have subgroups of two or three people focus upon particular forces and, after they have developed a number of concrete solutions, report them back to the larger group. If time permits, suggestions for new driving forces may also be developed.

20 min.

Step 6 Specific proposals including methods for implementation and group accountability are developed.

30 min.

Step 7 The total group is presented with the specific proposals, and a discussion follows (the group will probably not be able to handle more than 30 or 40 minutes after working for 3 hours). At this time, suggestions should be entertained for insuring that the various proposals are integrated into a strategy for action. This step is of utmost importance since it insures follow-up and commitment of further involvement by the very people who have developed the proposals. A cross-group steering committee may be a useful mechanism.

Step 8 An evaluation would take place at some agreed-upon date in the future and would provide the large group the opportunity to appraise what impact the various suggestions have actually had.

Obviously, there is no magic in these eight steps, or in this particular time frame. They simply provide a structure in which to implement the Force Field as a tool in the problem-solving process. It focuses on the building of constructive alternatives for action and attempts to draw out as many factors as possible that may inhibit potential solutions.

Exercise 4
Developing Feedback:
An Important Step in Open Communication

Rationale

Any system, whether it be an individual human being, a small group, or an organization, must have some source of information about itself (we are notoriously poor judges of our own performance). This process of receiving information about one's self is referred to as feedback. An examination is one source of feedback for a student even though more and more it is merely used as means of classifying individuals and often loses its value as a meaningful feedback instrument. In the course of a group meeting, thousands of verbal and non-verbal communications take place, thousands of internal responses occur within individuals, and a great deal occurs that is never recorded in the minutes. Yet, the next meeting of the same individuals may be dramatically influenced by just these events. Unless a feedback system is established within any working group, an enormous amount of time and energy may be poorly used as individuals attempt to cope with the many procedural and human problems that can hinder a group. The diagnostic process described in the previous exercise is, in fact, a form of feedback. However, if it is to really benefit the group over time, it must be legitimized as an important part of the work process. Feedback ideally is a welcomed source of information for the group as a whole or for individual members. If misused, it can be a destructive, inhibiting, and degenerative force; if skillfully integrated into the group, it can facilitate more effective communication and better working relationships. The following exercise represents one means of introducing the concept of feedback to a group so it can explore whether or not it is ready to be used more systematically.

Setting

There are many ways that information can be developed to provide a group with insights on its operating procedures and the consequences of its behaviors. Such information, however, will not be useful if it is imposed or if there is no opportunity for the group to do anything about it. The group, like the individual, must be ready to hear about itself and desire to act on what it hears. If the facilitator has evidence that the group is ready to deal more directly with its own process, the following exercise may be useful. One means of discovering readiness is simply to raise as a point of discussion whether or not the group would like to take the time to explore how it operates (that it will take too much time is an easy defensive response and suggests a rather low priority for the process efforts).

Action

The group is divided into subgroups of about three people, and each is asked to develop a set of rules that might be discussed and applied to any feedback efforts. For example, how can the group learn about its operation? How effective and ineffective is it? How does it facilitate and hinder the working process? Perhaps there are rules the group can agree on that will make the feedback more easily received and thus more easily given.

After 15 or 20 minutes, the results are posted by the facilitator on newsprint, with each group requested to give the most important recommendations first. The posted list represents a loosely grouped statement of rules and recommendations that have some priority to the various subgroups. To this list the facilitator may wish to add a few suggestions and integrate those already listed into a brief theory session. The key is that if people are going to hear about themselves, it must be done in a manner that creates the fewest possible defenses and insures a climate of acceptance. Some of the suggestions that may be forthcoming from the session are:

1. The information about the group is descriptive and not colored by value-laden adjectives of a good-bad nature.

2. The examples of group behavior being discussed should be specific and clarified through examples.

3. Whenever possible, the information should be given sooner rather than later. The longer the time between the behavior and its discussion, the less value.

4. The information must be confined to matters which are within the power of the group to do something about.

5. The group must seek the feedback. If it is not solicited, it will be met with resistance and probably have little positive impact.

6. A person and a group can only internalize a certain amount of information about itself at any one time. It is important not to overload the system with more than it can handle.

7. If a person presents his perception of how the group behaved in a certain instance, it is important to discover whether or not others share his view.

Following this, it may be useful to focus upon the areas of group activity about which information might be collected in a somewhat objective manner. A 5-minute brainstorming session might result in some of the following:

Communication patterns in the group (who talks and how much)

How problems are actually solved and decisions made

Problems that seem to keep the group from moving

The goals of the group (implicit and explicit)

The level of involvement and interest among the participants

Whether there is shared leadership in the group

The physical structure of the group

The roles taken by group members (constructive and destructive)

The degree to which the group is open or closed

Thus, in a matter of about 40 minutes, the group can establish some suggestions that it feels necessary for the presentation of feedback to be effective as well as useful. Now, following these guidelines, the final 20 minutes is designed so that the original groups of three reconvene and agree on one piece of feedback that should be presented to the larger group in a manner which will benefit the whole group in its future work together. It may be in the form of a comment on the group behavior that indicates the need for new behavior. However, it should be left for the large group to interpret the feedback and decide on any relevant action. The idea, at this particular point, is to get the group practicing the process they have been discussing. This gives them a good starting point for the next session.

Follow-up

If the group has been able to accept the notion of feedback with some equanimity, the way will be open for the facilitator to suggest (or, if time, have the group develop) a number of ways feedback within a group may be carried out. For example:

1. Appointing an observer[5] of the group's process who reports his systematic observations at the end of a meeting. A discussion of the implications would follow (it may take no more than 15 minutes).

2. Having the group fill out reaction forms to the meeting at the end of a session. These may focus upon various aspects of the group process.

3. Taping the meeting and then replaying a portion of the tape and briefly discussing its implications.

4. After building confidence in the feedback process and trust in one another, members look at the roles and specific behaviors of individual members to see how they influence the group. This level of feedback may take a long time to evolve, and it is best for it to

[5] A more detailed discussion of the process observer's role is given in the Appendix, including a description of a number of observational instruments and procedures.

develop naturally out of a deeper concern and involvement on the part of the members. In other words, a group is not just suddenly ready for individual feedback. It is simply a natural extension of the slowly developing willingness of the group to process its own behaviors.

Exercise 5
Post-Session Feedback

Rationale

Most task groups hardly have time to complete their business commitments, let alone spend much time exploring the process of the group. The comment is often heard, "If we get into that subject, we'll be here all night." This fear of personal overinvolvement outside the actual working agenda often can shut down all efforts to develop more effective working relationships. It is not necessary for a group to spend an inordinate amount of time in its process efforts, nor does it necessitate that members become overly personal. However, time must be allowed for the group to improve its own working relationships, or tensions and problems will subtly build up and eventually reduce effectiveness. Following are two simple suggestions for helping to keep the process level of group work legitimized.

1. After the working session, 10 minutes is set aside for a discussion, in pairs, of the question: "What are one or two ways that this group could improve its working procedures or relationships the next time it meets?" It is important that the participants focus on specific, constructive suggestions. If, for example, one member dominated the discussion and created hostility among many of the other participants, it might be helpful to establish a temporary mechanism for insuring that more individuals have an opportunity to share their views and also to help move the group past individual roadblocks. In a group where the level of trust and acceptance is high, it would not be inappropriate to share with an individual the problems created by his particular behavior. But, as suggested previously, the climate must be such that the individual desires the information and those giving it are skillful enough not to appear punitive or judgmental.

The group may also find the post-meeting session an avenue for suggesting a structural format in the meeting, for example, the role of the chairman. Similarly, the way the agenda is being formed may influence the feeling of individuals about participating, and a change in how this is accomplished may affect other aspects of the meeting.

The issues briefly raised by the individuals in the paired groups are then shared briefly with the total group. They are first shared without discussion in order to establish how much agreement there is among the different members. Then suggestions are taken to remedy the situation in time for the next meeting. The total process should take no more than 20 or 30 minutes. After the group has developed acceptance of the feedback idea, the first step of breaking into twos or threes will be unnecessary, and observations can be shared by the whole group. This would cut the process time down to 10 or 15 minutes, although, as groups become more open and communicative, there is a tendency to broaden the scope of the feedback process. It is possible that this can become a problem because many members may find feedback a fascinating and personally satisfying experience. Groups have been known to spend more time discussing their process than the task. Obviously, it is a sign of a mature group if it is able to use feedback in a constructive fashion rather than a means of meeting individual emotional needs which extend far beyond the purpose of the group.

2. If certain members of the work group are involved in establishing the format of a particular meeting (often this is a rotating responsibility in which agenda building and building procedures for a meeting change hands regularly), the following feedback procedure may prove useful: At the end of a meeting, a reaction sheet is passed out to the participants. They respond to a number of explicit questions concerning the operation of the meeting and also how it can be improved. The group responsible for the next meeting analyzes these responses (thus, it takes only about 5 minutes of the group's time), and they make plans to incorporate various changes in the format of the next meeting which they feel respond to the concerns and suggestions given. These new procedures or innovations are then evaluated in the reaction sheet developed for that meeting. In this way, there is a constant willingness to look at how the group is working together and an opportunity to develop new ideas. Theoretically, each person eventually has a chance to improve the meeting. It may be that a

certain format develops that is basically satisfactory to the members; this too will be found through the regular use of reaction sheets.

Exercise 6
The Force Field as a Means of Generating
Personal Feedback in a Work Group

Objective

To provide a group with a mechanism for generating personal feedback

Setting

For this exercise to be successful, it is necessary that the group members want to seek information about their own behavior, which assumes a willingness to expend time and energy in this effort. It is not necessary that the group have great cohesion or that individuals feel openness and trust toward all the other members. They should have one or two other individuals in the group with whom they feel comfortable and with whom they feel free to share. The participants should also be versed in enough of the theoretical and practical aspects of Force Field Analysis (see Exercise 3 in this section) so that they will be able to apply the concepts within the framework of the activity described below.

Action

The group is requested to form trios composed of individuals who have mutual confidence and are willing to work on an exercise designed to focus upon an aspect of their own behavior that they would like to change in order to be a more effective participant.

First, the individuals spend 15 or 20 minutes (or as much time as necessary) defining a problem condition for each person in the trio. This usually results in discussing particular behaviors that the person would like to change and which he believes would improve his effectiveness within the group. It is for the other two members to help the individual clearly define the problem. Once each individual has had a problem condition defined, he is asked to build for himself a personal Force Field Analysis in which he outlines the pushing and restraining forces impinging upon him. Each member of the trio works independently on his own problem. In approximately 20 minutes the individuals return to the trio for the second phase of the task. Solutions are not developed during this phase of the exercise.

Then, without alluding to his own Force Field, one of the three volunteers to work on his problem. One of the other individuals lists as many pushing forces as he can that seem to be forcing the person to desire change. The third person outlines as many of the restraining forces that he sees impinging upon the person, forces that keep him from changing in the desired direction, and, as a result, limit his effectiveness with groups. As candidly as possible, the two talk together to determine if they have described as many of the forces as possible, given only what they know of the individual. When this is done, the person whose problem is being discussed shares his own view of the problem, and the three then discuss any discrepancies among their views.

Together the individuals search for specific ways of altering the existing problem condition. They do this by focusing on the restraining forces that have been outlined and systematically build strategies that will help eliminate them. The key is to: (a) tackle those forces that offer the best possibility for solution, (b) discuss the possible consequences of any strategy, (c) be as specific as possible in terms of behavior, and (d) help establish the support and follow-up necessary so that the chance for real impact is enhanced.

For groups that are skilled in the use of interpersonal feedback, it is often meaningful to share the personal learnings of the trios. This, of course, must be a voluntary part of the exercise designed to increase an attitude of openness and support in the group.

REFERENCES

Adams, J. K. and Adams, P. A. Realism of confidence judgments. *Psychological Review*, 1967, *68*, 33–45.

Bergum, B. O. and Lehr, D. J. The effects of authoritarianism of vigilance performance. *Journal of Applied Psychology*, 1963, *47*, 75–77.

Bouchard, T. J., Jr. Personality, problem-solving procedure and performance in small groups. *Journal of Applied Psychology*, 1969, *53*(1, part 2), 1–29.

Brehm, J. Post decision changes in desirability of alternatives. *Journal of Abnormal and Social Psychology*, 1956, *52*, 384–389.

Campbell, J. P. Individual versus group problem solving in an industrial sample. *Journal of Applied Psychology*, 1968, *52*, 205–210.

Collaros, R. A. and Anderson, L. Effects of perceived expertness upon creativity of members of brainstorming groups. *Journal of Applied Psychology*, 1969, *53*(2, part 1), 159–164.

Crombag, H. R. Cooperation and competition in means-interdependent triads: A replication. *Journal of Personality and Social Psychology*, 1966, *4*, 692–695.

Deutsch, M. An experimental study of the effects of cooperation and competition on group success. *Human Relations*, 1949, *2*, 199–231.

Deutsch, M. Socially relevant science: reflections on some studies of interpersonal conflict. *American Psychologist*, 1969, *24*, 1076–1092.

Edwards, W. Behavioral decision theory. In W. Edwards (Ed.), *Decision making*. Baltimore: Penguin Books, 1967, 65–95.

Edwards, W. The theory of decision making. In W. Edwards and A. Tversky (Eds.), *Decision making*. Baltimore: Penguin Books, 1967, 18–40.

Ferguson, C. K. and Kelley, H. H. Significant factors in overevaluation of own-group's product. *Journal of Abnormal and Social Psychology*, 1964, *69*, 223–228.

Festinger, L. Informal social communication. *Psychology Review*, 1950, *57*, 271–292.

Festinger, L. *Theory of cognitive dissonance*. Evanston, Ill.: Row, Peterson, 1957.

Festinger, L. and Aronson, E. Arousal and reduction of dissonance in social contexts. In D. Cartwright and A. Zander (Eds.), *Group dynamics research and theory*. New York: Harper and Row, 1968, 125.

Festinger, L. and Carlsmith, J. Cognitive consequences of forced choice alternatives as a function of their number and qualitative similarity. *Journal of Abnormal and Social Psychology*, 1959, *58*, 203–210.

Fouriezos, N. T., Hutt, M. L., and Guetzkow, H. Measurement of self-oriented needs in discussion groups. *Journal of Abnormal and Social Psychology*, 1950, *45*, 682–690.

Gibb, J. R. The effects of group size and threat reduction on creativity in a problem solving situation. *American Psychologist*, 1951, *6*, 324–325.

Goffman, E. *The presentation of self in everyday life*. Garden City, N.Y.: Doubleday Anchor Books, 1959, pp. 76–105.

Guetzkow, H. and Gyr, J. An analysis of conflict in decision making groups. *Human Relations*, 1954, *7*, 367–382.

Hackman, R. J. and Vidman, N. Effects of size and task type on group performance and members' reactions. *Sociometry*, 1970, *33*, 37–55.

Hall, J. and Williams, M. S. Group dynamics training and improved decision making. *The Journal of Applied Behavioral Science*, 1970, *6*, 39–68.

Hammond, L. and Goldman, M. Competition and non-competition and its relationship to individuals' non-productivity. *Sociometry*, 1961, *24*, 46–60.

Heider, F. *The psychology of interpersonal relations.* New York: John Wiley and Sons, 1958, pp. 75–82.

Hurwitz, J. I., Zander, A. F., and Hymovitch, B. The effects of power on relations among group members. In D. Cartwright and A. Zander (Eds.), *Group dynamics: research and theory.* (2nd ed.). New York: Harper and Row, 1960, 801–809.

Idnik, B. P. Organization size and member participation: some empirical tests of alternative explanations. *Human Relations*, 1955, *8*, 121–152.

Katz, I. and Benjamin, L. Effects of white authoritarianism in biracial work groups. *Journal of Abnormal and Social Psychology*, 1960, *61*, 20.

Kelley, H. H. Communication in experimentally created hierarchies. *Human Relations*, 1951, *4*, 39–56.

Kelley, H. H. and Thibaut, J. Group problem solving. In G. Lindzey and E. Aronson (Eds.), *The handbook of social psychology.* (2nd ed.) Vol. 4. *Group psychology and phenomena of interaction.* Reading, Mass.: Addison-Wesley, 1969, 1.

Lewin, K. *Principles of topological psychology.* New York: McGraw Hill, 1936, p. 25.

Lewin, K. *Resolving social conflicts.* New York: Harper and Row, 1948.

Lewin, K. *Field theory in social sciences.* New York: Harper and Row, 1951.

Luce, R. D. and Raiffa, H. *Games and decisions: introduction and critical survey.* New York: John Wiley and Sons, 1957.

Maier, N. R. F. *Problem-solving discussions and conferences.* New York: McGraw-Hill, 1963, pp. 193–195.

McClintock, C. G. and McNeil, S. P. Reward and score feedback as determinants of cooperative and competitive behavior. *Journal of Personality and Social Psychology*, 1966, *4*, 606–613.

McCurdy, H. G. and Lambert, W. E. The efficiency of small human groups in the solution of problems requiring genuine cooperation. *Journal of Personality*, 1952, *20*, 478–494.

Moscovici, S. and Zavalloni, M. The group as a polarizer of attitudes. *Journal of Personality and Social Psychology*, 1969, *12*, 125–135.

Napier, H. Individual versus group learning: note on task variable. *Psychological Reports*, 1967, *23*, 757–758.

NTL Institute for Applied Behavioral Science. *Reading book: laboratories in human relations training*, Washington, D.C.: NTL, 1969, 33.

Phillips, D. J. Report on discussion 66. *Adult Education Journal*, 1948, *7*, 81.

Robert, H. M. *Robert's rules of order*. Chicago: Scott, Foresman, 1943.

Rotter, G. S. and Portergal, S. M. Group and individual effects in problem solving. *Journal of Applied Psychology*, 1969, *53*, 338–342.

Scodel, A., Minas, J. S., Ratoosh, P., and Lipetz, M. Some descriptive aspects of two-person non-zero-sum games. *Journal of Conflict Resolution*, 1959, *3*, 114–119.

Sherif, M. and Sherif, C. M. *An outline of social psychology*. New York: Harper and Row, 1956.

Stuls, M. H. Experience and prior probability in a complex decision task. *Journal of Applied Psychology*, 1969, *53*(2, part 1), 112–118.

Tolela, M. *Effects of T-group training and cognitive learning on small group effectiveness*. Unpublished doctoral dissertation, University of Denver, 1967.

Von Neumann, J. and Morgenstern, O. *Theory of games and economic behavior*. (2nd ed.). Princeton, N.J.: Princeton University Press, 1947.

Voytas, R. M. *Some effects of various combinations of group and individual participation in creative productivity*. Unpublished doctoral dissertation, University of Maryland, 1967.

Vroom, V. H., Grant, L. D., and Cotton, T. S. The consequences of social interaction in group problem solving. *Journal of Organizational Behavior and Human Performance*, 1969, *4*, 79–95.

Watson, G. Resistance to change. In G. Watson (Ed.), *Concepts of social change*. Washington, D.C.: NTL Institute of Applied Behavioral Science, 1967, 10–25.

ADDITIONAL REFERENCES

Asch, S. E. Effects of group pressure upon the modification and distortion of judgment. In H. Guetzkow (Ed.), *Groups, leadership and men*. Pittsburgh, Pa.: Carnegie Press, 1951, pp. 177–190.

Asch, S. E. Studies of independence and conformity: I. A minority of one against a unanimous majority. *Psychological Monographs*, 1956, *70* (9, Whole No. 416).

Bouchard, T. J., Jr. and Hare, M. Size, performance and potential in brainstorming groups. *Journal of Applied Psychology*, 1970, *54*, 51–56.

Brehm, J. Increasing cognitive dissonance by a fait accompli. *Journal of Abnormal and Social Psychology*, 1956, *58*, 379–382.

Bridges, E., Doyle, W., and Mahan, D. Effects of hierarchical differentiation on group productivity, efficiency and risk taking. *Administration Science Quarterly*, *13*, 305–319.

Cohen, A. *Attitude change and social influence*. New York: Basic Books, 1964.

Durham, L. E., and Gibb, J. R. A bibliography of research: 1947–60. In *Explorations: Human relations training and research*. Washington, D.C.: NTL Institute of Applied Behavioral Science, 1967.

Gordon, T. *Group centered leadership*. Boston: Houghton Mifflin, 1955.

Julian, J. W., and Ferry, F. A. Cooperation contrasted with intra-group and inter-group competition. *Sociometry*, 1967, *30*, 79.

Knowles, E. S. A. A bibliography of research: 1960–67. In *Explorations: Human relations training and research*. Washington, D.C.: NTL Institute of Applied Behavioral Science, 1967.

Lifton, W. M. *Working with groups*. (2nd ed.) New York: John Wiley and Sons, 1966.

Schutz, W. What makes groups productive? *Human Relations*, 1955, *8*, 429–465.

Serraf, G. Les techniques de groupes, les recherches de motivations. *Revue Française du Marketing*, 1965, *14*, 25–48.

Wrench, D. The perception of two-sided messages. *Human Relations*, 1964, *17*, 227.

Zajonic, R. B. Social facilitation. *Science*, 1965, *149*, 269–274.

Zajonic, R. B., and Sales, S. M. Social facilitation of dominant and subordinate responses. *Journal of Experimental Social Psychology*, 1966, *2*, 160–168.

Mark Silber

7 the evolution of working groups: understanding and prediction

The complex weave of relationships that comprise any small group eventually become rooted in roles, norms, problem-solving procedures, membership criteria, communication patterns, and a number of other conveniently labeled intellectual concepts. These concepts provide us with a means of establishing some order in viewing what might otherwise be a confusing labyrinth of factors that impinge upon the group and determine its success. However, what makes group behavior difficult to predict, even when one has a firm grasp of these concepts, is the never ending stream of personal needs that individual participants are seeking to meet and which can invariably influence the entire group process. In the following pages we look more closely at some of these needs which appear to be shared within most groups. Then, with an understanding of these needs in mind, the developmental characteristics of many working groups are discussed. Finally, distinctive qualities of successful groups are examined as a means of integrating many of the facts learned to this point.

The Task and Emotional Aspects of Groups: A Source of Unresolvable Tensions

Societies, institutions, and small groups are the breeding grounds for tensions generated from contradictory forces. The forces are real, and their nature must be comprehended if one is to understand the sources of many stresses that originate as a result of human interaction. Several examples will help describe the nature of these forces (Cooley, 1909; Parsons, 1951).

> The large mental health hospital is built on a model of informality, individual care, and attention. Its brochure describes the atmosphere of love and consideration that is cultivated in the hospital wards. There the patients are called "residents," and many of the features so common to institutional living have been purposely removed. Still,

one has merely to walk down the corridors, go into the staff lunch-rooms, or observe the interaction among the staff to feel the strain that exists. The informality so clearly outlined on paper fails to permeate the roles and expectations of the staff. Psychiatrists have little to say to psychologists, nurses to social workers, social workers to teachers, and no one seems to talk with the day-care workers who spend endless hours with the ward patients. The administration, composed mostly of ex-psychiatrists, attempts to maintain the open doors of informality in the tightly run staff hierarchy, but the tensions remain, and those who suffer most are the patients.

The trouble is that the family-oriented treatment center is built on a power-based status hierarchy and a set of clearly established behavioral norms that more than offset the good intentions. Staff roles are rigid and narrowly defined, respect is based on years of learning rather than experience and performance with patients, and staff relations are based primarily on role stereotypes rather than knowledge of one another.

Another example of countervailing forces follows:

The young religious novice enters the convent in an order that specializes in medical services. Her goal is to be a missionary and to work as a hospital administrator in one of the developing countries. Her personal training focuses on two areas; one is the technicalities of hospital administration (accounting, deployment of services, supervision), and the other involves her own personal growth as a sister dedicated to virtues like love, charity, and faith. Her relations with the other novices and sisters are warm and affectionate, and she finds it difficult to leave for her first assignment in a small Ghanaian hospital. The transition proves to be overwhelming. From the nurturing atmosphere of the convent where acceptance was immediate and unqualified, where gentleness and consideration for others was rewarded, she enters her new environment. Here, there is not enough time, every day is a new crisis, decisions are immediate and based less on human feelings than on expediency and efficiency. Her value to the hospital has little to do with Christian virtues. It depends how effectively she can keep the hospital out of the red, how efficiently she can keep the illiterate workers working, and how well she is able to marshal the limited resources available. Failure means transfer, perhaps into an even less desirable situation and very likely into another area of work.

Thus, from an atmosphere of trust, openness, and acceptance the young sister finds herself in a highly competitive, crisis-oriented situation in which she is vulnerable and where virtues of work far outweigh the personal dimensions so important in her previous life. There can be no right or wrong labels attached to these two situations. Each is real and must be understood in its own context. What is important here is to look carefully at the source of tension that results and its implications for the goals inherent in the particular situation.

In both the example of the convent and the mental health hospital there developed a large discrepancy between expectations and reality, between what was desirable and the conditions that prevailed. What stands out is the constant struggle between work efficiency and personal needs, between measured success in terms of task roles and success in terms of emotions. The dichotomy, of course, will be less apparent where the dual set of expectations is not present. In the army the rules, regulations, and codes of behavior are clearly detailed. A career soldier is fully cognizant of these and can accept the depersonalized nature of many of the relationships that exist. Similarly, a young man applying for a job with a Wall Street bank will find a complex set of rules (both explicit and implicit) that govern his behavior, clothes, hair style, language, accepted level of feelings to be displayed, and relations with other workers in the bank. If the individual accepts these rules and knows fully well what is expected of him, he will probably experience little tension, since the personal-emotional factor will have been screened from most of his work involvement.

In most groups and organizations, however, no such clear dichotomy exists, and this is exactly where the stress often originates. For example, in most groups, people wish to be accepted for themselves and not because of academic degrees, superficial knowledge, or other artificial standards; but most groups tend to define success in terms of some visible achievement. Material wealth (how much do you earn?), status (executive assistant to whom?), power (how many men under you?), or tenure (you mean you have 25 years with this department?) are much easier to grasp than the hazy variables that form the basis of most personal relationships. Thus, most groups and organizations are simply not established in such a manner that personal acceptance is not conditional and based upon some implicit or explicit achievement criteria.

Work-oriented task groups tend to be high in control, depend on material rewards for motivation, stress accuracy, organize their use of time, and minimize the range of free expression and autonomy allowed. Similarly, such conditions encourage individual competition rather than interdependence, and conformity rather than individuality.

Tension occurs when informality creeps in, when personal relations begin to get in the way of efficiency, and when regulations are altered to meet the peculiar needs of particular individuals. The fabric of army life would break down if exceptions were made to the rule. The same could be said for big business, the organized church, and, to some degree, large school systems.

For example, it is difficult to imagine the following situations occurring:

> On the day of a major battle, a young private remarks to his field sergeant, "I hope you won't mind, but I probably won't be going to the front today. This headache is killing me." The sergeant looks on with great sympathy and says, "That's all right Joe, we all have days like that; why don't you just rest and take it easy today and save yourself for tomorrow?"

> "Miss Jones, you mean you didn't get that rush report in like I asked?" "No, I'm sorry," she replied, "but Johnny surprised me last night, and we went out for the most heavenly lobster thermidor you can imagine." "Well," he said, "I know how you feel about John, and there will be other contracts. After all, we're only young once."

> "Well, Mr. Gibbs, how are you today, and did you like my sermon?" The minister waited expectantly for the usual monitored reply. "To tell the truth, I really felt you were talking down to us, and if there is one thing I don't appreciate, it's being lectured to in a condescending fashion. Also, you tended to stray from the point by bringing in humorous asides which, although interesting, tended to distract me from the issue."

Criticism to a minister, sympathy from a field sergeant, acceptance of gross inefficiency from one's boss are difficult to imagine within the context of expected role behaviors and institutional demands. But multiplied a thousand times these expectations condition our behaviors in nearly all groups in which people are involved. They are tied to the strands of a Puritan ethic and to years of involvement in schools, businesses, and churches where acceptance is linked to one's output, dependability, efficiency, and conformity.

Implications for Work in Small Groups

When entering a group we look for familiar hooks on which to hang our hats, signs that make the unpredictable predictable, sure ways of being accepted. Even in a social group one will begin with credentials, strengths, or skills in order to establish a tone of respectability. When working on a task, meeting a deadline, or in some way remaining highly task-oriented, there tends to be an order and safety in working relations; but if the curtain of formality is drawn away, one can almost feel the strain of another set of forces pushing for greater intimacy and the personalizing of behavior as well as greater authenticity. It implies increasing one's vulnerability and willingness for risk in a group where trust is typically built around performance. Indeed, it is the rare group that can effectively combine social-emotional interests with those necessary for getting the job done. It is not so much that they cannot be combined, but that the combination necessarily increases the complexity of the existing relationships and the risks for the participants. They simply may not be worth the trouble and, in fact, efficiency may decline and overall problems increase.

At this point the question is not how personal or impersonal, formal or informal, efficient or inefficient a group is. The issue is that the individual interested in understanding groups must be aware that underlying much overt, symptomatic behavior will be causal factors reaching far beyond the particular incident. In many cases the nature of the group or organization will simply not allow the legitimate expression of even basic social-emotional needs. If the resulting pressures and frustrations do not find release outside the group or if informal avenues are not created within, it is likely that tensions will be released indirectly. Usually this occurs by creating interpersonal conflicts around the task issue at hand. Thus, the task itself becomes the outlet for nontask-related tension release. Strange as it may seem, the very presence of restrictions to minimize extraneous issues from undermining the group's work creates new areas of stress that may be even more insidious and difficult to deal with. Exactly how the weave of interpersonal forces influences a group in its development can be understood by following what appears to be a typical group from its inception through various stages of its growth.

The Stages of Group Development

People working with groups often fall into a trap because groups appear to evolve through a series of discrete and visible stages in much the same way that children appear to move through rather specific periods of physical and emotional development. While in both cases there do appear to be rather clear patterns of development, it would be unwise to take them too seriously. Each group like each individual is unique and must be understood in terms of exceptions, and in terms of when, how, and why changes in development occur. True understanding results in grasping the subtle variations in time and place and in recognizing the nature of the precipitating factors and how they contribute to the uniqueness of the individual organism.

The following description of the events that may occur as a group develops, and the accompanying driving forces, is a composite of many views.[1] It is presented not as a model for all groups, but as an example of events that may take place and needs that may exist. By becoming more keenly aware of the changes in group behavior and raising appropriate questions in relation to them, the facilitator should be in a better position to respond effectively to the group's present needs. The following case assumes an ongoing group, one with a reason for being, relatively little personal information about fellow members, differing perceptions of task, and methods for reaching the goals. Finally, it assumes a group that is starting out, although much that is suggested will have relevance for groups at various stages of development.

The Beginning   People have expectations of what will occur in a group even before they attend. They flavor their first perceptions with these expectations and their personal needs. They bring with them their individual histories and experiences in previous groups. It is these factors that provide the glasses through which the group is perceived. First, it is necessary to survive, to protect themselves, and to be relatively secure in an unknown situation. For some this means acting out, almost immediately attempting to gain a measure of control through a strong offense. But for most it appears to be a time for waiting, for observing what lies ahead, for sorting out potential dangers and acting with discretion. Thus, there is a period of data gathering and processing through the screen of our own previous experiences, biases, and stereotypes. Like a child on the first day of school, we tend to:

[1] The composite is drawn from the views of many men working with a wide range of experiences and types of groups. They include: W. Bennis, W. Bion, R. B. Cattell, V. Cernius, E. Erikson, J. Gibb, C. C. Homans, T. Mills, F. Redl, C. Rogers, W. Schutz, H. Shepherd, C. Theodorsen, H. Thelen (see References at the end of this chapter).

Feel inadequate, but afraid to show it.

Feel tentative, but often need to appear fairly certain.

Be watchful.

Lack a feeling of potency or sense of control over our environment.

Act superficially and reveal only what is appropriate.

Scan the environment for clues of what is proper: clothes, tone of voice, vocabulary, who speaks to whom.

Be nice, certainly not hostile.

Try to place other participants in pigeon-holes so that they become comfortable to us, able to be coped with in our own minds.

Worry about who "we" should try to be in "this" group.

Desire structure and order to reduce our own pressure to perform.

Wonder what price it will take to be "in" and whether the rewards are worth the effort.

Find it difficult to listen and look beyond our own immediate needs.

So, it is a time for testing, a time of inhibition guided by the rules of other places and experiences. It is not a time for heroics, but for first impressions. Often, it is an environment based more on suspicion than trust, partly because of our initial discomfort and partly because we simply do not know. However, because people always want something better and seek to reduce tensions, more often than not they will risk involvement, and at least a minimal sharing. Our needs to be liked and accepted tend to light the way, and, though seldom satisfied, there usually are indications of better things to come. On either side of this position there are, of course, the groups that from the first minute are so tightly controlled that one's very breath and individuality are lost. Then, too, there are those equally rare groups where a sense of openness and security prevails immediately. However, it appears that most groups are a mix of hope and trepidation, where our own needs and the mixed views of others provide the ingredients for an initial climate of doubt and hesitation.

Movement Toward Confrontation   It is not until the initial probing into the boundaries of appropriate behaviors has taken place that façades are dropped and individuals establish personal roles and reveal more characteristic behaviors. Much of the new movement in the group relates to the patterns of power and leadership that are being established. The initial period of unfamiliarity often leads to an acquiesence to authority and a seeking of structure which allows members to move with a certain ease in the strange environment. However, for many this soon results in a desire for more influence in what is happening and focuses attention upon those with power. How to be liked and accepted by those with influence becomes of central importance to some, while others begin to seek personal recognition and their own spheres of influence. Suddenly the leader becomes not only a source of dependency and admiration but also an object of criticism whose inadequacies become a source of discussion. How things are to be done, how decisions are made and by whom, as well as issues of freedom and control all become preeminent issues. Whether there is a leader focus or a member focus, influence and so-called territoriality among the participants is central. It is the assertive seeking of one's place in the group that bares behavior formerly hidden, and, thus, it is a period of new behavioral dimensions for various members and a period in which stereotypes are often disconfirmed. This springing forth of new behaviors creates suspicion and mistrust in some and forms the basis for new alliances within the group. It is bound to cause tensions and conflict. Not uncommon are such statements as: "I wouldn't have suspected that of John"; "I knew there was more to him than that soft voice and smile"; "I didn't know he was capable of being so angry."

Within this more assertive environment, members begin to take more definite stands, and issues become polarized. Instead of an argument being looked at in terms of data and facts, it also becomes a testing ground for personal influence and prestige. Tenacity may be as important as rationality in winning, and for some it is winning or losing and not the issue itself that is important. The tentativeness is gone, hostility is legitimized, and in many ways the group is much more real than it was in the beginning. Alliances within the group are redrawn based more on experience and behavior than on expectations and wishful thinking. Along with the increased amounts of anger being shown there is also probably more laughter as well and a generally wider range of affective behaviors.

During the first phase it is often difficult to concentrate one's energies upon task issues as long as one's own role and secure position in the group has not been established. Now, however, the task becomes a means of exercising other spheres of influence and expertise. Underlying issues facing the group may involve such things as status, prestige, and power. With increased signs of rigidity among the participants and an unwillingness to compromise, less assertive members tend to withdraw as others in the group now bring personality issues into what had been previously content or task issues. If the group is able to face its own destructive tendencies, there will very likely be a confrontation and an effort to get people together and back on the track.

Compromise and Harmony   A confrontation over work and personal issues will usually occur when individuals who are more willing to compromise recognize how self-defeating the present course of events seems to be. Acting as intermediaries, they reopen issues and help to get individuals talking again. It may also result when some of the more aggressive members realize that their own personal aims are not being met as a result of their present course of action. They begin to see a more amicable climate as essential to any further movement or growth on the part of the group.

The result is a countermovement to shut off the growing hostility, to reopen communication, and to draw the group together into a more smoothly working body. It is often this effort that ushers in a period of goodwill and harmony during which time there is a reassessment of how people have or have not been working together and how conditions for work might be facilitated. The dissensions are eased, deviations in member behaviors appear to be more readily accepted, and self-expression is encouraged. Collaboration is more readily sought and competitiveness is played down, if not rejected, by the members. The group tends to exude a new confidence and begins to actually see itself as an integrated unit that can be facilitative when it wishes to be. There is a genuine effort to look at issues, discover appropriate resources, and avoid the personalizing of issues that occurred earlier.

After the nearly destructive series of events and the mistrust previously generated, members are careful not to step on one another's toes, to avoid signs of hostility, and to make sure everyone is heard. Real honesty and openness are encouraged on the one hand, but, on the other hand, there is a subtle pressure to not raise any problems that might break down the harmony that has been so difficult to obtain. Thus, everyone is given "air time" and encouraged to voice his opinions. There is a tendency to let people talk (even extraneously) rather than cut them off. Joking and laughter are common, and personal irritations, unless couched in veiled sarcasm, tend to go unnoticed. An increasing discrepancy develops between feelings and behavior, but even so the group may increasingly talk of its openness and ability to work together. Yet the denial of personal issues tends to increase tensions that remain unexpressed. With this submergence of issues there is less participant involvement, stimulation, and overall interest.

Thus, while fences have been repaired and wounds covered, it has been done at a cost of some of the group's integrity and efficiency. Instead of the anger and overt blocking that had occurred previously, issues are overdiscussed, and it is very difficult to make decisions. Resistance appears to be more covert. Instead of leading to greater productivity, this harmony often leads to even less efficiency. Eventually there is the realization that the behaviors within the group are actually inhibiting authenticity and directness. One reason it takes so long to reach decisions is that covert resistance and passivity block progress. The initial elation shared during the beginning of the period gives way to disillusionment and increasing tension. The group's efforts toward harmony simply have not succeeded as they might.

Reassessment: Union of Emotional and Task Components   Having worked under a period of relative structure and under conditions of less control with neither resulting in a satisfactory climate for work, the group seeks a new alternative. One obvious solution is to impose greater operational restrictions to insure a more rational approach to decision making. Such a thrust would streamline work procedures and redirect the group toward the task with greater efficiency. It would not, however, face the source of many of the problems created within the group. As with many life problems, this approach only attacks the symptoms and eases the pain of the current situation, but it may be enough to insure a smoother decision-making process.

If, however, the group decides to delve more deeply into the problems at hand, into causal factors, then considerably more time, energy, and involvement will be the cost. It requires a sizable risk on the part of the members since many issues that have long been submerged will be forced to the surface. Member roles, decision-making procedures, and leadership and communication patterns are likely to come under close scrutiny as are the personal behaviors that facilitated or inhibited the group. Thus, this becomes a period of reflection on goals and performance, means and ends. There is usually a recognition of how vulnerable the group is to the personal needs, suspicions, and fears that can determine how successful the group is in reaching these goals.

If the group chooses this latter course of action, it must build a mechanism that allows it to appraise its own ongoing operations and to alter its pattern of working behaviors when it is obvious that current methods are not proving effective. The group must face the question of how honest it can be and just what level of personal intimacy must be reached before the group can accomplish its goals in the most effective manner. It makes sense that a third-grade classroom will demand greater intimacy than a Marine Corps platoon. Thus the period of harmony and compromise, while not allowing all the issues that needed to emerge, did prove to be of great importance in the development of the group. Because it was a period of reduced competition, greater informality, and increased familiarity among members, it provided a needed foundation upon which to build. What had been missing was a means of legitimizing the feelings that were not positive, the communication of feelings and ideas that might create conflict or force the group to consider alternative approaches.

Often at this same time there is a realization that as the functions of the group become increasingly complex and there is a need for more resources, greater interdependence is necessary. Greater participation through the division of labor becomes essential, and with it accountability and personal responsibility are spread throughout the group. With greater freedom to communicate and methods of feedback built into the group's operations, necessary tasks are increasingly undertaken by those with particular skills and interests, leadership is shared, and participant involvement is generally increased. The notion of accountability is crucial here, and it suggests that individuals know what is expected of them, that their expectations are shared by the group, and that they are to some degree measurable.

There is, of course, the possibility of a temporary period of intense conflict resulting as tensions and stresses previously withheld are brought out. If the group can overcome the fear of such conflict and realize that it can be put to effective use without being destructive to individuals, then there will be less reluctance to deal more openly with such issues in the future. Thus, during this period the group realizes that if it is to survive, it must increase shared responsibility as well as personal accountability. This in turn will increase trust and insure more individual risk-taking as well as a willingness to devote the necessary time to resolve working issues of both a substantive and personal nature.

Resolution and Recycling Effective working groups are not necessarily harmonious and free of tensions and conflict. There seem to be periods of conflict resolution and harmony and even times in which the group tends to regress into a pattern of indecisiveness and floundering. As a group matures it should find itself resolving conflicts more quickly and with a minimal expenditure of energy. And, like any mature person, it should be increasingly able to recognize its own limitations and build effectively around them. It has, however, been found that if the group is suddenly faced with a crisis, a series of critical deadlines, a number of new participants, or even a controversial new idea, it may usher in a period of readjustment and a reappearance of old and not necessarily helpful behaviors. For example, special interest subgroups might develop and inhibit the efforts of the entire group, or the group could enter into a period when lines of communication break down, feelings and emotions are denied, and tensions begin to build. Such tensions, quite often, will be released toward other members, thus creating further points of stress.

It is not a sign of group immaturity that such tensions develop, but the degree of maturity is revealed in how effectively the group is able to cope with these very natural problems. A new, influential person being added to the group will be a threat to some member's security, for another he will represent a potential ally, and for a third a competitive rival for leadership in the group. Since personal needs are involved as well as various levels of the group's working relationships, conflict is inevitable. Too many groups deny the various reasons for the increased tensions and proceed as if nothing has happened. This denial begins to decay further existing levels of trust. A mature group will stop the deteriorating cycle of events by openly exploring the possible causal factors and then providing at least temporary solutions during the period of adjustment. By confronting the issues that tend to debilitate the group, a norm of positive and constructive problem solving will be reinforced, and this will reduce the length and intensity of the regressive cycle.

Groups, like people, can become immobilized at certain levels or stages of their development. Some individuals can never break away from dependency on their parents, and it carries into nearly every other relationship they have. Others fail to resolve their own needs to fight authority. Still others cannot tolerate conflict and the fear of being rejected. In a similar manner, some groups never move beyond a particular stage of development because of various unresolved issues among the members or external factors out of their control. Whatever the reason, such groups will find it difficult to reach an adequate level of functioning. For example, many groups develop a norm that inhibits the expression of anger. As a result, many emotions are bottled up, and the group remains at an artificial level of interaction where harmony inhibits the development of authenticity. Similarly, compromise may become a mechanism for escaping the true resolution of issues. Instead of tensions being reduced, they are increased by the passive behaviors used to cope with individual feelings of anger and aggression.

Other groups have other problems which, unless dealt with directly, will influence nearly every aspect of their work. If members do not feel involved in the decision-making process and are constantly having to respond to edicts from various sources outside themselves, they will build characteristic response patterns to counteract the new edicts or regulations. Because this group is treated as immature and not responsible, it will tend to respond in an immature fashion. If it lacks the feeling of potency, it will not express itself through power. Rather it will respond through inaction or denial. Members may spend a great deal of time angrily discussing the issue among themselves, but never actively and overtly taking a position against the particular source of power behind the edict. Such in-group catharsis may reduce tensions momentarily, but in the long run it will tend to lead to only more feelings of frustration, impotency, and perhaps guilt. One would hardly expect such a group to move smoothly through the various stages of development and on to resolution of its own problems.

Group Process:
A Continual Adaptation to Stress and Tension

If a person wishes to understand another individual quickly, it is often helpful to ask, "What are his needs and the sources of tension he is trying to reduce?" Similarly, groups represent the composite needs of a number of different people and the attempt to reduce the level of existing tensions. Usually it appears that if there is a choice between facing such tensions and the conflicts that often accompany them, the tendency will be avoidance. However, by minimizing the disruption and agitation of the moment through such mechanisms as denial and avoidance, underlying sources of tensions tend to multiply, and tremors of dissatisfaction erupt into even greater turbulence later. It is the inclination of a group to maintain the status quo that severely hinders the development of a dynamic and flexible working group. Disproportionate energy is often spent on issues of little relevance and minimal controversy while emotional concerns focus on issues that may never be formally placed on the agenda. An example of this follows:

During a recent rather volatile spring, racial conflicts flared in a number of schools of a large eastern city. Many of the secondary schools waited for the incident that might ignite demonstrations, strikes, or even riots. It was during this time that a special faculty meeting was called at a special school for academically superior students. Because of their status within the school district and the reputation of having the best teachers and most talented students, an "it's their problem" sort of smugness had settled among this faculty group. Racial issues were seldom even the topic of conversation.

A brief incident of racial conflict several months before, however, had stimulated an interested group of teachers, students, and community members into action. Without publicity, they decided to discover whether, in fact, they did have serious problems within the school and, if they did, what constructive steps might be taken to alleviate them. Thus, it was at this particular meeting that these data were presented. Questionnaires, interviews, and discussion groups had been conducted in an effort to tap the representative views of students, faculty, and the community. As might be expected, the study uncovered areas of tension that had been denied or glossed over lightly by the faculty and revealed a potentially dangerous situation developing between a particular student group and certain faculty members. The proposal was met with immediate denial and anger and was voted down with almost no discussion. The only response to these concerns and the supporting information was an irate negation of the report and of the individuals who had developed it. The idea that such a literate, sophisticated, and learned body could be guilty of having even the seeds of racism or prejudice was inconceivable to the group.

Clearly, the single best indicator of the depth of this problem was the highly symptomatic denial of the issue, a refusal to even explore the problem at a time when schools were literally burning around them. The lack of positive response might have been the result of the faculty's own guilt, fear of imperfection, or discovery of their intellectual dishonesty. Whatever the cause, the denial of the present reality almost precipitated the chaos the faculty was so desperately trying to avoid. The hope was that the momentary overt expression of discontent expressed in the report would soon pass and a semblance of the previous peace and tranquility would again appear.

Similarly, it is not uncommon for a group or organization to handle a period of conflict or severe crisis by developing a commission to study the problem or by devising an experimental study to explore the parameters of the problem. What usually occurs is a reduction in the immediate level of tension, an avoidance of a direct confrontation, and a redirection of participant energy. Often what then occurs is a diluting of the issue over time as it loses immediacy and becomes entangled in the bureaucratic ritual of meetings and reports. Even with good intentions, such task forces frequently prove ineffective since the recommendations for action will be presented at a point in time far removed from the crisis and when there is less pressure for change.

It appears that a group will often be willing to sustain a gnawing source of tension and conflict over time rather than to dig the issue out and place it in the open. Dealing with the problem directly will inevitably rupture the status quo. Thus, to really understand a group, an individual must look beyond superficial behaviors and into the underlying stresses that exist but are not being dealt with. More often than not these tension points lie behind those concepts and values being most vociferously defended within the group and which, if altered, would force a change in the imaginary point of equilibrium around which expectations are built and habits are forged.

The Successful Working Group

To talk of an ideal or perfect group is to walk on very thin ice. Nevertheless, it may be worth the risk since it will allow an exploration of certain dimensions of group behavior that seem to result in a productive work climate and where both emotional and task needs are given necessary consideration. It will, at the very least, provide a list of pertinent questions to be used in helping to diagnose a group and the internal working relationships that develop. Special circumstances and particular demands require groups with specific orientations and skills, but, from what has been said to this point, there appear to be certain conditions that facilitate the involvement of people in groups, and there do seem to be generalities that can be drawn. Depending upon the group and the unique circumstances prevailing, the following summary will make sense and have application.

1. The group should have a shared sense of purpose, and its members should be aware of common goals. Their participation should be voluntary if at all possible.

2. Roles in the group are varied and differentiated according to both interest and performance. In other words, there is a concerted attempt to discover appropriate resources, depending upon the particular need at a given time.

3. Communication channels are open, and there is a specific effort on the part of members to listen and clarify what has been said. An interest is shown in what others have to say or feel. This also implies that the vocabulary and any special jargon is familiar to the group.

4. Similarly, dissent is freely expressed, and silence is not taken as consent; opposing opinions are sought as part of the clarification process. In this manner, inputs are seen as shared ideas, and they are not evaluated in terms of the presenter. On the other hand, each member assumes responsibility for himself and his own ideas and is willing to stand accountable to the group for these ideas.

5. In this light, there is an acceptance of different participant styles, although the group is not dominated or controlled by the personality characteristics of a few members. Thus, the whole group, rather than a few powerful individuals, is in charge of its own destiny, and there is a sense of shared leadership based on changing needs and varying according to particular situations.

6. Since to not decide is to decide, the group makes decisions. Most of these decisions, however, are seen as provisional and are to be evaluated by the group with particular members being held accountable for assignments accepted. It is this assurance of reappraisal and accountability that enables the members to accept a consensual method of decision making in many instances.

7. Nevertheless, the decision-making process is flexible enough so that a number of decision-making procedures may be used, depending on the peculiar nature of the problem under consideration. Under-

lying this process is an awareness that an apparent decision (regardless of method) is not a real decision until it has been initiated, and members of the group are made responsible for its implementation.

8. Failure does not immobilize the group or its interest in experimentation. Thus, innovation is encouraged and support given for the implementation of reasonable ideas. However, success does not shut the door to further evaluation and exploration. This assumes that the group is willing to look carefully at its own productivity and, equally important, how it works as a group to accomplish its agreed-upon goals.

9. Thus, the group has developed the skills and interest necessary to diagnose those problems that minimize its effectiveness. This includes the collecting and processing of a variety of data which provide the group as a whole and individual members with information relating to their own behaviors and their impact upon others in the group.

10. It is important that impersonal problems are seen as issues that influence the entire group and do not become "member" problems which can easily result in an evaluative and even punitive climate. This also assumes that the group is fully involved in establishing its own system of rewards and is able to identify and maximize its strong points.

11. The group is responsive to its own changing needs and goals, able to create new functions and roles, work in subgroups or as a whole and, if necessary, assimilate new members with a minimum of disruption. This takes for granted a well-balanced interdependency while maintaining necessary flexibility.

Conclusion

Most people have never experienced true participative decision making within the kind of problem-solving climate described above. It is a relatively rare and difficult process because those with successful previous experience are usually in the minority in a work group. Most of us are used to strong leaders who control rewards, establish the ground rules of the particular task, and provide the necessary push to get the job done. We expect to be directed, motivated, intellectual, impersonal, and rational in our approach to problem solving. As a result, we tend to see ourselves as separate from the group, often competing with other members for recognition and responding to authority rather than to member peers. Such a climate is not conducive to establishing free and open communication, role flexibility, and a truly nonevaluative atmosphere. It is this kind of atmosphere that helps to predetermine the kind of development possible for a group. We are used to being dependent and, even though we do not like it, will often demand behaviors from those in control which insure its presence. Even when a work group is responsive to democratic principles, members too often become the victims of the majority vote, the conflict-reducing option which, if used indiscriminately, may polarize a group and erase the vital thread of compromise upon which the effective decision-making group must be based.

If a group has never had experience outside the confines of a rigid time schedule, agenda, and parliamentary procedure, it is doubtful that it will ever develop the trust necessary for processing its own behaviors or for the interdependence necessary to see issues as other than politically expedient and strategic. Certainly decisions will be made and groups will function, sometimes in an extraordinarily efficient manner. The price paid, however, will be in terms of participant involvement, interest, cooperation, and member accountability. The group, like a growing child, responds best to patience, freedom within limits, concern from others, and a climate that encourages spontaneity and authenticity. It is a nonquantifiable mixture that varies from group to group, with intangibles often determining the difference between success and failure. Yet, more and more success can be assured if the leader-facilitator is able to formulate the necessary questions to help him understand the group with which he is to work. This, added to a familiarity with diagnostic techniques and a few basic approaches to working with the task and emotional problems that inevitably face any working group, is essential. Much more than the use of gimmicks and techniques, success seems geared to how effectively the group is able to respond to its very human needs in a manner that exploits no one and maximizes its own potential.

Exercise 1
Tinker Toy Exercise

Objectives

To help focus a group upon the importance of nonverbal communication in its developmental process

To familiarize the group with how easily the group climate is influenced by particular behaviors of the participants

Setting

As in many of the other exercises, competition between groups can be used as a means of bringing a sense of reality to a particular task. How individuals behave and what their impact is upon a group will tend to be characteristic of other situations that stimulate, annoy, challenge, or bore them. In this example, it is assumed that there are two groups of randomly selected participants with from 7 to 10 in each group. (Note: if the group has been working together for some time, an interesting dimension may be added by assigning the individuals who tend to verbally dominate a group—gathered from previous data—into one subgroup and those who are less active in the other.)

Each group is placed around a table (no chairs). The two tables are close enough so that each may see what the other is doing (about 10 to 15 feet apart). There is nothing on the table. They are told to await instructions.

Materials

One can of Tinker Toys is needed for each group.

Action

The groups are told that they will have 45 minutes to develop the best possible product from the materials distributed to them. It is important that the product represent a group effort. The groups may begin as soon as they have the assigned materials, but the members may *not* speak to one another during the exercise.

At this point, the Tinker Toys are spread on the center of the table. The can and all instructions are taken away. The participants must use *all* of the materials in their project. They may also use any materials they have on their person, although they may not leave the table to obtain such materials.

Observation of the Task

It is assumed that the observers have some skill and experience in observing groups. If there are three for each group, they should have

15 minutes prior to the beginning of the exercise to decide what observation procedures will give the participants the best picture of what actually happened. The following questions may help the observers in selecting their observational instruments and strategies.

1. How do individuals in the group arrange themselves around the table (randomly, friendship subgroups, etc.)?

2. At the end of the task, how has this initial ordering been changed? In front of whom is the final product? Why? Has this person the most skill? Is he the best organizer? Is he the most popular? Does he have the most power?

3. To which people in the group was most of the nonverbal communication directed? Were others encouraged to share their ideas in some manner?

4. Did members "jump" on one of the first ideas communicated or did they seek to explore alternatives? Did all the participants really understand what they were building when they started, and did they seem to agree with the idea?

5. How were tasks distributed during the work period? Was there any organization of labor or did individuals just do what came naturally?

6. Were particular roles (facilitating and inhibiting) identified within the group?

7. What did individuals who were obviously not directly involved in the decisions or perceived as resource people do to compensate for feelings of noninvolvement, impotency, or even inadequacy in this particular group?

8. Did particular behaviors by individuals (no names are necessary, but it is helpful if the group can accept direct feedback) create defensive responses in other members? Responses should be specific about the action and reaction parts to this question.

9. How did the group respond to the pressure of time and to the pressure of the group working next to them?

10. What norms developed as the group began to work together? Did these change as the task progressed?

11. What types of leadership were exhibited within the group and what impact did these have upon the developing group climate?

Other observations relating to membership, subgrouping patterns, tension release, reward, and punishment in the group may be explored. It is also important to observe how the two groups use each other as outlets for their own feelings.

Follow-up and Discussion

Depending on the particular objectives of the facilitator, there are a number of possible interventions that may be used following the action phase of the exercise.

Option 1:   Still within the nonverbal framework, each group is asked to move to an opposite end of the room and in a relatively open space ideally, about 15 × 15 ft.), form themselves into a "group shape" which should symbolically represent a picture of how the individuals within the group feel about their own participation and the product of the group. They should try out as many shapes as they feel are necessary until they can all agree on one. Again, this activity should be observed in terms of group pressure, decision making, leadership, etc. Do the members really have the courage to represent the feelings generated during the activity? Once the shape is formed, the members sit down where they are and discuss the implications of their shape and how it reflects the process of their work together. After this discussion, the observers may wish to bring the group into a circle and share with them some of the data (again, there may be a tendency to overwhelm them with too much information) they feel is most useful. They should help draw the participants into the discussion and to have them, using their own experience from participation, respond to the questions the observers were asking. Observers are most effective when they are used to supplement the insights of the participants themselves.

Option 2:   The facilitator announces that the groups will now have an opportunity to present their products to the other group. Each group will be asked to explain briefly what the product was and how the idea was arrived at. Then they will be asked to make a number of observations about their work together. The observers should carefully note who responds for the group, how this was decided, and how accurate the description is in terms of what actually happened. Also, it should be noted which behaviors occur while one group is listening to the other and while participants in the group being described hear a version of what happened according to their representative. Often the product is not what some of the participants thought, nor is the description of what happened the same as their own. After both groups have presented their product to the other group, each group meets to discuss the observers' data and explore what happened during (and after) the activity.

Summary

It is quite possible that the discussion period after either of the two options may take as much as an hour, but it can take much less if there is a more systematic presentation of the data and discussion is minimized. Time should be allowed at the end of the program so that each group can share with the total group specific learnings that seem to have developed out of the particular activity. Special emphasis should be placed on those behaviors characteristic of most groups as they develop during a specific task.

Other Possible Materials

The same basic design can be used with a wide range of materials. If the group is outdoors and near a wooded area, it is possible to build interesting products from only what is available in nature. Or, a brief trip to a dime store or supermarket can result in a seemingly endless supply of materials that could be distributed to the groups (clothes pins, tape, paper, plastic hair curlers, hair pins, rubber bands, crayons, pipe cleaners, etc.). The main thing is to give the group enough so that decisions must be made as to the allocation of materials, but the materials should be different enough so they do not naturally form a product.

Exercise 2
Developing a Helping Attitude Within a Group

Rationale

Many individuals have an extremely difficult time giving help to others. Perhaps because of a competitive atmosphere, a need to dominate or control, or even a belief in the independence of others, there is often a tendency to withhold help that we could give. Similarly, for many the difficulty is in receiving help. In this case the need to stand alone, to be strong in the eyes of oneself, or others, and a desire to not become involved can all be reasons to avoid a helping hand. While some individuals may succeed in achieving their goals without being good givers or receivers of help, a lack of either one will restrict the line of communication, limit the most effective use of those individuals with special skills, and, in general, curb the potential effectiveness of the working group. This exercise is designed not only to legitimize the giving and receiving of help but also to provide practice in how to do it more effectively.

Setting

The group is divided into groups of three. Although the task is designed to assist individuals in developing a helping relationship, there is no need to divide the group into what might be called "friendship" trios. In this activity, it is better that the groups be randomly mixed (there are exceptions, however, particularly when deep animosities are present in the group). No preliminaries are required and no special materials necessary.

Action

All the participants are requested to write down two very different problems that influence their effectiveness in this or other groups or in relationships generally. The participants should avoid being so general in their descriptions of problems that nothing can be done with them, and they should be problems that they want help in resolving. Having done this, the following phases are suggested:

Phase 1:   The members of the trio are labeled 1, 2, and 3. Person 1 is to receive help from person 2. Person 3 is to observe the attempt at giving and receiving help, noting anything that might be helpful in a later discussion. A time limit of about 15 minutes is recommended. At this point, person 2 states his problem to person 3, and person 1 observes the helping process. Finally, person 3 states his problem to person 1 with person 2 observing.   (Total time for three persons is estimated at between 45 and 60 min.)

Phase 2: At this time, the members of the trio discuss their efforts at helping one another and from their observations suggest some of the facilitating and inhibiting behaviors that resulted. Then they consolidate a number of general learnings that can be shared with the total group about the helping process. (Approx. 20 min.)

Phase 3: The facilitator draws from the various trios the learnings they have experienced thus far in terms of specific behaviors. He may wish to supplement these, but this may not be at all necessary. Whenever possible, the participants should be given a brief behavioral example. (Approx. 15–20 min.)

Phase 4: Having had a round of practice and a round of theory, the final phase has the trio back at work, this time using their second problem. Person 3 receives help from person 2 with person 1 observing. If at some time in this process, person 1 feels he can be of help to person 2, he should feel free to interject briefly. Again, after about 15 minutes, person 1 receives help from person 3 and person 2 observes and tries to help. Finally, person 2 receives help from person 1, and person 3 observes.

A brief period should be allowed at the end to enable the trios to discuss how their approaches changed and whether or not those receiving help actually could feel the difference. The facilitator may wish to bring closure on the exercise by asking the large group how, if at all, the practice and theory session facilitated the ability to give help during the final phase of the activity.

REFERENCES

Argyris, C. *Interpersonal competence and organizational effectiveness.* Homewood, Ill.: Irwin Dorsey, 1962.

Argyris, C. The incompleteness of social psychological theory. *American Psychologist,* 1969, *24,* 893–908.

Bales, R. *Interaction analysis.* Reading, Mass.: Addison-Wesley, 1950.

Bales, R., and Strodtbeck, F. L. Phases in group problem solving. *Journal of Abnormal and Social Psychology,* 1951, *46,* 485–495.

Bion, W. R. *Experiences in groups.* New York: Basic Books, 1961.

Bennis, W., and Shepherd, H. A theory of group development. *Human Relations,* 1956, *9,* 418–419.

Cattell, R. B., Sanders, D. R., and Stice, G. F. The dimensions of syntality in small groups. *Human Relations,* 1953, *6,* 331–336.

Cooley, C. H. *Social organization.* New York: Charles Scribners' Sons, 1909.

Erikson, E. *Childhood and society.* New York: W. W. Norton, 1950.

Goffman, E. *The presentation of self in everyday life.* New York: Doubleday, 1959.

Homans, G. C. *The human group.* New York: Harcourt, Brace, 1950.

Homans, G. C. *The nature of social science.* New York: Harcourt, Brace, 1967.

Mills, T. *Group transformation.* Englewood Cliffs, N.J.: Prentice-Hall, 1964.

Mills, T. *The sociology of small groups.* Englewood Cliffs, N.J.: Prentice-Hall, 1967.

Parsons, T. *The social system.* Glencoe, Ill.: The Free Press, 1951.

Redl, F. *When we deal with children.* New York: The Free Press, 1966.

Schutz, W. *The interpersonal underworld.* Palo Alto, Calif.: Science & Behavior Books, 1966.

Stock, D. and Thelen, H. *Emotional dynamics and group culture.* New York: New York University Press, 1955.

Thelen, H. *Dynamics of groups at work.* Chicago: Phoenix Books, 1954.

Theodorsen, G. A. Elements in the progressive development of small groups. *Social Forces,* 1953, *31,* 311–320.

Wechsler, I. R., and Reisel, J. *Inside a sensitivity training group.* Los Angeles: University of California, Institute of Industrial Relations, 1959.

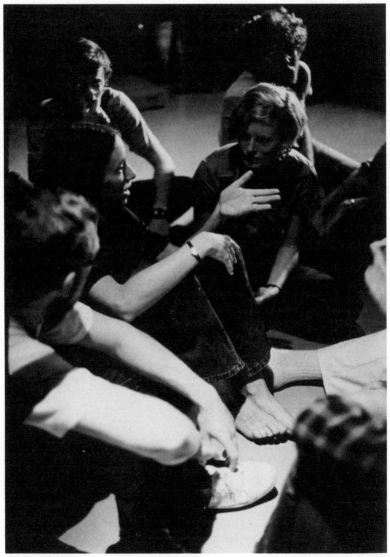

Mark Silber

8 the current status of groups

There have always been groups: family groups, communal groups, committee groups, task force groups, groups of every conceivable shape, size, and purpose. It has only been in the last 20 years, however, that there was any significant growth or change in what people think of when they think of groups. In the past it appeared that most groups had been one-dimensional. Except for the traditional family, most groups had a rather specific purpose, and their members could adjust themselves to that purpose with relative ease. If a person joined a social group in a church, a single visit could easily reveal acceptable patterns of behavior and the depth of the relationships that could be expected. It was relatively simple to decide whether the group would be beneficial. Similarly, a bridge club, though social in nature, exists within a very particular task and behavioral framework. While different groups might have their own individual flavor, one could anticipate a degree of similarity. In the realm of task groups an unmistakable sameness resulted during the course of the last century as parliamentary procedures dictated the style, rhythm, and order of thousands of institutional meetings throughout the country.

The intensive study of human behavior within the group framework during and after World War II resulted in an awareness of the variety of benefits groups could have as well as their potential influence and power on both members and others outside the group. Industry and the military were quick to take advantage of many of these learnings and applied them in more effective decision-making processes, especially in relation to the development of "think tanks" and ideation centers.

Changes were also occurring on a very different level as the study of group dynamics began to look beyond the traditional structure of work groups and into the groups as a unified organism. New ways of looking at the behaviors in these groups were needed as well as ways of understanding both the social and task aspects of group life and their interrelationships. A prime instrument in this exploration and learning process both for participants and theorists was the T-group (training group).

The T-Group   The group of about ten individuals and one leader (trainer) would meet together regularly over a stated period of time. Unlike other groups, there were no stated goals other than to become a group, and the participants were left to their own resources. Having no appointed leader and usually not being familiar with one another, the group found itself with all the difficulties facing any new organization or community. There were no rules, guidelines, structures, no means of even making a simple decision or solving the most basic problem. Not only would goals and procedures have to be established, but the group had to face the social dimension (getting to know one another) that is often avoided in other groups. As the group proceeded to write its own history and resolve its many and varied problems, it experienced the wide range of feelings, tensions, and frustrations that would naturally evolve. Leadership struggles, different levels of competence, interest and participation, gaps in communication, role conflicts, personal competition, and a thousand issues had to be dealt with. The group would grow and suffer and even enjoy the intensity of involvement together. As interdependence was generated and trust developed, it was not uncommon for such groups to become intensely personal. Individuals would share their own strengths, weaknesses, and views, and open channels of feedback that they had not previously experienced.

Although the initial aim of these groups was to help individuals learn about how groups and organizations function and how their behavior influenced that process, an added dividend often resulted. For the first time many of the participants found a group in which they were accepted for themselves, in which façades were dropped, and in which they were even free to experiment with new behaviors that might help them in other groups. While there is some question concerning how well these individuals were able to transfer their learnings to other groups, many returned with an experience that was deeply personal and difficult to explain. True, there were unsuccessful T-groups, as individuals occasionally pushed too far too fast. But, for the most part, groups proved to be self-protective and tended to develop only as fast as their members could tolerate.

The T-group is still used extensively in a wide variety of training programs, and it is considered a laboratory for helping individuals comprehend group process. It has also proved to be the wellspring for a movement that has spread throughout the entire United States in a period of 10 years. Building on the learnings of group therapy and concepts developed out of the human relations movement (T-groups, laboratories in human relations), and in the broader area of sensitivity training, there has been a rapid proliferation of what might be generally called "personal growth" groups.

Group Therapy   It was inevitable that with the shortage of psychiatrists and psychologists qualified to give psychotherapy, the notion of practicing therapy in groups of individuals with similar problems would eventually be initiated. At first, during the late forties and early fifties, the tendency was to conduct the therapy session as nothing more than individual therapy in a group setting. The therapist in a rather traditional role would help a particular individual work through a problem while others looked on and occasionally added their perspective. In many cases, the group was only a convenience, and its success was dependent upon the wisdom and interventions of the therapist. As the therapist began to be less intimidated by the prospect of being outnumbered eight or ten to one, he was able to alter his role and begin to tap the extraordinary resources of the group. Instead of merely framing individual therapy within a group setting, the group began to be seen as a means for testing reality, a microcosm of the real society, an accumulation of the very personalities and problems that occur on the outside. Thus, group therapy, looking only at the personal growth dimension, began to discover that groups had enormous qualities of support and love, of anger and tension, that could be used to benefit those who participated in them. It was also true that group therapy began to attract a population less severely disturbed than might be expected, a population of individuals seeking a better adjustment within an increasingly impersonal society.

At the same time that increasing number of "normal" individuals were experiencing the excitement and benefits of T-groups, another large number of individuals were grasping the value of groups within the confines of an intended therapeutic environment. It appears that these two forces working at different ends of the social spectrum and being developed in a period of social turmoil helped to stimulate a third movement in the group area, which could be described as personal growth groups.

Confrontation Groups   Confronting ourselves with the honest views of others can be disconcerting and even traumatic. Many of us tend to spend our lives screening ourselves from realities we might not feel comfortable with, building on our strengths, and rationalizing our limitations. Others, of course, do the opposite. These people concentrate on their limitations and avoid accepting their own areas of greatest potency. However, by limiting our view of the total picture, it is possible to exist from day to day without realizing the impact we are having on those around us and how we shape our lives to fit our own limited perceptions of reality. The confrontation approach to personal growth is based on the assumption that a person needs to be shaken out of previous patterns, awakened from his lethargy, and made to face his own self-created realities. Because we are encased in defenses of our own creation, it is believed that they cannot be soothed away and that it requires more than gentleness and understanding to grasp the true self from which we have been hiding. Only then will a person have a chance to visualize alternative behavioral patterns that may strengthen and enrich his life.

This approach to change and personal growth was begun in therapy sessions with hard-core drug addicts and alcoholics, where unless change occurred immediately, a self-destructive cycle of events would continue. Thus, almost anything outside of physical violence that would help the individual face his own problems and develop new choice points seemed warranted. Anger, support, open hostility, even taunts, might precede a point of self-realization, after which an outpouring of love and affection might result. Whatever the course of events, the aim is to help an individual break through his own resistances so that he at least has a choice of new behavior. Absolute honesty within the group is demanded, along with a discarding of the pretensions and social postures often carried into the group.

Confrontation is a vehicle used for facilitating change in a wide variety of personal growth groups. It may form the major part of the reeducation process that is taking place, or it may supplement a variety of other approaches. It has been widely adapted as a method of raising critical issues between opposing groups or factions. For example, it has been used extensively in meetings between white and black community groups as a means of drawing forth critical issues and moving away from the social niceties that often inhibit the expression of true feelings and attitudes.

The idea of personal confrontation, as a means of facilitating awareness and dropping inhibitions, has much to offer. Too often, however, it is used indiscriminately, and the repercussions can be severe. For example, the entire approach can become patterned or routine where the implied aim is to help each person in the group have some kind of "breakthrough." Group acceptance may require self-denial, tears, or dramatic efforts toward new behavior. The group may be used as a coercive tool to intimidate the individual. In a sense, the approach itself can become highly ritualistic and un-authentic, which of course is the opposite of what is desired. Further-more, it is not uncommon that individuals later feel used, even victims of the process, and react against what they see has happened to them. Nor do all individuals have the same needs or respond equally to the same stimuli or pattern of help. Too often individuals find them-selves open and vulnerable, shorn of their defenses, and without clear-cut alternatives. This can be a frightening experience indeed. Since many of the confrontation groups last for only a period of several intensive days, there is often little time to internalize new behavior or even the impact of one's personal discoveries. Removed from the support of the group, a person may be faced with fears and conflicts much greater than before entering the group. If he has no access to further help and understanding, the experience could pre-cipitate a most difficult and unsatisfactory period of adjustment.

Thus, because of its apparent anybody-can-do-it flavor, this par-ticular approach has been picked up by a great many untrained opportunists who fail to understand the complexities of human per-sonality and the reasons defenses and characteristic behaviors exist. It can polarize entire groups and create greater barriers than existed before. Again, this is not to deny its value, but to suggest that its present use is often highly questionable.

The Basic Encounter Group   Probably the most publicized arm of the group movement has been the encounter group. It has been sensa-tionalized, misinterpreted, and subjected to scathing attacks and boundless praise. Certainly in terms of the traditional experiences of most people in society, encounter groups do represent a radical de-parture from the daily routine and, taken out of context, they could easily appear sensational. Furthermore, they take on an aura of the mysterious when participants attempt to explain their experiences to the uninitiated. As for the attacks and the praise, it is very difficult to talk about them descriptively and with some sense of objectivity. Research is extremely limited in relation to the therapeutic or social benefits these groups produce, but, in the meantime, they continue to meet the needs of a large population of people and will probably continue to proliferate.

Unlike the traditional T-group in which personal goals range from an intellectual interest in how groups function to developing greater personal skills while relating to people, most encounter group participants join with the intent of being personal and at least exploring areas of personal growth for themselves. The thrust is toward intimacy and sharing, and although personal needs and goals quite obviously differ, expectations seem to point toward therapeutic objectives.

Basic encounter groups differ in relation to their duration, facilitator style, participant populations, and mode of operation. For example, in some groups nearly all communication is verbal, and the focus is on what is said or not said, tone of voice, characteristic style of speaking, and, of course, verbal content. In essence a person encounters in the group a mixture of human beings and himself. At first he has only his own narrow field of reference and the vague words of others to guide him. But as trust and openness are developed on a bedrock of similar and increasingly personal experiences, words take on new dimensions, perceptions are clarified, and one's awareness of the shades and variations within the group are enhanced. As authenticity is encouraged and content is less intellectual and more emotional, it becomes appropriate for an individual to experiment with new behaviors and to take the necessary risks that such change entails. At some point the group will inevitably respond to these new behaviors and, as a result, help the individual gain a clear perception of the impact he is now having upon the group.

In other encounter groups the focus may be much more on nonverbal behaviors and activities that involve the group in physical ways. It is believed that we hide so effectively behind words that by responding more to physical cues a great deal of the smoke screening and game playing can be avoided. However, even though the questions of intimacy, personal acceptance, and authenticity are so vital to most participants, the feeling of many group leaders is to avoid the anxiety which accompanies an exploration of the nonverbal and the physical, which in turn is to deny a source of great concern.

In such a group, a person who reveals hostility with another group member may be asked to encounter the person in a physical way (arm wrestling, for example), which encourages a release of tension and then a relating to feelings. It also avoids talking intellectually about the feelings involved. Or the group may be encouraged to express feelings nonverbally, to communicate without words one's own views and attitudes. The process is difficult but often rewarding, if the aim is to open new levels of awareness and channels of communication.

Finally, the spread of intensive encounter groups has resulted in a desire to explore other ways of helping individuals get back in touch with parts of themselves that have been programed out of their lives. The routine of work, commuting, and restricted organizational behaviors has tended to reduce our awareness of the environment in which we live. Sounds, textures, and colors lose their variations as we pattern our lives in a narrowly defined manner. Thus, many encounter groups spend time in an attempt to reawaken these other dimensions of life. Participants may be asked to express themselves through dance or sculpture; to create fantasies around music; to experience darkness, cold, physical fatigue, and dependency on others by exploring a cave or perhaps spending a night in the woods. Whatever the means, the aim is to share the essence of old experiences reborn and to encounter a side of life and ourselves that may help to reestablish old priorities or create new ones. The belief is that for many there are no longer even choices, that our lives are so routine that we forget the alternatives available.

Thus, an encounter group may be a variation upon many themes. With a primary focus on personal growth and little interest in the dynamics of the group (norms, roles, membership, decision making, etc.), it differs from the theoretical notions of the T-group. With a much broader conception of personal growth and ways of facilitating increased awareness in people, it differs significantly from the confrontation group. Nevertheless, many of the dangers and problems mentioned previously certainly apply to the encounter group as it multiplies many times under the guidance of individuals whose skill, training, and motivations may be questionable.

The Human Relations Laboratory   A laboratory environment is one in which experimentation can occur, data analyzed, and new ideas encouraged. In a sense, each of the previous types of groups discussed —the T-group, group therapy, the confrontation group, and the basic encounter group—is based on experimentation, data gathering, and new ideas, which often means new behaviors. Many human relations laboratories, however, are geared to an understanding of groups and focus less on personal growth and more on understanding the group processes. This is not to say that individuals do not grow personally from such experiences, only that it is something gained as a result of the other focus. For example, such a laboratory may extend over a number of days and combine problem simulations, games, and various other activities, all created to help the participants understand how groups and organizations respond to a variety of conditions. In fact, part of the time in such a laboratory setting might very well include T-group sessions as another means of exploring how groups develop. In addition to experiential activities, it is not unusual to supplement these with brief, intellectually oriented theory sessions which attempt to tie perceived group behaviors into a more comprehensive theoretical framework. Thus, by looking carefully at how the group responds in a variety of conditions and generalizing such learnings to other groups, the participants begin to draw conclusions which may very likely relate to their own participation in other groups or with other individuals. The range of activities and the attempt to inject intellectual understanding into the process may tend to reduce their intensity and provide less focus on building the intimate personal relations that might occur in other types of groups.

There are, of course, other types of groups that could be discussed, but most of them would only represent dimensions of the same picture. For example, marathon encounter groups increase tension, intimacy, and the possibility for confrontation by extending group sessions over a long period of time. Instead of stopping after 3 or 4 or even 7 or 8 hours, these groups will often continue 20, 30, or even 40 hours. As layers of defenses slip away with time and fatigue, issues that might have never risen to the surface appear and are dealt with. Similarly, there are now institutes of psychodrama in which individuals work through personal problems within a group setting by involving themselves in intensive role-playing situations with other participants taking significant roles in their lives. Some of these same techniques are used in various encounter and therapy groups. Gestalt workshops, Tavistock groups, programs of reevaluation counseling, transactional analysis, and rational-emotive workshops—all add important "chapters" to the personal growth movement. Interpreted by skilled leaders, each provides new ways of understanding individual behavior and human potential. All are relatively new and await empirical measures of their effectiveness.

Finally, such a discussion should not be concluded without at least alluding to the "sensitivity group." In fact, the term no longer has any meaning since it has become an umbrella under which almost all types of personal growth groups, human relations laboratories, and group dynamics programs are labeled. For those in a mood to criticize groups in general, sensitivity has become a convenient handle that can be pushed and twisted to fit the particular argument. Thus, a series of stereotypes have developed around the term which may or may not be applicable to the particular group being discussed.

An Increasingly Impersonal Society: A Source of Tension and Alienation

The gratification gained through intensely personal relations is less and less possible within the complexities of a modern, urban society. Moving an average of five or six times during an adult lifetime, it is increasingly difficult to develop deep and emotional ties. Just as a relationship becomes intimate, one of the parties leaves. When the fear of moving does not inhibit involvement, often personal relations are tied into the job, and a cover of wariness is implied in any relationship. Even within one's own neighborhood, relations tend to remain at the most social and cordial level with limited opportunities to develop the intensive and intimate relations that many people apparently need.

Another source that may account for the increasing depersonalization of the urban culture is the increasing dependency upon visual stimuli to satisfy tactile needs. Games, dances, and other participative activities have become less a part of our lives, and also gone are the physical involvements that these produced.

Similarly, as we become more sophisticated and worldly as a culture, it becomes less and less acceptable to reveal emotions, to portray the feelings externally that we carry on the inside. Stray a bit too far from the behavioral norm, and one may be labeled as hypersensitive or even eccentric. With little opportunity to develop close personal and emotional ties and caught in a web of social norms that prohibit a full range of emotional responses, many individuals are left with a mounting sense of frustration and guilt. This is particularly understandable since there has never been a time of so many uncertainties, a time when lives are touched with so many common points of tension. Yet, more than ever, people are feeling a sense of isolation from one another.

The Personal Growth Movement

Movements spring from human needs. If the needs are deep and entrenched enough, the movement may become an integral part of the cultural system to which it is attached. If not, it will vanish as a moment in time, a symptom of other problems perhaps, but it will not be a means to any solution. At this time there is a movement that involves the proliferation of groups, all kinds of groups, as an answer to some of the very basic social needs discussed previously. In the past, cocktail parties were a social invention that helped meet a variety of needs, and they have remained an integral part of the social life among several levels of society. In a like manner the pot parties of the youth culture have become socialized and ritualistic, supplying this group with avenues for meeting needs that were either met in different ways previously or had not been clearly defined. Actually behind the pot smoking is a struggle for identity, a reprieve from isolation, a ceremonial process that seeks to personalize relationships and legitimize the emotional or affective side of ourselves.

The personal growth movement appears to provide a means of filling the same societal void. In some ways it is an attempt to retrieve a dimension of the person that has been lost in the smooth mechanization of industry, in the rush to urban or suburban anonymity, in the loss of family, and in the glossy, superficial, material life. It responds to the need for individuals to be seen for themselves and to savor the acceptance and openness found in a few of the one-dimensional groups that run the wheels of the larger society. The new groups appear to fulfill a need, although they may cause problems or be a blessing. At either extreme they are symptomatic of issues that are tearing at the very fabric of our social system. Whether such groups can be helpful in the long run is still difficult to measure.

In reality, the personal growth movement in groups seems to represent a kind of social and individual therapeutic process aimed at a greater personal awareness and sensitivity to others and the surrounding environment. Although generalizations are difficult to make because of the diversity of the many groups, they seem to have a number of things in common. First, these groups remove the imposed restrictions of most work groups and encourage a responsiveness to the moment. The desire is to move away from preplanned, patterned behavior and to cultivate an aspect of spontaneity that might have been lost over the years. Second, there seems to be more interest in dealing with what is happening within the group rather than with past experiences unfamiliar to its members. It is assumed that participants are more open, honest, direct, and intimate in their behavior than normal society allows. These groups differ significantly from a T-group since the assumption of intimacy is implied in the former while in the T-group it is quite possible that the group will spend a majority of its time analyzing process and little time on personal growth. Thus, through its own natural process of development, a T-group may or may not resolve the tensions that surround the question of personal intimacy. It is quite conceivable that a person could leave a T-group having reached his own personal learning goals even though the group might have failed to resolve a number of important issues.

But what is actually meant by a personal growth group? Can there be a definition for a phenomenon that seems to encompass so many diverse experiences ranging from what might be called total immersion marathon groups to a relatively short but intense confrontation session in the community? It seems important to attempt to define the differences between a number of different approaches to personal growth. Even this, however, must be done with considerable reservation since no single definition is acceptable to everyone, and new labels seem to be developing daily. Nevertheless, it may be useful to explore at least the surface differences that exist among these various approaches. Beyond this, much is dependent upon the unique training and philosophical approach of the facilitator,[1] who is, to some degree, responsible to the group as a resource person. In some instances he leads directly; in other situations he may clarify what is happening; sometimes he may interpret events; or in some cases he may play a passive member role.

Personal Growth Groups: The Dangers

Some of the dangers have already been expressed. Many of those who hold serious reservations about the increasing involvement of people in these groups have well-founded criticisms, and they should be heard. On page 280 is one example based on stereotypes, untested assumptions, and half-truths.

[1] Facilitator, leader, trainer are a few of the names used by individuals working as leaders in personal growth groups.

Sensitivity groups are seen as a method of social control through social pressure that is used by every Communist regime in the exact form now spreading throughout our nation. Only it is never called group criticism, but something dear to the hearts of guilt-ridden liberals: human relations perhaps, or operant conditioning. Most often of all, however, you will hear it called "sensitivity training."[2]

Beyond the sensational and irrational, what are the sources of most criticism, and do they appear justified? Following are a number of questions that should be considered when considering the value of personal growth groups.

Question 1: Isn't the entire personal growth movement just another way of talking about therapy?

Therapy is basically a means of reducing a problem condition. Talking intimately to a friend during a period of personal crisis may have great therapeutic value. Similarly, taking a vacation can ready a person to face challenges that might not have been possible without it. Certainly, going to a therapist, a counselor, a valued teacher or confidant may have benefits. But what may be a therapeutic experience to one may be disruptive to another; one source of help may only magnify the issue for another. For many people, groups themselves have a therapeutic value. Almost regardless of their purpose they seem to reinforce the individual's concept of personal worth and esteem. For others, a group of individuals may be an immobilizing factor in which he finds little confirmation of his own worth. Similarly, therapy for one is a strong confrontation, a facing of reality, a demand that he look at alternatives. For another it is simply being totally accepted as one is, without having to perform or compete with others. In the latter case one might suspect that a strong confrontation could be destructive, while in the former case acceptance is taken for granted and would lead to few insights. Yet there appears to be considerable therapeutic orientation in the group movement, and groups will differ dramatically in the degree that personal growth (almost by definition, therapy) occurs or is even intended to occur.

There are, of course, important differences. The personal growth movement has tended to attract a population which is relatively well adjusted to societal norms but who wish to alter certain patterns of

[2] *Sensitivity Training*, San Diego Patriotic Society Bulletin no. 1162, p. 1.

behavior, or gain insights about groups and their behavior in them. In many cases there is an involvement by individuals who, although coping adequately, desire to maximize their own effectiveness in an interpersonal situation or in other ways actualize their own potential. Individuals who enter group therapy are probably less able to cope and adjust to societal norms or are facing a personal crisis. Their level of ego strength may be lower than in the first group, and they may find what occurs in a personal growth group highly threatening. However, just as a definition of therapy has become a very relative issue in recent years, so too has our concept of "adjusted" and "normal." One interesting observation is that the personal growth movement has sprung out of a need for societal therapy, a reappraisal of basic values and behaviors so that unnatural restrictions of behavior and ideas that have been imposed may begin to break down. It is conceivable that the reduction in societal constraints around clothes, sexual mores, the amount of facial hair, the use of "proper" language are all outcomes of a therapeutic process that has been occurring during recent years, and groups have been one instrument in this process.

Question 2: But isn't it possible that the intensive nature of these groups could be destructive to some individuals unless a careful screening process is carried out?

There is no doubt that some individuals are not capable of coping effectively with what occurs in some of these groups. Most people realize that for learning to take place children or adults must be ready, motivated, interested, and desirous of the experience. If the experience is premature, frightening, or considered coercive, it will be thrown off, and a counterreaction may very likely set in. The best way to combat this situation is to make sure that participants, as much as possible, know the nature of the experience in which they wish to participate. A session that helps them focus on the risks and commitment and possible expectations of the group will inevitably act as a self-screening device for those not ready for the particular experience. Individuals contemplating therapy or already undergoing therapy should seriously consider the implications of such an intensive and involving experience, preferably with a therapist or one of the group facilitators. In this same light, it is imperative that participants are aware of the different kinds of groups that are available and that they seek the kind of experience most appropriate for them at a given time.

It should also be noted that groups tend to be highly protective of individuals and if allowed to move at their own speed (this is particularly true of the traditional T-group), there is little chance of an individual's being pushed into an emotional crisis. Precipitating such a crisis is more likely under coercive leadership and when therapeutic goals have not been developed and accepted by the group.

Question 3: Isn't it possible, even with an understanding of what is going to happen and a desire to learn more about oneself, that a person may get in over his head and leave the intensive experience more unsettled than when he entered?

Personal change is nearly always unsettling, since a variety of adjustments must be made at various levels of one's life. It is difficult to implement new behavior because there are many people who are comfortable with us the way we are, since we are predictable. Changing predictable patterns requires others to make adjustments as well. More often than not the glow of a personal growth group will be lost when it comes to implementing one's own goals for change. This is particularly true in a brief 2- or 3-day experience where ideas of change are raised but where there has been little opportunity for the individuals to practice new behavior before returning to their work-a-day world. This inability to live up to rapidly built dreams can itself produce guilt feelings and anxieties. Like anything else, one gets what he pays for. If a person undertakes a bargain-priced 2-day encounter group, there is little chance for new learnings. If such an experience is followed up with further meetings and continued support, chances for success obviously improve. This does not suggest that all 2-day experiences are negative; they may be a valuable first step for many, but their goals and methods should be carefully scrutinized by the participant to determine whether they are, in fact, realistic.

Thus, the opportunity to engage in a supportive follow-up program should be built into any short-term and intensive personal growth group experience. The availability itself provides important security to many individuals and a much-needed opportunity to further integrate learnings and explore the reality of personal goals arrived at in the group. Also, it should be pointed out that increasing numbers of people enter intensive group experiences as an alternative to more traditional, expensive, and time-consuming therapy. Actually, for some individuals, therapy provides an important complementary experience. It is not unusual for participants in personal growth groups to wish to explore at greater depth the causal factors behind certain behaviors or problems. The personal growth experience may help clarify the issues and give them the motivation to undertake a constructive period of therapy. But, because of limited time, limited goals, and limited facilitator expertise, one should not harbor the illusion that such groups are an alternative to intensive psychotherapy.

Question 4: Is it true that no certification is required in this field and that virtually anyone can run a group? Isn't this dangerous and likely to result in a possible backlash against a potentially constructive movement?

This is true, and the danger suggested a very real one.[3] The problem with certification is that the experiences being offered to the public differ radically. Participants often enter the experiences of their own free will and, as suggested previously, it is virtually impossible to define therapy by those who would become accrediting bodies. To make matters worse, some of those without traditional credentials (Ph.D., clinical training, formal education in mental health) have proven to be highly effective as facilitators and leaders in a wide range of programs for numerous goals. Presently a number of certification courses are being developed, but these hold unofficial status and have been created by private organizations as a means of controlling some of the problems already mentioned.

There does, however, seem to be general agreement among those in the field that a leader of any intensive group should have considerable sophistication as a clinical diagnostician in order to be able to screen successfully participants who might find it difficult to cope

---

[3] The American Psychological Association appointed a committee to examine training and qualifications of those who lead groups as well as examining the ethical issues of what happens in groups. A preliminary report of the committee appears in *American Psychologist*, July 1971. The NTL Institute for Applied Behavioral Science, which has been the leading organization concerned with training for behavioral science, is currently reorganizing. NTL will continue in the education, training, and research. However, there will be a different organization that will develop criteria and certification for practitioners. The International Association of Applied Social Scientists (tentative name) will be a certifying organization—the first official one.

with the stress and vigor of such a program. Also, it is difficult to conceive of how a person without having had appropriate supervision as well as certain conceptual understanding about personality, human development, and group processes would begin to undertake work in groups. A person may be extremely sensitive and helpful and still not be aware of any destructive forces in a group or what is happening to an individual. For this reason it appears essential that intensive training under supervision become an integral part of the field.[4]

In the meantime, the responsibility for selecting effective leaders and group experiences lies totally in the hands of the untrained consumer. Few know the risks, the alternative programs available, or even the questions to ask about a particular program. Brochures and descriptions of programs often provide little relevant information about what is to occur, what specific objectives are to be considered, and what expertise the facilitators have in the field. It is true, however, that lately the consumer participant has himself grown more wary and is beginning to demand more information about the various programs as well as assurances of such things as selective screening of participants and appropriate follow-up experiences. With pressure increasing on state and local legislative bodies, it is almost certain that accrediting networks will be established within the next few years. Until then, it is imperative that the public be educated concerning these training programs and develop at least a knowledge of important guiding questions. This chapter has been a step in that direction.

---

[4] NTL has developed several intensive intern programs for leaders specializing in human relations training, T-groups, and planned institutional change. An intern can expect as many as 350 hours of intensive training followed by a 2-year period of supervised group work and program designing and ending with a final 30 hours of evaluation and appraisal.

appendix:
a guide for facilitators

No one consciously plans a disaster. On the contrary, facilitators hope that their presentations or interventions will be helpful to their group members. Often, subconsciously, however, the informality of a model facilitator's style is equated with informality in the facilitator's preparation; casualness in manner is construed as a casual approach; and a spontaneous bit of humor is regarded as a spontaneous attitude. Such reasoning invites trouble. The facilitator's effectiveness depends on adequate and frequently extensive preparation, involving a careful diagnosis of himself and his role; the group, its readiness and expectations; and the situation. He will have considered and discarded several alternative plans prior to determining which approach would be most likely to help the group; and he may even enter with several other alternatives that could be activated under varying conditions. The casual manner and informal approach are typically part of the facilitator's design to elicit a climate more conducive to the learning and sharing of both information and feelings. His spontaneous humor is a personal plus, as is his ability to shift a portion of a design or appropriately change a program. Effectiveness as a facilitator requires careful diagnosis, planning, knowledge, and, always, consideration of alternatives.

The following pages are meant as a guide for facilitators. We will present a number of factors of which the facilitator should be aware. Hopefully the mere listing and brief discussion of some of them will serve to remind both the experienced facilitator as well as the neophyte of the multiplicity of factors to be considered and evaluated in designing a presentation, program, or intervention.

Some Basic Understandings

Let us assume the facilitator is planning an intervention for a group. Prior to determining the theory input, the exercise to be used, or the design to be developed, there are some basic questions that must first be asked. They may sound commonplace, but failure to consider them is most frequently the cause of frustration for the facilitator and the group when the goals intended are not attained.

Who Am I?   First, there is the question of personal identity in relation to the group being considered. The facilitator must seriously and analytically ask himself who he is with regard to this group. Does he have a legitimate role in the group? What is it? How will it influence his effectiveness? From that vantage point how and what kind of intervention can he make? The answers to these questions determine at what level he begins. For example, a teacher in a typical elementary school classroom can legitimately design interventions (an activity, project, special program) for his class. He might set up a role play based on fighting among the children. He might explain the situation and ask for role players to enact the problem. The role play begins, the children enact the fight sequence with a rare opportunity to "fight" in class, and the teacher stops the role play. Now he is ready to discuss alternative methods for resolving fights with the role players and the other students. The students fidget, or reexamine the floors or ceiling, or become suddenly absorbed in other activities. They know that discussing ideas on fights, or alternative methods of coping with hostility, are "exercises in futility." They know from previous admonitions that "fighting is bad, people shouldn't hate each other but love each other," etc. They know that the teacher does not really want a discussion of what they feel, but rather a moralistic conclusion that fighting is bad.

If the teacher has previously made known his opinions in certain areas, and would like to have the students reconsider the subject themselves, he will need to reexamine his position or indicate some meaningful change before his intervention can be effective. Or, a teacher who has previously been interested in "facts not opinions, please," may encounter great difficulty when he attempts to encourage students to express their feelings. Frequently there is a norm that only feelings related to school are appropriate in school and that other subjects (sex, dating, relations with family) should be avoided in teacher-student interactions; if this is the norm, a teacher must be especially aware of who he is in planning such a discussion.

Often the person making the intervention is an outside consultant, a person outside the organization hired to work on a specific project or with that organization. Outside consultants can be effective because of their special expertise in their subject and because they will be able to influence without being involved in the intricacies of cliques and power groups. However, the outside consultant, hired to work with a new organization, must carefully consider the level of trust that members will have in him initially, and he should design an initial experience that allows the members to test him.

Interventions may also be made by an inside consultant (someone employed by the organization). Who he is also is the basic consideration. He is not unknown. He comes into a group with a reputation developed through the grapevine as to his style and his effectiveness; if his reputation is one of being well-liked and effective, he has much greater latitude in being able to make interventions he sees as needed. It cannot be stated too strongly that who you are greatly influences the manner of your approach—your legitimacy, and, consequently, the degree of potential influence.

Who Is the Group?   Consideration of the facilitator's role is not enough. It is equally important to know the makeup of the group. What kind of people are they? What are their ages? How receptive are they to change? Have they been a group for some time, or is this the first time they are meeting? How can they be expected to regard you? (Some groups have immediate distrustful reactions to university professors, or men with beards, or women in facilitator roles.) These questions are important since they relate to the crucial question of whether the group is ready for what is being planned. The plan may be premature or anxiety-producing because it is beyond the experience of most of the members. It may require work at regular intervals, but the group may not be willing to commit themselves to regular segments of time.

Are My Goals as Facilitator Clear?   A third factor is whether or not the facilitator has clear goals. To say, "I want to be helpful," or "this is a good exercise to give them data," or "this worked in a group I was in and will be stimulating here" are insufficiently clear goals. Wanting to be helpful and being helpful is the difference between fantasy and reality. An exercise that focuses on a problem with which the group is unconcerned is frequently viewed as a waste of time or meaningless "game playing," and what was a stimulating exercise in one group may be an inappropriate bore in another. Thus, a facilitator must ask, "What are my goals?" and be able to state them explicitly to himself; frequently it is helpful to state them to the group. At the beginning of the session, the facilitator may state simply and directly what his objectives are, how they will be accomplished, and in what time. This serves as both a framework and a guide for achieving goals. The facilitator develops his objectives on an understanding of the first two factors, his own role and the appropriateness of doing what he has planned, plus the third factor, the readiness, composition, and expectations of the group in that situation.

This third factor can rarely be determined by the facilitator alone. It is developed through involvement and participation as the group sets its goals and expectations given the realistic constraints of time, money, and resources. The goals which then develop, and which the facilitator may state, become the group's goals.

Communication Pitfalls   Although an entire chapter is devoted to communication and perception, it is not belaboring the point to state again that situations are perceived and words are heard uniquely. Too often it is assumed that the facilitator's words mean to the group what they mean to him. *It is imperative that both have the same understanding of words.* A term frequently used to refer to the person who professionally works with groups is the word "trainer." For many the term conjures up impressions of mechanistic animal trainers or other forms of compulsory training, and they may well generate defenses in the participants. A more acceptable word presently in vogue is "facilitator." Obviously almost any word for leader may evoke different meanings, just as behavioral science jargon may also be a source of anxiety and frustration for those involved. Recently, a group was told that there would be an intervention designed for them the next week. This statement meant that time would be set aside for the group to examine its processes of making decisions, since it seemed to have limited skill in this area. Several members, after hearing of an intervention, became visibly anxious. When asked why, the members said that they interpreted intervention as meaning a confrontation, and they were terrified at the possibility of such an experience.

Many of the words which facilitators take for granted or which have an accepted meaning for people "in the trade" have little or different meanings for laymen and those unfamiliar with these terms. The facilitator must either explain the meaning of the term or use a term familiar to the group. Asking a group to form into dyads generally produces raised eyebrows but little movement; however, asking them to form into groups of two, or to select a partner, produces the desired response. Frequently, the facilitator only learns afterwards that there was a misinterpretation. This is usually too late and results in a less than optimal learning situation. However, the facilitator can minimize some misunderstanding by being aware of facial expressions of members as checks for inadequate comprehension, and he can ask at frequent intervals if there are any questions. Generally, after directions have been given, the facilitator will ask, "Are there any questions before we start?" If understanding is valued, this cannot be asked as a rhetorical question. The question is asked, and there should be a sufficient pause for questions plus time allotted for answers. Obviously questions before are more productive than discussions of "I thought you meant" afterwards. Since questions are often seen as signs of ignorance, they are often difficult to elicit from a group with whom the facilitator is not familiar. By breaking the group into clusters of three or four and asking for a few questions from each at appropriate times, there is a greater assurance of questions that will help the group and the facilitator in their efforts to understand each other.

In summary, a facilitator should begin with some basic understanding of himself and his role, the group with which he is working, and a clear formulation of his objectives. These are specific considerations that require careful previous study by anyone working with a group—by a facilitator working with a new group, by a staff member or teacher examining his group at regular intervals, and by facilitators and groups working together in each planning session.

Time as a Dynamic Variable

Too often time is perceived as a given rather than a dynamic component in planning. Typically, we think in terms of having a day to present a specific program, or 2 hours, or a period, and we design in terms of filling up that time space. We diagnose our group, develop a plan, and attempt to "guesstimate" how long it will take to present it. We allow time for an introduction, a theory input, an exercise, and discussion and implications at the end. Then the inevitable, but it is so frequent it should almost be anticipated, occurs. The program does not start on time, someone has an announcement, or we run late and are forced to cut out the most important part of the learning experience—the sharing of information and the implications. In reality, we tend to overplan and assume that we will get more in than we actually can. At one level, time should be viewed as the limits within which learning takes place, and it should be allocated so that both the initial as well as the more important concluding aspects are timed within the unit.

Time can also be a facilitator's tool. It can be used as a means to implement the training goals. If the facilitator wishes to increase involvement, he shortens the time allotted for a task; the micro aspect compresses action—there is less time for small talk and a greater motivation to accomplish the given task in the given time. This breakdown of the time component for greater involvement and increased productivity can be formulated in many ways. A number of them will be briefly stated and described.

Micro-lab   As the name indicates, a micro-lab is a condensed version of a total laboratory or workshop experience. Because the time is shortened, usually about 2 hours for the entire experience, the session is intensive. It is designed to give participants a taste of a laboratory experience that involves them immediately, raises issues, and provides diagnostic data for later analysis. It is especially effective because it can be geared and designed towards the goals of that laboratory. And for the participants it provides experiential data from a number of different approaches to a subject which then allows them to personalize implications. Out of the time pressure, out of the many senses and feelings generated in the micro-lab, people internalize more than they would in a typical introductory program or initial lecture. The micro-lab, designed as a series of short interpersonal experiences, is especially effective as an introductory session to get people directly involved yet simultaneously working on the issues to be raised in the longer workshop. Micro-labs are frequently designed around getting to know others in a group of strangers, interpersonal communication, an examination of stereotyped roles as males and females, or increased sensory awareness. The possibilities are limitless. (See Micro-lab examples at the end of Chapters 1 and 5.)

Micro-lecture   At times the facilitator may consider it desirable to speak on the theoretical or research findings related to a particular subject. He is frequently in a bind: he values participant involvement and wants to encourage discussion of the issues he raises, yet he knows a lecture will reduce involvement to passive listening at best with little subsequent exchange. The micro-lecture uses time pressure for both involvement and integration of material for participants. The facilitator prepares his lecture so that it can be presented in 5-minute segments. He may present his thesis in the first segment, and the substantiating points one by one in subsequent segments. The participants are divided into small groups. The procedure is a 5-minute lecture, followed by a 10-minute discussion on that point, and the pattern continues three or four times—a 5-minute lecture on one point, a 10-minute discussion of it. The result is a continued involvement, discussion, and integration of the material in a limited time. Obviously presentation and discussion time blocks are flexible, depending on the particular situation and the need that arises.

Micro-discussion On a given topic, frequently only a few of the more verbal individuals participate. Others never get a chance to express their views, or feel that they are peripheral members and not really meant to participate. Sometimes talk is bogged down to a discussion of a tangential point, and there is difficulty in returning to the main subject. Once more time is used actively to promote the facilitator's objectives of enlarged participation. The group is divided in half (and with a larger group, even in thirds). One-half the group comes into the center of a circle and discusses the topic for 10 minutes. At the end of that time, the other group comes into the center, and the first group recedes. The discussion continues on the same topic for another 10 minutes. Every 10 minutes there is a reversal of inner-outer groups. What happens is that with half the number in the circle, there are more opportunities to speak for the more reticent or less involved members. The 10-minute limit on discussion allows the new group to build on previous discussion and not to be stymied by a personality conflict or a peripheral view of the discussion. Once more the limiting of time produces greater involvement, a leap-frogging of ideas as one group builds on the discussion of the previous group, and members build on the resources of members in both groups.

Just as time should not be taken for granted but viewed as a tool to implement the goals of the facilitator, so are other aspects a means to help the facilitator accomplish more of his objectives. Grouping especially will influence both the process as well as the outcomes.

The Many Ways to Group

It is frequently stated in the exercises of this book, "Divide the participants into groups of 6 to 8." That sounds simple enough, but a consideration of the methods of grouping can produce not only units small enough for conversation but may also be critically important for insuring implementation of the training goals. By failing to have effective procedures ready for such a simple part of the design, the facilitator may make the group and himself uncomfortable and reduce the rapport so essential for a successful intervention.

Random Grouping This is the simplest. First it must be decided how many groups are desirable, let us say five, and participants are asked to count off (1, 2, 3, 4, 5, 1, 2, etc.). Then the facilitator specifies a location for each of the groups (the ones go to one corner, the twos to another, and so on as all of the groups form). Sometimes names are pulled from a hat, with the first five names being group one, the second five being group two, and continuing until the desired number of groups is attained. Yet another method is to group people by their birthday month—all January and February birthdays would be group one, etc. The advantages of random grouping are that whatever diversity there is in the population is likely to be spread among the groups, friendship groups are split, and participants view each group as having equal resources. There are no higher and lower status groups. Random groups are especially effective in a new group where some enter with friends and others are alone and feel like outcasts. The random group requires that each individual build a relationship in the group alone and anew. Sometimes, an especially hostile group will perceive even a random grouping as being manipulative. It is the wise (and experienced) facilitator who accepts their suspicions and is sensitive and responsive to their fears. He may simply ask that participants get together in groups of five with others they do not know and form groups in this manner. Of course, it is unlikely that such a suspicious group will move into stranger subgroups. The key is to get them moving and caught up in the plan of the day, which should reduce their doubts or anxieties.

Homogeneous Grouping For some purposes a homogeneous grouping may be more suitable for the design. There can be one table for elementary school teachers, another for secondary school teachers, a third for higher education, another for administrative staffs. Or there can be women at one table and men at another, or parents at one table and students at another. Homogeneous groupings may be utilized to permit groups with common concerns to work on joint problems, or they may be used in an initial grouping to be followed by a pairing of members from each group, or they may be the basis for discussion with a representative from each group.

Stratified-Random Grouping   In some designs it is desirable to have a planned mix in each group, i.e., a given number in proportion to diverse populations. Here each group may be composed of a representative from each school, or representatives of different occupations may form a group. This grouping is frequently used to attain diverse populations within a group who might not ordinarily distribute themselves in such a manner: blacks and whites, adults and students, inner city residents and suburbanites, Christians and Jews. There is the predicted tendency for like to sit with like; this form, by design, places representatives of the diverse segments within each group. It is important to let these groups understand how they have been selected so the feelings of manipulation are minimized.

Ad Hoc Grouping   Often involvement itself is the goal, and the type of grouping matters little. In an auditorium, the facilitator will ask that those in the front row turn their chairs so that they can speak to those in the next row, and those in the third row turn so that they can speak to those in the fourth row. Sometimes, he begins by having the room arranged with round tables and chairs. Persons enter, and as they seat themselves they are self-grouping. The facilitator then proceeds on the basis that those at a table become a group. These are some of the types of grouping facilitators use. However, at other times there is a very different rationale for grouping.

Dyads and Triads   In a new situation, a whole group looks frightening. Talking to one other person, who may be equally apprehensive, becomes a way to enter the group and feel less alone. Dyads are frequently used in initial micro-labs, in pairing for observations, in sharing of perceptions and reactions. Dyads, used in the micro-concept for a stated short time, increase involvement as well as personal reactions to the subject under discussion.

Triads are frequently effective in discussing an issue. Triads permit a flexibility of relationships: two may side against one on one issue but align differently on another; in three-man groups there is high involvement, a possibility of utilization of multiple reactions and resources, and a variety of relationships. Groups of four are infrequently used since they permit a formation of sides that could remain deadlocked. Groups of five are used in decision-making or problem-solving groups, but they are used less frequently where the goal is personal reaction and involvement. In a group of six or more, there is a likelihood that two people will take over; therefore many facilitators will give two groups of threes 15 minutes to discuss a problem rather than assigning a group of 6 half an hour.

Clusters   Sometimes an anchor group or support group is helpful to achieve the goals of the program; these are termed "clusters." In a program in which there are representatives of many schools, the team from a particular school becomes a cluster and meets at specified times to discuss their reactions, or the applicability of the program to their school, or other questions based on implications of the current program. Clusters may be trios or larger groups who share an interest and discuss it together; they cluster out of the large participatory body.

Fishbowl   Fishbowls are like the micro-discussions described earlier. The group is divided into half, or an even number of units. One-half comes into the center and discusses a question while the others listen. After 8 to 10 minutes (or a predetermined length of time), the other group comes into the center and discusses either the same question or another issue. In either event, the group builds as each unit in the center assimilates and responds as if continuing the previous discussion. Thus, by listening to the previous group and then participating, there is a tendency to move over roadblocks encountered in the last period.

A fishbowl is also used in decision making. A representative group may be the inner circle as in a fishbowl, with the other participants listening to the negotiations as in the outer circle of the fishbowl. Sometimes the "tap in" is used to allow those on the outside to express their views directly. If someone has something to say which he feels is pertinent and thus far unsaid, he taps the person with whom he disagrees, or another, who has been silent or uninvolved, and takes the place of the person tapped. He then presents his views, and depending on the rules, continues to stay until he is tapped out or leaves after his comments, thereby permitting the displaced member to return. Instead of tapping out, another variation is to place an empty chair in the inner circle. Someone from the outer group who has a comment seats himself in the empty chair, speaks, and then returns to his former place. A fishbowl has the advantage of allowing all to participate in the decision-making process either directly or at least by hearing the negotiations firsthand. Since decision making and discussion of recommendations are often conducted in secrecy and privacy, the fishbowl frequently has great impact on persons who are witness to this procedure for the first time.

Which grouping is used depends on the basic understandings described earlier in the chapter. The method of grouping will be governed by the goals of the facilitator and the kind of problem being examined.

Using Techniques Effectively

A number of techniques are described in training exercises throughout the book, and they are usually self-explanatory to experienced facilitators. To the newcomer, however, a brief review of what is involved in using a technique effectively may be appropriate.

Posting on Newsprint   Using newsprint, large sheets of cheap paper typically purchased in tablets, is one sure way of increasing participant involvement. The newsprint, which is written on with broad felt-tipped marking pens and mounted on the walls with masking tape, is an effective device for having data available and readily evident to participants. It is used to record the reports presented by various groups, to list recommendations, to describe aspects of a situation, and to provide feedback to a group. The newsprint on the wall even serves to remind participants of how much they have accomplished as they see the layers of newsprint surrounding them by the end of a 3-day workshop. Like anything else, newsprint can be overused, and it will never save the poorly prepared or unskilled facilitator. But it can help increase idea visibility, reduce credibility gaps, and focus attention of groups from two to several hundred.

Role Playing   Role playing is an especially effective method for having participants experience a situation in its concrete reality, as against a discussion in abstraction. It permits analysis of behaviors as well as a possibility for a replay with certain roles enacted in another way. The benefits of role play are inadequately stated here, but there are two good books that will provide the reader with additional information.[1] For our purposes the emphasis will be on frequently ignored steps in a role play that undermine the effectiveness of the technique. Prior to the role play there might be some warm-up activities to help people feel less self-conscious; for example, how people coming to a protest meeting walk in, where they sit, etc. Such activities create an atmosphere and environment for a realistic role play. After some warm-up activities, a role play situation is identified, the players are selected, and the role play takes place. First, it is important that the role players have an opportunity to read their roles, become familiar with them, and feel able to perform the behaviors indicated. The players might try imaginary monologues to get them in the mood of the character, or stand outside the room and practice how the role player might act in a given situation. There might even be one or two coaches help the role player become more aware of nuances and styles. The facilitator checks that all are familiar and comfortable with their roles; if not, he further clarifies the role or attempts to be helpful to the insecure role player. If there are to be observers gathering data during the role play, the facilitator instructs them in detail, or distributes and reviews an observer's guide which provides the information needed. Having ascertained that the players are ready and the observers know their instructions, the facilitator asks that the role players enter and seat themselves according to the role-play situation. He once more establishes the situation, and the role play begins. Too often role playing becomes boring, because the facilitator does not cut soon enough. The facilitator terminates action as soon as a decision is made, or when it becomes evident there will be no decision. The role play is the focal incident. After it ends, the discussion enlarges from individual reactions often to implications or alternatives for that situation. The facilitator might ask each role player to respond to how he felt in that role: "Were you comfortable, was it familiar, how did it feel?" Then the debriefing continues as he asks each to respond to the character out of role: "How different was this from your usual role?" Only then are there reports called for from the observers and other participants. Finally,

[1] M. Chester and R. Fox, *Role-Playing Methods in the Classroom*, Chicago, Ill.: Science Research Associates, Inc., 1966; A. F. Klein, *How to Use Role Playing Effectively*, New York: Association Press, 1959.

there is a discussion of generalizations or implications of the role play, in which all enter. As is evident, the role play is only a small portion of what is involved in a training design. The preparation and debriefing are important but often overlooked aspects, and enough time must be allowed for reporting and generalizations.

Role Reversal The objective of role reversal is to understand to what extent one person perceives and can enact the role of another. Usually it is very difficult, or done at a level of superficial mannerisms. It becomes evident that we often see others through the narrow view of our own limited experience. Prior to the role reversal, each person in the group has before him either a name tag or a card with his name on it. In the midst of a discussion, the facilitator abruptly cuts the activity. He explains that people frequently are concerned only with what they are thinking or trying to say, and not what others feel. He asks that those across from each other exchange seats and name tags. The participants are then asked to continue the discussion as if they were the person in the seat opposite them; they are to attempt to be faithful in their body movements and emotional tone as well as continue the discussion from their point of view. After a few minutes the discussion is again terminated and participants share their experiences. Sometimes, this is done a second time. The second time members will have become more aware of each other's verbal and nonverbal behaviors and will be better able to attempt the role reversal. Obviously the activity can be extended to a variety of situations in which individuals are concerned with how they are being perceived. It is ideal for opening communication between two individuals who are no longer capable of listening to each other.

Alter-Ego An alter-ego is basically the other persons within us, the "voices" who might urge us to speak when we are silent, or express feelings we dare not openly express. The alter-ego as a technique may be used in a modification of a role play, or it may be used to illustrate the conflicts within a person. In a role play, a given character will have two (or more) others who stand behind him in the role play and enact hidden parts of him. The football captain who is a member of a committee to decide on a new dress code may have his alter-egos behind him. One may remind him that he should vote for short hair; if he votes that way, his regulation short hair will seem less conspicuous. Another alter-ego will remind him to vote for long hair, because that is what the students want, and if he is planning to run for class election, a vote in that direction will enhance his popularity. The role player continues, but every time the alter-ego (inner voice) wants to speak, he puts his arm on the shoulder of the role player, who stops talking. The alter-ego speaks, and then releases the role player's arm, signaling the continuation of the role play. It is especially important that the alter-ego and the role players thoroughly understand and are comfortable in their roles. There should be adequate time to warm up and explain the alter-ego concept. Following the role play, the debriefing includes the alter-egos as well as the role players. The prime understanding that develops in an alter-ego role play is empathy for the person who is trapped, who is placed in the position of not being able to express what he feels. At times we all experience this, and can remember the pain and the frustration.

An alter-ego role play is also a prime example of all the things that can go wrong; those viewing the exercise may be confused about who those people are in the back, alter-egos may not be sure when or how to come in, role players may be confused about how to respond to them. It takes preparation for an alter-ego role play to come off. However, it can demonstrate in physical terms that sometimes we intend to side with one group and act with another, or sometimes we seem to vacillate and others have difficulty understanding our behavior, and sometimes we are quiet when we have much to say.

Sociodrama, Psychodrama. Both are "acting out" techniques without written formal roles as is usually the case in a role play. In a sociodrama, members will act out a social situation, i.e., a mother, a father, and a child discussing the anticipated move to a new city; or a job applicant being interviewed. In a psychodrama individuals volunteeer problems they would like to work on. One is selected. The person can "play" to another person he chooses or to an imagined person. The participants, in each kind of drama, may change roles as a means of further implementing understanding. The sociodrama is used to increase understanding and skill in certain situations; the psychodrama is frequently used to examine and work on unresolved relations with other people or personal issues.[2]

To be effective, there should be a warm-up, or a series of practice activities, so that members feel less self-conscious, and the situation

[2] For more information on psychodrama, read J. L. Moreno, *Psychodrama*, New York: Beacon House, 1946.

must be clearly presented. After the drama, both participants as well as those observing are asked to respond. It may be in terms of feelings to this situation, or a sharing of similar experiences in their lives, or suggestions for an alternative method of enacting the role or viewing the situation.

Replay Drama   Situations occur in which the members are caught off guard, where an incident occurs that is typical, and the response is anxious and defensive. For example, two Black Panthers were invited to present their platform to a mostly white college graduate class in psychology. In the question-and-answer period the discussion became personal and heated. At the next session of class there was a replay drama; the situation of the previous week was replayed with class members enacting all of the roles. The scene was rekindled, but now the group started where the previous week's discussion ended. Replay drama is a powerful technique that permits people close to a situation to reexamine their behaviors less defensively and more objectively. The replay is different from the original, and some of the most important learnings come from a discussion of what is different and why. Although a relatively new technique, it holds promise for allowing persons to reexamine their behaviors in highly emotional areas. This attempt to help the participants to know, to replay, and to understand is fundamental in the facilitator's efforts to help his group.

Gathering Data on Groups

Gathering data is the scientific basis for understanding what is happening. There are a number of methods for observing aspects of groups, but only a few will be described here. Which method is used depends on the training objectives and the readiness of the group to diagnose its situation. It is less threatening to observe a role play than an ongoing group, and comparable resistances are to be anticipated when an ongoing group is to be observed. Groups frequently are fearful of observations because of the assumed implications that the leader might be a poor one or that the group might be viewed as a failure. It is very difficult to ask a group to consider examining its own behavior. The fears are enormous. It is easier in a laboratory group or classroom, where the learning aspect can be heightened and the evaluative aspects muted. Sometimes beginning with a simple observation form, like a post-meeting reaction, and allowing the members to discuss the results among themselves and draw conclusions or consider modifications allows the group to begin the observation process without fear of expectations from the facilitator.

Post-meeting Reactions   A series of questions are developed dealing with the degree of involvement of each member, the amount of participation, the amount of perceived conflict, and the amount of movement toward goals. Each question is followed by a rating scale going from 1 (not involved) to 5 (highly involved). The sheets are prepared by the facilitator. He explains that they may be a useful instrument to help the group diagnose its present situation. If the groups are agreeable, one sheet is distributed to each member who then records his responses. The results are determined and read back either by a volunteer, or the group itself analyzes the results. It is a useful device for helping a group diagnose its present state and possibly may lead to more effectiveness as members become aware of the responses of others and find areas of agreement or disagreement.

Task-Maintenance Observation   Frequently groups understand their work in the problem-solving areas, but they rarely know of the socioemotional areas of equal importance—the harmonizer, the gatekeeper, etc., the roles that influence how members feel about one another (see Chapter 5). One kind of observation focuses on task-maintenance behaviors. It may begin by dividing the group into thirds. One group performs some experimental task assigned by the facilitator. One group has sheets listing task behaviors, and one group has sheets listing maintenance behaviors. Following the exercise, the observers report their findings. The reporting of this data helps participants become aware of the variety of roles in a group and the limited number used by each member. As a result, some members may endeavor to attempt new behaviors. Frequently, the ensuing discussion prompts members to talk about groups they find effective and in which they are comfortable, and it leads to a discussion of implications for that group.

Process-Content Observation   When a facilitator asks, "What are they talking about?" he is asking a content question. When he asks, "What is happening; what do they seem to be doing?" he is asking a process question. Who is listened to and who is ignored can be determined by process observations, who has high status and who has low, who is friends with whom—all of these are process questions which, as we obtain answers, permit us to understand the dynamics of a particular group.

A *sociogram* is an instrument that measures interpersonal relations. It may measure productivity; it may ask a member to rate the three hardest workers in the group. It may measure a friendship dimension, and ask, "Who are the three people you like best in the group?" Questions can be designed to obtain information in the area desired. The replies to the questions are tallied and, based on the number of times mentioned, people are rated. The most often rated is the "star," the least rated may be the "unchosen." The results yield information on members' perceptions of individuals on the dimensions studied, i.e., who is viewed as an isolate, who is the most popular, which are the subgroups. The facilitator might encourage members to design their own sociograms for data they feel is pertinent. Afterwards, members discuss the findings as well as their feelings about them. The sociogram is easy to design, administer, and interpret. It is a form of data a group readily understands. It can also be misused or used too lightly in situations that may prove threatening.

A *who-to-whom* is an instrument for collecting information recorded by an observer which completely disregards content. The recorder (this could be the facilitator or a selected observer) tallies each time a person speaks (one tally per sentence) and notes to whom the statement is addressed. The observations are recorded in a matrix, which indicates who spoke to whom. The matrix is illustrated on page 302.

On the left side are listed the names of the members of the group, or if the recorder is unfamiliar with them, he lists them by number. This left-hand column represents the list of possible speakers. Across the top are listed the members, or numbers representing them, in the same order. Now, however, these numbers indicate to whom the speaker addresses his comment. If person #2 speaks to person #5, a tally is recorded on the row with #2 at the left and in the column under #5, or in the cell 2–5. If the person continues to talk, tallies are continued, one for each sentence. In the illustration #2 spoke about six sentences. Tallies are recorded in this fashion for a given time unit, usually 10 minutes at the beginning, and 10 minutes at the end of an observation period. There is a cell for a member ad-

To Whom Spoken
(the recipient)

		Name (1)	Name (2)	Name (3)	Name (4)	Name (5)	Group	Total
Who Speaks (the speaker)	Name (1)							
	Name (2)							
	Name (3)							
	Name (4)							
	Name (5)							
	Total							

dressing the entire group (in the illustration, the Group column). Note that there is a diagonal line in the cell in which #1 might be speaking to himself, or #2 to himself—it may be possible, but it is unrecorded. Following the observation period, the tallies are totaled, and frequently percentages are computed. The totals at the right represent the number of units (or the percentage) of the total amount of verbal interaction that one person spoke. The totals at the bottom represent the number of times a person was spoken to.

Although content is disregarded, the who-to-whom yields a great deal of information on the relationships within a group. The high-status person is typically the one who is spoken to much more than he speaks; the low-status person is typically the one who speaks a disproportionate amount in comparison with the low proportion of times he is spoken to. Subgroupings are seen as two members who speak almost exclusively to each other, or speak to each other much more than others. Someone not sure of his membership role may rarely speak.

A who-to-whom is an especially valuable instrument for collecting data on a variety of aspects of a group and in analysis allows members to develop new understandings of the dynamics of their group. It should be mentioned that one observation may be atypical, as is a single measure unreliable in many instances; several observations over time are required for a more reliable description of the dynamics of that group.

Feedback

Another method for obtaining data on individuals and groups is through feedback, i.e., the individual asks for certain information, and others answer him based upon their perceptions of him. For example, if one person notices people looking at him during all of the discussion and thinks he has been informally designated the leader of the group, he may ask the group whether they see him as the leader. Their reply is feedback to him. The whole concept of feedback may be viewed as threatening since it is so alien to the norms of our society. People are really secretive in their feelings toward others and do not tell others how they see them. They not only feel threatened by the prospect, but may view it as harmful. Yet feedback is the means by which we can be more honest in groups and deal more effectively with one another as our behavior is consonant with our thoughts. But feedback can be harmful to individuals or to the development of an entire group. The facilitator should be clear on the rules of feedback. The feedback should be requested, be descriptive rather than evaluative, be specific rather than general, be behavioral rather than total, and preferably should be constructive. To illustrate: If someone asks why no one wants him in the group, a person responding might answer that the last time they were in a project together he never came to meetings and did almost none of the work.

Where appropriate, the facilitator can encourage feedback among members, and there are a number of exercises in Chapter 1 that deal with feedback more extensively. There are many kinds of feedback. Results of observation instruments are a kind of feedback. Reports of observers are feedback. There are many kinds of observations that provide members with data about themselves and their roles in a group.

1. *Feedback on descriptive behavior.* Two people are paired. One, P (Participant), works with others in the performance of an experimental task; the other, O (Observer), observes his behavior. The observer then describes the behavior he saw—how often P spoke, on what subjects, his body motions, etc. The two then reverse.

2. *Feedback on nonverbal behavior.* A pairing similar to the situation above is made, except the person doing the observing watches only for nonverbal behaviors. Frequently nonverbal be-

haviors give us greater clues to what the person is feeling than his verbal responses. The observer shares his findings, and the participant listens. The partners then reverse.

3. *Feedback on coming closer, being more distant.* Yet another version of the observation feedback techniques described above is one in which the observer focuses on his partner in terms of behaviors that help people come closer to him (looking at them, listening) or those that make people more distant from him. In each of these observational schemes, the facilitator instructs the observers as to what to look for and preferably develops a list of descriptive behaviors to be checked.

Groups are encouraged to make up their own observational systems. The limitation to be emphasized by the facilitator is that the observations must be descriptive or based on behaviors that can be described.

Ongoing Feedback and Readjustment by the Facilitator It is so obvious it sounds trite, but the facilitator's effectiveness is directly related to his receptivity and sensitivity to feedback. In planning a session he may meet with other members of the group to get feedback and to ascertain more realistically how the group sees his role, and where they are as a group. He may test tentative ideas by submitting them to the planning group and carefully watching for their reactions. If they say, "That sounds too much like sensitivity training to be in a teacher's workshop," the facilitator might propose other means for achieving that objective. Even after a preliminary training design has been developed, the facilitator may still be considering others. He may meet a hostile "show me" group and decide to alter his opening. He may find the first part of his design did not meet with the anticipated reactions and may revise the design to get more group discussion in the second phase. He may find, as is typical, that he will not have time to develop his design as planned and will decide which section to eliminate. In a break in the session, he might ask some of the participants how they feel about what is happening. Following the program, he might "hang around" so that he is available to hear comments. Of course, the facilitator is routinely "reading faces" even when he is not consciously aware that he is observing.

Summary

Being a facilitator sometimes looks easy; it never is. The facilitator must constantly be aware of himself, his expectations, and his role in a group; he must be sensitive to that group and where it is; he must be clear about his goals and objectives with that group in its current state. Skills are required, and with experience they can be enhanced through observation, gathering data, giving feedback, and developing training experiences. Most important, he has to be sensitive to the feedback he receives. He plans for a group but does not arrive with "the plan." He has other resources at his disposal so that if he notes a change in a group, he can activate an alternative plan as appropriate. With experience and ever increasing sensitivity to what is going on, he learns how he can be effective.

index